The Thunder and The Sunshine

Paula de Somoggy, the mysterious "Rita" over whom Conrad fought a duel. In this 1880 Paris photograph she wears the arrow pin of his autobiographical romance, *The Arrow of Gold*.

The Thunder
and The Sunshine

A BIOGRAPHY OF JOSEPH CONRAD

JERRY ALLEN

G. P. Putnam's Sons   New York

© 1958 by Jerry Allen

*Published simultaneously in the Dominion of Canada
by Longmans, Green and Company, Toronto.*

Library of Congress Catalog
Card Number: 58-7441

MANUFACTURED IN THE UNITED STATES OF AMERICA

There lies the port; the vessel puffs her sail:
There gloom the dark broad seas. My mariners,
Souls that have toil'd, and wrought, and
      thought with me—
That ever with a frolic welcome took
The thunder and the sunshine, and opposed
Free hearts, free foreheads—you and I are old . . .

                    —*Ulysses* Tennyson

Preface

◇◇◇◇◇◇◇◇◇◇◇◇◇◇◇◇◇

When illness ended his career as a sea captain Joseph Conrad sought the seclusion of the English countryside and until his death in 1924 "Young Ulysses" wrote his own odyssey from that retreat. Some of the world's classics were written there, stories that were, on the surface, about the sea. Resembling in their far view Tennyson's untraveled world "whose margin fades for ever and for ever when I move," they have stirred continuing wonder, with more than three thousand items by one late count published in Western languages alone.

As complex a man as the tales which for sixty years have called out a flood of notice, Conrad has long sheltered under the word heard like a footfall through all his work—mysterious. His friends over the years made repeated efforts to define him. None succeeded. With a mind so inexhaustible others flagged at the end of an hour's talk, so restless of movement photographers despaired of holding him for a pose, he was a wind-swept personality. Terms he once used to classify his work, Calm-pieces and Storm-pieces, applied also to his volatile temperament. He could be, and often was, a fascinating storyteller, infinitely charming, endearingly tender. But he was also a man of tempest, developing through the refining furnace of his own experience his great compassion for a mankind so limited. "Conrad understood everything," the artist Sir William Rothenstein concluded of the "proud, overwrought spirit" who had been his friend for twenty years.

Among early friends to attempt a portrait of him was Edward Garnett, then a publisher's reader in London who recommended the book so strange for its times, *Almayer's Folly*. Meeting Conrad in 1894, a sea captain in pointed patent-leather shoes, Garnett saw a "stranger who charmed one by something polished and fastidious in the inflections of his manner," a man with "brilliant eyes, now narrowed and penetrating, now soft and warm, with a manner alert yet caressing, whose speech was ingratiating, guarded, and brusque turn by turn. I had never seen before a man so masculinely keen yet so femininely sensitive."

John Galsworthy wrote sympathetically of the friend whose pains were intolerably great but who was nevertheless no stranger to humor. Darkness and light were in him, blackness of brooding dissolving when his sense of fun would leap up and "take charge with a shout."

In the bewilderment which twelve years of knowing Conrad had not lessened, Richard Curle spoke of "the abiding mystery of his fascinating and enigmatic personality." Bertrand Russell, awarded the Nobel Prize for Literature in 1950, met Conrad in 1913 and forty-three years later in *Portraits From Memory* told of the haunting quality of the man for whom he named his eldest son.

"At our very first meeting, we talked with continually increasing intimacy. We seemed to sink through layer after layer of what was superficial, till gradually both reached the central fire . . . I came away bewildered, and hardly able to find my way among ordinary affairs."

Drawing about himself a shielding screen, living beyond the public's reach, Conrad proved no less difficult for critics to capture. From his books, refracting prisms changing with each new reading, they culled a variety of meaning. But the author, so elusive, was baffling still.

"There was always an air of mystery about him," Virginia Woolf wrote of the novelist whose "reputation of later years was, with one obvious exception, undoubtedly the highest in England." One hears, she says, in his "rather stiff and sombre music, with its reserve, its pride, its vast and implacable integrity, how it is better to be good than bad, how loyalty is good and honesty and courage."

Courage was often a theme in Conrad's work, and a question. From the usually critical H. L. Mencken it drew lyric praise. Mencken was an early Conrad enthusiast and in *A Book of Prefaces* gave his summing-up of the mysterious teller of tales.

"He may think, as Walpole argues, that 'life is too strong, too clever and too remorseless for the sons of men,' but he does not think that they are too weak and poor in spirit to challenge it. It is the challenging that engrosses him, and enchants him, and raises up the magic of his wonder. It is as futile, in the end, as Hamlet's or Faust's—but still a gallant and a gorgeous adventure, a game uproariously worth the playing."

A natural reticence and strong sense of privacy were inherent in Conrad. But the scars of a tragic childhood and the long-healing wound of a love affair early added to his need of barricade. Poor health hampered him always yet he spent twenty years at sea in a day when sailing ships relentlessly tested the men who alternately courted the winds and fought them. He was a Pole who knew no English until he was twenty, yet he wrote all of his books, twenty-seven, in that language. His English, spiced with ironic humor and vivid with a painter's colors, never came easily. He wrote eighteen volumes, books always highly praised, before he made a living from them.

His work has won for Conrad the current designation of "the greatest British novelist of the early twentieth century," a standing reached in steady mounting since the publication of his first novel, chosen then by such critics as H. G. Wells. By the time of his death he was winning the acclaim described on August 4, 1924 by *The New York Times*:

"In recent years Joseph Conrad had received such high titles as 'the greatest living writer of English' and 'the most arresting and the most romantic figure in English literature.' And as his fame increased among the critical, so did his position with the general public, so that from being merely the idol of the discerning few when *Almayer's Folly* appeared in 1895, after the publication of *The Rover* last year, he became, or very nearly became, a popular favorite."

Today reviews of his books are appearing again as if they were new. *Nostromo*, fifty-three years after it was published, was recently given a full-page criticism in *The New Republic* because it was still a "magnificent book, a beautiful book," and timely. The rediscovery of an author earlier and too narrowly identified as "the greatest of sea writers" is due less to the sea content of his books than to the current in them, the "life-stuff" of his own term. For it was with "The Secret Sharer," *The Shadow Line, Lord Jim,* "Youth," *The Nigger of the Narcissus,* and "Heart of Darkness" that Conrad became an acknowledged master of the psychological story.

Like "Youth" and *The Shadow Line,* his fiction was frequently, and admittedly, autobiographical. In *The Arrow of Gold* he appeared in his own love story under the French-English name of Monsieur George. It was a *nom de guerre* cloaking both his youthful gunrunning adventure in France and his love affair with the "woman of all time."

A duel, in life as in the novel, ended his romance with *l'amie du Roi* and from Marseilles Conrad became a rover of the seas, embarking on a life of voyages from which his books were drawn. His first twenty years, from a childhood in exile to his departure from Marseilles with an "incurable wound," were the molding years of the writer who was an artist in prose, a writer who, as the New York *World* said, was like no predecessor and left no followers behind him.

The subtlety with which an author uses experience, transmuting fact to fiction, is an indefinable process. With Conrad, one of the most personal of writers, the landmarks of events stand out, however intangible the art by which he wove them into greatness. In this history of his exile years and of his romance with the girl whose name he was to vary so slightly for the heroines of his stories may lie a major key to the mystery of one of the great narrative artists, whose nostalgic thought returned again and again to Marseilles.

From Polish letters written by Conrad and his family, to date largely unpublished, and from new material drawn from European sources, this biography attempts a fresh portrait of the paradoxical, nattily dressed seaman who sought the violent winds; the artist unlike any other whose mind and understanding were awesome in compass; the man hurt, scarred deeply, who repeatedly stood into challenge—who so often, like his own Leggatt, "lowered himself into the water to take his punishment: a free man, a proud swimmer striking out for a new destiny."

J. A.

New York
February, 1958

Chapter I

◆◇◆◇◆◇◆◇◆◇◆◇◆◇◆◇◆◇◆

THE rain, a winter London rain effortless and quiet, seeped into pools on the cobbled street. Water trickled in the gutter, a quivering thread under the gaslight that, like some trapped and weary moth, fanned in pulsing trys at brightness. The night in its cocoon of fog and soot smudged over the row of low brick houses, merging roofs and chimney pots and sky. Occasionally a horse clopped by and the wheels of a carriage on its way from Victoria Station slurred with a deadened sound over uneven stones cupping the rain.

In the Pimlico lodginghouse at 17 Gillingham Street on this raw winter night of 1895 a light spluttered in an upstairs window where a man sat writing. His serious lean face, the wind-tanned face of an outdoor man, was lengthened by a close-cut tapered beard. Dark brown eyes under heavily folded lids shone in brilliant reflection of each swiftly changing mood. Encased by the rain-padded silence of the street and by the shrouded tone of a private seclusion which others knew as the mark of him, he wrote with deep attention.

He was absorbed in the story of Stephen he was creating, a slowly, painfully growing story that, with recent news of Paula, was fresh in his mind. Six months before, he had walked in the Passy neighborhood of Paris where Paula had had her fame and, as recently as August, again in Paris, he had talked with Pascalis of *Le Figaro* and with the Deputy Jules Guesde about the town of their youth, the haunting town of his unforgotten love, the Marseilles of seventeen years ago. Now Paula was married, a Marquise, living in Paris—and he, a Master in the British merchant marine.

Since "neither his fellows, nor his gods, nor his passions will leave a man alone," he was also a man writing, bringing into fiction the unrelenting ghost he schooled himself to call "Rita." In close privacy he held the real name—nor in his whole life did he ever give it—of the mysterious girl over whom he had fought a duel, his exotic "woman of all time." Yet a special world knew her as *l'amie du Roi.*

He had hesitated to go back into the deep shadows—"one does not undertake such a journey without misgivings"—to recall the love affair from which, as from his first boyhood love at fifteen, he had emerged "seamed, scarred, almost flayed and with a complete mistrust of himself, an abiding fear." So strongly was she before him now that he wrote in the memory of hearing her talk of her childhood in the Hungarian hills.

She had been "an unruly minx," a wild child running about the crags in tattered clothes, an orphan receiving the austere, unloving care of a priest. The priest, a brother of her mother, ruled over a hamlet of peasants whom he "endeavored to keep in the path of godliness with fierce denunciations, with menacing words, with gloomy fanaticism, knowing nothing of the world; hating it." A zealous Royalist, he was equally violent in his religious views, "ready to leap . . . like a sword from the scabbard in the hand of an unforgiving God."

So he wrote, hearing the girl talk as they had talked together in Marseilles. He was nineteen then, and she a year younger. Now at thirty-eight he was a mirror of his own Stephen, a questioner of guides hawking the sure routes, an unpersuaded listener who "heard, right and left, the vociferations of idle fanatics extolling this path or that with earthly and hoarse voices that rang out, untrustworthy, in empty darkness."

An uprooted wanderer since childhood, he had known the ports where clippers called, the migrants of the waterfront, their tentative settling. If he doubted the existence of bliss and the gold of it, if he had learned in the bargaining of life "that a sacrifice must be made, that something has to be given up," yet he stood for the courage of search. Passionate and intense, he accepted the shadow line, the part that was not all, and never clear. He might have in him the canny knowledge spoken in a peasant's proverb heard long ago—"happiness that lasts is no more to be found than ice which never melts"—but he had lived in challenge.

A slight, short man, with the broad shoulders and long arms of a strong man, his movements were quick and restless. His friends knew him as a fascinating storyteller, zestful, vivid— his hands, his knees, his feet carrying the story, some part of him always in motion.

Tapping his pipe nervously, pacing light-footedly about the room, he appeared ill at ease in any house. Twenty years at sea spent on moving decks forever pointed at some far horizon had made him a stranger on the rigid land. Illness contracted in the Belgian Congo had ended—he hoped temporarily—his sea days. On shore for more than a year, he was impatient for another ship he could command.

He was a seaman and wished no better life than that. In his land time he had turned to writing, with pages of his first book written in many ports over the years. That novel of a trader with the Dutch name of Olmeijer whom he had known in Borneo had recently been published. *Almayer's Folly*. It came out under the name he had grown used to, a name known for ten years in the Sailors' Homes of his ports of call—Joseph Conrad. Shipping records might list him since his last command as Captain Conrad Korzeniowski but his Polish name, proving too much for the tongues of English sailors, had been shortened by those men of clipped speech who had been his shipmates for seventeen years.

Another novel of Eastern waters, *An Outcast of the Islands,* was completed, and as he wrote this new story, one he was never to finish, *The Sisters,* he thought back to the days of his life before he had ever seen a sail, to a land of plains, one as vast as the sea.

As his pen scratched over the thin ruled paper, hesitating, picking the words, the pages filled with the picture of a remembered country.

"In the shallow folds of the plain dammed streams overflowed into an unruffled glimmer of small lakes, placid, as though soothed by the whispering tenderness of encircling reeds. On their banks dark willows and slim, unsteady birches stirred in the gentle and powerful breath of the indolent steppe. Here and there a clump of low oaks looked sombre and stolid, planted firmly above the dark patch of its own shade. On the slope hung a village, scattered white huts, with high, ragged, thatched roofs under which small unequal windows twinkled, like small eyes of a band of deformed and humorous dwarfs winking under high caps cavalierly aslant . . ."

His wrist stung with rheumatic pain, the incurable gout that along with the fevers formed his legacy from six crippling months in the Congo. He laid his pen down, pushed his chair away and listened to rain falling with velvet steps on the mud-deadened stones below. At this late hour so silent, the street was bedlam by day. Then a barrel organ tremulously ground out the new and popular *Cavalleria Rusticana,* children shrilled as they dodged about the feet of horses straining in harness as they pulled heavy wagons to the Vauxhall Bridge Road. Chimney sweeps wiped ale from blackened faces in the seamy taverns where blowzy women picked up trade. Ten blocks away the Thames moved in sullied water, its burden of working ships charging and discharging cargo. Draymen, publicans, blacksmiths, roustabouts of the docks and the railway lived in this backwater off Belgrave Road.

An earthy corner of hard-living men, noisy and bleak, Gillingham Street was the dark underedge of that other part of London where Oscar Wilde sat elegantly at the height of his fame. The author of *The Importance of Being Earnest,* produced for the first time early this year at the St. James's Theatre, twigged London's ear with blasé quips, dismissing an ocean with "I am not exactly pleased with the Atlantic." Rolling off aphorisms the smart set was quoting—"the man who can dominate a London dinner-table can dominate the world"—Oscar Wilde was the pet of London.

Around him were England's end-of-the-century writers who, like the century, seemed tired. Peacocking elderly youths who delighted in their name of "The Decadents," their slender volumes were lush with purple patches, jingled with a toy life. Shunning the sound of life and the feel of it, they were unknowingly making way for a seaman whose aim was "to make you hear, to make you feel—before all, to make you *see.*" The settings he knew, the faltering people he knew, moved into place on the handwritten pages. So much were they out of his own life that, as he had written his aunt, "What bothers me most is that my figures are so real. I know them so well that they fetter my imagination."

The fog outside, more solid than that of Borneo, more stifling than that of Marseilles, gave the house the chill of dankness. Conrad turned back from it to another place and time. He warmed his stiffening hands at the open coal fire lighting the snug bachelor's quarters of a man trained to neatness by a life at sea. Sitting with his back to the screen-hidden bed, he faced links with the past he was recalling, the mantelpiece row of French novels, two fading photographs of his parents. He dipped his pen in an inkstand crusted with use and wrote again.

"The uniform level of ripe wheat stretched far out into unbounded distance . . . one unbroken murmuring field, as big as a world . . ."

That world, which he was remembering in sunlight, had held tragedy for a boy. Its cutting edge had entered when, a child in exile, he was four. It had then been a world of forests, of the ominous noise of snow.

Chapter II

✧✧✧✧✧✧✧✧✧✧✧✧✧✧✧✧✧✧

FROM the last Russian posting station the heavy traveling carriage lumbered through the storm, its wheels churning the axle-deep mud of the country road. For some time the steppes had been free of snow but sleet, "the son coming after the father," lanced down on the wind and scythed this night of early summer. In reminder that northern Russia with its summers of blazing sunsets and long twilights was a winter land, needles of ice sped like flung darts from a sky dense with their stampede. The squeaking of leather traces, the sucking of mud, the jingling bells on the yoke over the shaft horse gave the sounds of movement to the carriage crawling in the blurred darkness of storm. The fields, the road, the great hemlock forests that fringed it were invisible in the dense air which obliterated depth and distance and like the inside of a cloud made all directions equal.

The driver's rain-soaked *murmolka* dripped into his peasant's beard as he sat rigid on the box, bent against the wind lashing in a savage sweep from the White Sea. His small eyes, screwed to gimlets, searched for landmarks, for some cluster of huts rare enough in the wide country. His three horses in troika harness ploughed through clinging mire, now skidding down sharp slopes, now passing under towering fir trees where clattering branches rocked in the wind. At each lurch the passengers in the coach—a man, a woman, and a child—were thrown against each other. But for the sick woman's cough and the boy's fretful cries, they rode in heavy-hearted silence.

For weeks they had been traveling in the uncertain weather of spring, first westward toward the Ural Mountains, then north. They had come, this family of three, more than fourteen hundred miles in horse-drawn carriages, finding warmth by the red-hot stoves of posting stations where the horses were changed, and the drivers. In the cramped stations and inns offered by the small villages they passed through they had found food and such beds as there were for the night, primitive lodgings the more miserable for the contrast they made to the luxury of their home in Warsaw. That home now so far behind them—with its rich comforts, its staff of family servants, its scarlet-and-white salon where so many friends had gathered, with his writing table where she had liked to come upon him, working—was a home forfeited. On this day, severed from the literary circles which had known them in Warsaw, they were political prisoners.

The end of the long trip across Poland and Russia was near for the convoy being taken into exile, for the Polish poet of forty-two, Apollo Korzeniowski, his ailing wife Evelina, thirty-one, their four-year-old son Conrad. The Czarist military escort had hurried them from the posting station, a room crowded with rough travelers speaking a northern tongue they did not understand. At Vologda, 350 miles south of Archangel, they would stay, by order of Czar Alexander II, an indefinite time.

In this year of 1862 Poles were deported from their homeland in an increasing stream which reached a peak in 1863 when the Czar hanged 128 Polish leaders, exiled 18,672 more. Some, like the Korzeniowskis, were sent to exist, if they could, in the bitter 50-below-zero air of Vologda, an ancient town set in dense evergreen forests and since early days a way-station to the White Sea.

In one of the low-browed log houses where the cold was to stand with a wall's force the Korzeniowskis settled to eke out time. The father, cut away from his work and unable to earn a living, sat by candlelight and wrote the days away.

Recognized in Poland as an excellent playwright and a gifted poet, Apollo Korzeniowski had known considerable success as a writer. His play *Because of the Money* had been produced in Zhitomir, had won a prize in Warsaw. High praise had been given to his satire on manners, *A Comedy,* a five-act drama in verse. He had also the reputation of being a spirited, just critic and an unequaled translator of Victor Hugo and Heine.

A man with a "soft, sensitive heart, and much compassion for the poor and oppressed," Apollo felt bitterly about Poland's subjugation, about the slavery of his serf-holding times. Like Mickiewicz and Dostoevsky, he held thoughts objectionable to the Czars and, like them, had been punished for it.

Sensitive and dreamy, he was a brooding man with a disposition that soared to extremes—at times gloomy, bitterly ironic, mystical, despairing; at other times witty, charming, brilliant in conversation. His face "in repose sombre, lighted all over when he smiled," his son remembered.

Born in the village of Honoratce near Kiev on February 21, 1820, Apollonius Nalecz Korzeniowski came of a middle-class family of landowners descended from a line first recorded in 1584. In their long history the Korzeniowskis had proved to be impractical romantics with vivid imaginations; they had often been soldiers, sometimes officials, most often gamblers of the long chance, incurable dreamers.

Apollo's father, Theodor Korzeniowski, was a moody and spark-tempered fighting man who in his early youth had been a lieutenant in Napoleon's forces, the 1807 conquering armies, the disastrous 1812 Moscow campaign. As a cavalry officer rising to the rank of captain, he had served in the Polish Army from 1817 to 1820. Twice wounded in action, his bravery in battle had brought him the Polish cross of valor, *Virtuti Militari*. At forty-two he went to the wars for the final time, joining the Polish forces against Czar Nicholas I in the 1831 uprising. When Poland revolted again in 1863 Theodor was seventy-four and, regretfully, no longer a cavalryman able to "get into the saddle and drive them out."

He was also the author, this daring, breezy, boastful man, of a five-act tragedy in verse which he had had privately printed. His grandson Conrad called it "so extremely dull that no one was ever known to have read it through. I know I couldn't, notwithstanding my family pride and the general piety of my disposition."

Theodor had a passion for speculating and through it lost most of his inherited property in the Ukraine. He retired after that economic defeat to his wife's estate in Volhynia where, for a living, he administered the vast lands of a neighbor, Mme. Melanie Sobanska.

On those rolling plains of the Ukraine where an estate of fifteen hundred acres was considered small, serfs, counted as so many owned "souls," worked the land, supplying their masters with the expansive life American plantation owners knew in ante-bellum days. Theodor Korzeniowski was critical of his times and talked admiringly of the social theories sifting through from France—the Utopian ideas of Proudhon, Saint-Simon and Fourier which attracted, in America, such followers as Horace Greeley.

In one of the columned mansions set apart from the thatched-hut villages Theodor Korzeniowski and his wife brought up their three sons. The eldest, Robert, was a hard-drinking, gambling gay blade; the youngest, Hilary, a "Utopian" like his father, spent his life as an estate-manager until 1863 when he was arrested by the Czar for his Polish-patriot activities and exiled to Tomsk, dying there in 1878. The third son, Apollo, was a scholar.

Apollo was educated in private boarding schools and at the High School of Zhitomir, an old Lithuanian city founded in 1240 whose streets were lined with the mansions of Polish nobles. In those salons Apollo's courtly manners and stimulating talk made him a popular guest. Wanting to know more of the world beyond Zhitomir, more than he could learn from avid reading, he applied for a passport while still in his teens to go to Berlin and on to France and Italy. When it was refused by Nicholas I in his ban on foreign travel, Apollo attended St. Petersburg University for six years, first entering the Department of Oriental Studies and Philology, changing to the Faculty of Arts to study his favorite subject, French literature.

Like other educated sons of the gentry admitted to the university in the early 1840's, he strolled the Nevsky Prospect in the cap and uniform of his Faculty, ate oysters at Smurov's, danced the English waltz at the many social affairs of the court city, talked the nights through in students' rooms in the preferred tongues of French and German.

Turgenev and Dostoevsky were both university students in St. Petersburg, Dostoevsky studying at the School of Military Engineers. A thick-set boy with reddish hair, snub-nosed and freckled, he was struggling with algebra, physics, ballistics, in the sternly regimented school where errors brought the punishment of whips. To win fame some twenty years later with *Crime and Punishment,* Dostoevsky was a serious, nervous student, a year younger than Apollo.

Another student beginning his college courses as Dostoevsky and Apollo were finishing theirs was Tolstoy, a sixteen-year-old boy entering the faculty of Oriental Languages at Kazan University. A wealthy nobleman, his mother a Princess, Tolstoy wore expensive clothes, had his own droshki, sat in examination rooms on the benches reserved for princes, counts and barons. With his personal serf Alexis to attend him, his coachman to drive him, the sword of a student at his belt, Tolstoy plunged into the social life of Kazan, dancing at all the balls, attending concerts, soirees, tableaux vivants, seen everywhere with friends he was to use for models in *War and Peace*. After three years of a social round Tolstoy left the university without his degree in 1847.

Apollo Korzeniowski, by far less wealthy, also left the university without his degree that year and returned to his father's estate in Volhynia where he passed the time as a country gentleman, reading French literature, dancing at balls, writing turbulent poetry. The indolence of his life, if not his scholarly use of it, was usual for Ukraine landowners. Living in isolated manor houses, surrounded by unending miles of forests and wheatfields where work was done by serfs, they struggled against boredom. Their days were dissolved in hunting, gambling, drinking, their evenings in family games of whist, patience, *l'hombre*.

Entering that tedious round in what he called the cultural "desert" of the Ukraine was a famous Frenchman, a short stout man of forty-eight visiting at a Volhynia estate a few miles away. Cholera was striking down fifty people a day in Kiev but in the mansions of the countryside the exciting news, the drawingroom news, was the arrival of Balzac.

Chapter III

❖❖❖❖❖❖❖❖❖❖❖❖❖❖

HONORÉ DE BALZAC had been courting Madame de Hanska for fourteen years. As the Polish Countess Rzewuska before her marriage she had been a famous beauty but when Balzac made his first visit to her estate in Volhynia in September, 1847, she was a widow only a year or two younger than himself, an educated and pampered woman of great wealth whose figure had rounded into the plumpness of middle age. In a final attempt to win her to marriage he had dashed across Europe in an eight-day non-stop journey from Paris.

Arriving at her estate of Wierzchownia, Balzac was overwhelmed by its incredible size and the luxury of the enormous mansion.

"This house is exactly a Louvre, and the lands are as great as our *départements*," he wrote back to his sister Laure in Paris. There were three hundred household servants and, attached to the house, all the shops that one needed at hand, including that of a tailor where winter cloaks of Siberian fur were made for his comfort. On another of the estates in Count Mniszek's domain of a thousand households was an equally imposing chateau, "the Versailles of Poland."

Balzac had his own apartment, a three-room suite of a salon, bedroom and study, in a house so great that "in this Louvre there are five or six apartments of this sort to give." One of the larger properties of Polish landowners, Wierzchownia had been turned over by Evelina de Hanska to her daughter when Anna married Count Georges Mniszek. To work his combined estates Count Mniszek owned, in 1847, more than 40,000 serfs. And yet, Balzac calculated, it would take 400,000 to cultivate all his land.

The nearest town, Berdichev, was thirty-six miles away. When letters were to be posted a servant was sent that distance on horseback, one of the horde of serfs who Balzac declared "literally throw themselves on their stomachs when they come into one's presence, beat the ground three times with their foreheads, and kiss one's feet."

Balzac spent four months at Wierzchownia and before the winter brought its sub-zero weather made calls with Madame de Hanska at other mansions in the neighborhood where she could display her enthralled suitor, her amusing *"bilboquet."*

On an estate not far off and one much less pretentious was a serious young man reading Balzac's books. Apollo Korzeniowski was twenty-seven in that year of 1847, the year of his meeting Evelina Bobrowska, the beautiful sixteen-year-old sister of a university classmate, Thaddeus Bobrowski. Apollo immediately fell deeply in love. For nine years he sought her parents' permission to marry. Her father, looking upon him in spite of his social advantages as an "undesirable pretender," a young man living with his father, doing nothing, possessing nothing, urged him to find some other bride.

Evelina loved as devotedly as Apollo. She was, however, sternly dutiful, an overly protected girl in a family whose four boys closed round her in what Conrad called "an extraordinary sister-cult." She could not persuade her brothers to accept the suitor who spent his days writing poetry, on love and spring, on the fiery, revolutionary theme of "There will be a Poland! There will be, there will be, as there is a God in heaven!" Nor could she persuade her father, Joseph Bobrowski. Out of love and respect for him she waited.

Joseph Bobrowski was firmly rooted in the land, thoroughly content in the narrow sphere of his estate of Oratov where he lived his life, and where he died. Above all things a practical man and never a restless one, he was an ardent lover of every sport, his attention keenly fastened on the famous stud of Steppe horses he owned. Landowners for generations—and of the same land, which no folly of gambling ever threatened—the Bobrowskis were stable provincial gentry, prosperous and economical, careful managers with a solid sense of proportion. Their interests had never led them astray into the dubious pursuit of poetry.

As a schoolboy Joseph Bobrowski had been taught by liberal-minded Benedictine monks and had read the authors of the eighteenth century but his taste in letters had narrowed to the concise forms of business, to loans, sales, receipts. A bald man with a thin hooked nose, he was popular for his quick wit and for a generally easygoing temperament. But he was also a man not readily budged. For years he had fought a lawsuit with his stepfather over the lands and the two villages he now owned. With that same determination he held his six children close, particularly the elder of his two daughters, Evelina. He stood fast against her marriage since to him, a country squire absorbed in hunting and the breeding of horses, Apollo as a son-in-law was all things wrong. He was an intellectual and not a sportsman; he had feelings too strong and a wit too sharp; he was changeable, impractical; he was a sincere democrat, an ardent patriot, a "revolutionary." He was likable enough, well-mannered and well-born, but he had no income, no settled position.

Apollo was popular with the sons of the family but more than ever after the deaths of the father and the younger sister Teofila did the brothers circle around the twenty-year-old Evelina in sheltering protection. Only when her health was seriously threatened, after nine years of struggle, torn between her love for Apollo and her family's stern objection to him, was she released to marry. She was twenty-five and Apollo thirty-six when they were married in the village church of Oratov on April 28, 1856.

To answer the complaint of the Bobrowskis that he was a young man "doing nothing"—and to win their final consent to his marriage—Apollo had taken on the management of an estate, a piece of the vast tract owned by Mme. Melanie Sobanska, and there he and Evelina spent the first year of their marriage. When her one-sixth share of her father's property was sold she received her dowry—eight thousand rubles, a fur coat, a large carpet, silverware, a dinner service, and an additional gift of a thousand rubles from her brothers—which enabled Apollo, without funds of his own, to rent another and more potentially prosperous estate. During the winter Evelina went to an uncle's estate near Berdichev, and there the only child she and Apollo were to have, a son, was born on December 3, 1857.

Christened Joseph Theodor Konrad Nalecz Korzeniowski, the heir of the line was to shorten that full signature many years later to Joseph Conrad. To the names Joseph and Theodor of his two grandfathers the Konrad was added as Apollo's tribute to Poland's great poet Mickiewicz and the Konrad hero of his verse. Further insuring a literary future for his son, Apollo on the day of the child's birth asked the best-known Polish novelist of the time, his friend Joseph Kraszewski, to give the boy a writer's blessing. On that day, too, Apollo wrote a poem to his newborn son. But the poem, not about a father's joy, dwelt on Poland's struggle for freedom and its fidelity to that cause. Poland had then been under Russian rule for eighty-five years; in his first stanza Apollo struck that sombre note.

> Child, son, sleep quietly,
> You arrive under a foreign cloud;
> You own only your heart

> And the strength of your arm
> Is your only crest.

For two years the young family stayed on the rented property, gradually losing their investment in a project that totally failed. Apollo proved an inexpert manager, being a man his brother-in-law called "passionate in his feelings, expansive, and a sincere friend of everybody, but impractical in his action and often even helpless."

The young wife had no more talent for practical affairs than her husband. Though brilliantly gifted and better educated than women usually were in that time, the wide-browed Evelina "whose eyes," as her son remembered, "had a sort of commanding sweetness," had grown up in a family where capable men made all the decisions. In the Bobrowski's expansive home innumerable servants had made life a time of leisure for the quiet girl whose health was never sturdy. She had a cultivated mind and unusual beauty which made her "exceptionally distinguished in person, manner, and intellect." But nervous, sensitive, and self-exacting, she was at times "at war with herself."

How extraordinary his mother was Conrad realized from the letters she wrote to her husband and brothers in the early days of her marriage, letters he read when working on his first book *Almayer's Folly*. The personality standing out in her correspondence, he wrote, "was a revelation to me; I shall never forget my delight, admiration and unutterable regret at my loss (before I could appreciate her), which only then I fully understood."

After failing with the rented estate the Korzeniowskis moved in 1859 to Zhitomir where Apollo had many friends. Having proved that he had neither the ability nor the inclination to be an estate manager, he undertook, at thirty-nine, work he liked. He joined a publishing firm called "Publications," translated Victor Hugo's *La Légende des Siècles* and *Hernani*, continued to write his explosive call-to-arms poetry, became an active leader of Polish patriots. In May, 1861 he was offered the editorship of a projected literary journal and left for Warsaw, eager to be in the heart of Poland where a new rebellion was forming.

For nearly a hundred years the hope of recovering independence had been a chafing dream in the split land. A monarchy till the middle of the eighteenth century, Poland had been destroyed as a nation by Frederick II of Prussia, Catherine the Great of Russia, Joseph II of Austria. Under them it had undergone partition in 1772, 1793, 1795. Young Poles, growing up in a country occupied by three powers, knowing by heart the heroism of their grandfathers in earlier attempts to free it, had grown savagely intolerant of foreign rule.

The fever of revolt, always fanned and always strong, was rising to white heat in 1861. Angry men were gathering in the capital of Warsaw which since 1815 had been in Russian hands. Apollo was among them. It was no longer enough to write revolutionary poems he could not publish—some not to appear until 1955—crying "Wake up from your sleep, raise your heads, your Motherland calls you!" Evelina, as fervent a patriot as her husband, accepted the need. Spending the summer with Conrad on her brother's estate in the country, she wrote constantly to Apollo of his political plans, not knowing her letters were being read by the Czarist police—letters which were shortly to help bring about his exile.

By the fall, established in Warsaw, Apollo sent for his wife and young son. Conrad, who was to know so much of wandering, came to his third home in the first three years of his life.

Apollo's editorial plans for a journal modeled on the Paris *Revue des Deux Mondes* moved ahead in a reading climate where literary papers were given prompt support. Dostoevsky was succeeding in a similar project, his St. Petersburg monthly *Time* having 4,302 subscribers in 1862, a year after its first issue.

But Apollo, joining in the political moves of his genial brother-in-law Stefan, had more than a literary paper in mind.

Poland, like Russia, was in ferment, impatient for reforms too long delayed. Although Czar Alexander II had issued an edict on February 19, 1861, emancipating the serfs in Russian territory, it had proved but a paper freedom—the serfs were to be temporarily bound for nine years, serving their landlords during that time with free labor. Alexander had relaxed his hold on Poland by granting it a Council of State in which Poles were permitted to serve in the administration of their own affairs; but that, too, was a concession exasperatingly mild.

The slowness of any real change in Russia's serfdom caused increasing peasant revolts, with 400 uprisings in 1862. In St. Petersburg students staged explosive protests; the university was closed, all public lectures banned. Anger mounted, secret societies formed. Mysterious fires broke out in St. Petersburg and the Russian capital, with one blaze after another searing it, was kept in flames for two weeks.

In Warsaw a national uprising was in the making. In the fall of 1861 crowds gathered for the traditional celebration honoring Thaddeus Kosciusko, Poland's national hero who had not only fought for the liberty of his own country but had taken part in the American Revolution, as a soldier, as chief engineer of the West Point fortifications, as an aide to Washington. On Kosciusko Day the Czar declared the city of Warsaw in a state of siege, sent troops into Polish churches to halt memorial services. Street battles resulted in which scores were killed and wounded, two thousand Poles arrested.

The thrust of revolt gained strength and a secret Central Committee, which was to direct the uprising of 1863, was formed, with Apollo as one of its founders. Its serious members met to talk of the sobering crisis in the Korzeniowski home where Conrad, nearing four, saw strangers with grave faces come and go, saw his mother in the black dress of national mourning.

News of the meetings reached the police and shortly after the Central Committee was organized Apollo was arrested. During the night of November 1, 1861 police searched the Korzeniowski home, terrifying the small boy who watched as his father was led away. Apollo was imprisoned in the citadel and for fifteen days waited for his first police questioning, waited three months for another. After six months—during which Conrad rarely saw his father, through prison bars—the long investigations ended in April, 1862. A hasty trial brought the conviction of conspiracy against the Czar, he who shared with God the supreme title of "Most High," and Apollo was condemned to exile.

Stanislas Bobrowski, Evelina's brother and an officer in the Russian army, was a friend of the Colonel who presided over the military court and through that connection secured for Apollo a relatively light sentence. He was not to be sent to eastern Siberia for thirty years doing hard labor in irons part of the time as had Tolstoy's cousin in 1825, nor was he to be given "eight years of hard labor in Siberia" as Dostoevsky's sentence had read. He was to be exiled to Perm, in the foothills of the Ural Mountains, sixteen hundred miles east of Warsaw.

Evelina asked for permission to go with her husband, to take her son. She was allowed to leave on the condition that she become a voluntary prisoner, submitting to a prisoner's treatment. The family left Warsaw under police escort at the end of April, 1862 for Perm. In a land having but 1,116 miles of railroad, the country was crossed in horse-drawn vehicles and in those cumbersome traveling carriages the Korzeniowskis moved slowly east. Spring thaws made the dirt roads impassable and, sinking in bogholes to the carriage windows, they waited in chilling rain while peasants with winches labored to drag their carriage free. Rain, sleet and mud turned a week's drive into a month's struggle to move on the heavy roads.

By the time the family had gone seven hundred and fifty miles, before they reached Moscow, Conrad fell seriously ill. The escort refused to stop for help but a passing traveler rode ahead to Moscow, sent back a doctor who saved the child's life.

The mother's health, too, broke under the long ordeal. Three hundred miles east of Moscow, at Nizhni Novgorod where new orders directed that the prisoners be taken north to Vologda instead of on to Perm, Evelina became too weak to walk from the carriage and had to be carried. Again an angry traveler lodged a complaint with the police, condemning the brutal treatment given the Korzeniowskis, and secured permission for them to rest.

Weakened by exposure from weeks of carriage travel in the harsh weather of spring—a journey such as twelve years earlier had brought on the death of Balzac—they reached Vologda in June, 1862.

Corroded time flaked off in months as "homesickness, like a rust" gnawed at the family shelved in exile. A year passed slowly. They were still in Vologda, beyond the hearing of a world violently moving, when, in a land half the earth away, 155,000 men were fighting one of the most savage battles of the nineteenth century on the hills surrounding Gettysburg, Pennsylvania.

Chapter IV

◇◇◇◇◇◇◇◇◇◇◇◇◇◇◇◇◇

THE NEWS of Lincoln's Emancipation Proclamation freeing 3,120,000 slaves upon its issue on January 1, 1863 had barely reached Europe on the slow boats of that time when newspapers in London, Paris and Berlin printed their first dispatches of the Polish uprising. On the night of January 21, 1863 open rebellion broke out in Poland as large bodies of armed civilians attacked the Czar's troops. Telegraphic communication with Warsaw was totally cut off. Railway and waterway transport ceased. By January 28 Warsaw was under martial law and the newly appointed viceroy of Poland, Grand Duke Constantine, brother of the Czar, asked for a reinforcement of fifty thousand Russian troops to cope with bands of civilians springing up all over Poland.

One center of the insurrection was Zhitomir where the Korzeniowski and Bobrowski sons were in the van of the fighting. Apollo's older brother Robert, then fifty, was killed, and his younger brother Hilary was sent to Siberia. Evelina's brother, Stefan Bobrowski, one of the founders of the Central Committee, had been killed in a duel with a political opponent, Count Grabowski, just before the uprising.

America was in the throes of its own Civil War but gave

front-page newspaper space to the rising in Poland. Europe watched the conflict with undisguised sympathy for the Poles.

"Everything that reaches us from Poland," the London *Times* said in an editorial on January 29, "shows that the importance of the Insurrection has not been exaggerated. That it may be put down by overwhelming military force we do not pretend to deny. But it will be not the less the furious rising of a people maddened by oppression against a Government which, besides being that of the stranger, has carried into our reflective and humane age the policy by which 50 years ago it was thought legitimate to overawe and exhaust discontented provinces."

By October, with fighting still intense, the Czar instituted savage reprisals. Polish populations of whole towns were deported to Siberia. Captured patriots were executed; their fathers too. Honoring these dead was prohibited. By a Czarist order of October 27 posted in Warsaw it was declared that "mourning, and in general every revolutionary sign in dress, is forbidden. Women, without respect to station, occupation, or age who after 10 November appear in mourning will be arrested and fined." The fines ran from ten rubles imposed on a woman wearing a black dress while walking, to one hundred rubles for a black-clothed woman driving in a carriage, to the loss of a month's salary for any official whose wife appeared in mourning.

But Polish women defied the order. On a single night in November forty-one women were arrested in Warsaw; girls of fifteen were imprisoned in the citadel. To strangle resistance, the Czar at the approach of winter prohibited the importation into Poland of furs, shoes and boots.

By December a year of the revolution had not seen its end. Arrests were unceasing, with 103 persons imprisoned in Warsaw in a day. In Lithuania the Russian governor, Muraviev, ordered his troops not to take prisoners and won for himself the name of "the hangman." General Berg horrified the world by his massacre of Poles at Fishau. Demonstrating against these atrocities, crowds gathered in London, Paris, Vienna. Napoleon III called from Paris for a conclave of emperors to seek a means of peace and, failing, prepared France for war. But the Czar was impervious to appeals, to representations from the Pope, to threats of armed intervention by France, England and Austria.

Little of this news trickled through to the Korzeniowskis in exile. Little of it reached the countryside of Russia—newspapers there discounting the massive Polish insurrection as the spitfire movement of a few hotheads—where Tolstoy on his estate of Yásnaya Polyána wondered about "the Polish business." He, thirty-five, had been married a year. The first of his thirteen children, his son Sergius, was born in the June that saw Union and Confederate troops converging for the Battle of Gettysburg. A happily married man, a new father, Tolstoy was occupied with his immense estate, "the bees, the sheep, a new orchard, and the distillery." Yet he was writing. He published *The Cossacks* and the serf's story *Polikoúshka* in 1863, completed two plays, *The Nihilist* and *The Infected Family,* which he never published, started his unfinished novel *The Decembrists.*

With the Polish revolution still on, with impatient Russian serfs in revolt—his own serfs, reflecting the country-wide discontent, had refused to cut the hay—Tolstoy began the laborious research of his six years' work on *War and Peace.*

"I am in the dumps and am writing nothing, but work painfully," he wrote to his friend A. A. Fet. "You cannot imagine how hard I find the preliminary work of ploughing deep the field in which I must sow. To consider and reconsider all that may happen to all the future characters in the very large work I am preparing, and to weigh millions of possible combinations in order to select from among them a millionth part, is terribly difficult. And that is what I am doing."

Meanwhile in St. Petersburg Dostoevsky's journal *Time* carried an article judged favorable to Poland and in 1863 the Russian Minister of the Interior suppressed the paper on the charge that its policy was "contrary to the intentions of the government and to Russia's interest."

The journal was never issued again. In its short two years it had won wide recognition largely for the installments of Dostoevsky's *The House of the Dead,* the novel in which he told of his own experiences in a Siberian prison, of what it had meant to be sentenced to exile.

Chapter V

◇◇◇◇◇◇◇◇◇◇◇◇◇◇◇◇◇◇

. . . the Punch of my childhood . . . with his spine broken in two and his nose on the floor between his feet; his legs and arms stiffly spread, in that attitude of deep despair—so pathetically comic—of toys thrown in a corner. He had no phosphorous; I know, for I licked all the paint from his scarlet cheeks, kissed, and even bit, his nose many times without being any the worse for it. He was a true friend. He heard my secrets sympathetically, regarding me with an affectionate eye. I say *an* eye because in the first days of our friendship I had put out the other one in a fit of mad tenderness. Yet he seemed never to give it any thought, for fear of causing me pain. He was a gentleman. . . .

—*Letter of Joseph Conrad to Marguerite Poradowska.*

There were twenty-one Polish exiles in Vologda, troubled and homesick men. Conrad was the only child. To the Korzeniowski log house they came to see a child, to see a Polish wife, one of the "great martyrs who had voluntarily followed their husbands" whom Dostoevsky described. Apollo, strengthened by the presence of his family, bolstered the spirits of the group and became their leader.

Conrad was a frail and sober boy in a world cut off from everything familiar, a child with no playmates. His only friends were the dejected men with bushy beards, permeated with melancholy, never far from despair. For a companion less dour the small boy turned to the wooden Punch with the painted face. The memory of his childhood loneliness was still vivid when, a seafaring man of thirty-four, he recalled it in a letter to his aunt, Marguerite Poradowska.

The Korzeniowskis suffered from extreme poverty in Vologda. What little money they lived on was sent by Evelina's brother Casimir who, without letting the rest of the family know of it, sent them all he had. The funds of the other exiled Poles, many of them priests, were as meager. Existing in a small, tight band, knowing too little Russian to talk to anyone in the town, they shared food, fuel, their talk of home.

"As a rule Polish exiles are not oppressed, but the position is awful for those who have no private means," Alexander Herzen wrote of his Siberian exile. "The government gives those who have nothing *fifteen rubles a month;* with that they must pay for lodging, food, clothes, and fuel. In the bigger towns, in Kazan and Tobolsk, it is possible to earn something by giving lessons or concerts, playing at balls, drawing portraits and teaching dancing. In Perm and Vyatka they had no such resources. And in spite of that they would ask nothing from Russians."

The Polish exiles he saw were political prisoners sent by Czar Nicholas I, men who had been deported in chains to remote towns, often waiting out the years in solitude. The people of the Russian countryside, showing them neither hatred nor goodwill, considered them outsiders. Peasants were "always on the side of those who are punished. The word 'convict' disappears near the Siberian frontier and is replaced by the word 'unfortunate.' In the eyes of the Russian peasant legal sentence is no disgrace to a man. The peasants of the Perm Province, living along the main road to Tobolsk, often put out kvass, milk, and bread in a little window in case an 'unfortunate' should be secretly passing that way from Siberia."

The son of a wealthy Russian nobleman, Herzen was a twenty-two-year-old student at the University of Moscow when he was arrested and, after six months in prison, was exiled for his manner of thinking "in opposition to the spirit of the government," being "imbued with the pernicious doctrines of Saint Simon." His wealth and high family connections spared him the treatment Dostoevsky received.

Dostoevsky was a writer in St. Petersburg, already the author of *Poor Folk, The Double,* and *The Landlady,* when he took part in the meetings of a literary group who criticized the Czar. For that he was arrested, held in prison for eight months, prepared for execution in a macabre jest of Czar Nicholas I, and at twenty-eight was sent in chains to Siberia. He was to do hard labor for four years at the fortress of Omsk, followed by six years as an infantry soldier in a labor battalion at Semipalatinsk. At Omsk his head was shaved, he was dressed in convict clothes, and, working with chains on his feet, spent the days carrying heavy loads of bricks in winter weather forty below zero. Each night he was locked up in a barracks filled with thieves, counterfeiters, murderers.

"We were squeezed in like herring in a barrel," he wrote his brother. "In vain did we put ten logs in the stove, there was no heat (ice could hardly melt in the room), only unbearable smoke. The convicts washed their clothes in the rooms, and there were puddles of water everywhere, one did not know where to set one's foot down. From nightfall till day it was forbidden to go out for any excuse whatsoever, and at the entrance a bucket was placed for the purpose you may guess; all night long the stench was suffocating. The convicts stank like pigs. . . . Two bare boards served us as beds. For blankets we had only our short coats that left our feet uncovered; all night long we shivered from cold. The bedbugs, lice, and other insects could be counted by the bushel."

With Dostoevsky in the prison at Omsk were four Polish

exiles. They included a professor of fifty who, for protesting "we are not bandits, we are political prisoners," received a hundred blows with a stick.

Life for Polish exiles was less harsh in Vologda. Though they had neither enough food to subsist on nor work to fill their days, they were treated with moderation by the governor of the city. Largely through Apollo's influence and Evelina's "uncommon gifts of mind and heart which compelled the respect and admiration even of our foes," the Polish group lived apart, unmolested outsiders. Poverty and the rigorous climate, as severe as that of the Yukon, supplied a greater punishment than the police could give.

Winter in the north closed in early. The men of the exiled band were weakened by scurvy and Evelina's health broke totally under the thin diet, the penetrating and frigid air. Conrad played in silence by the bedside of his mother as she lay ill with tuberculosis. For the sake of his wife's health Apollo appealed for a change of exile to a warmer climate, to Chernigov, where she would be nearer her family. The Korzeniowskis waited in the hopes of that release.

But the winter months like a frozen block of time disappeared slowly. Snow fell from an overburdened sky in the unrelenting cadence of a clock beat. The crunch of runners carried into the house from the white blurred streets outside. From the frozen Vologda River, used as a road in winter, the jingle of sleighbells drummed through the cushion of the never-ending storm. Sledge drivers called their insistent warnings.

"Beware! Beware!"

Answers floated back and the cries in the muffled air were like the foghorns of ships giving notice at sea.

" 'Ware, 'ware!"

At the family table suet candles perished in lazy flame as the Arctic nights passed in the North's long hours of darkness.

Another season came. Thawed days, alike "as one drop of water is like another drop of water," merged into spring. Spring closed the circle of a year in Vologda. July brought the change of exile to Chernigov, 120 miles north of Kiev, and summer under a cheerful sun gave Conrad "the very happiest period" of his life when, on a three months' leave with his mother, he lived on his uncle's Ukraine estate.

Chapter VI

◇◇◇◇◇◇◇◇◇◇◇◇◇◇◇◇◇◇

CONRAD was a boy almost six at harvest time. The great unfenced fields were yellow with ripened grain. Women with kerchief-bound heads moved through the fields reaping; sheaves were pitched onto carts as horses, waiting command, shrugged off flies; grain spurted out under flails on the threshing floor. Evening sounds reached the big house: of peasant girls singing on their way home from the fields, of cows lowing at late milking time, of dogs barking in the village as they herded sheep running in wooden gallop to their home gates.

Conrad rolled in the grass stippled with clover and dandelions on the wide lawn in front of the house at Nowofastow. On drives with his uncle through the "gentle and powerful breath of the indolent steppe" he caught the dark fragrance of the woods, of the heat of carriage horses fluffing the dust of the road. He saw the sun set, a clear red ball lowered over the edge of the plain as it would one day look setting at sea.

For three months he had the companionship of children near his own age. After tumbling about with them outdoors, he was scrubbed by Francesca and taken to the drawing room where his grandmother sat behind the samovar and his mother smiled at the boy growing hardy.

These far-stretching acres where Conrad spent the happiest months of his childhood were lands Thaddeus Bobrowski had inherited from the Volhynia estate of his father and to which he had added adjoining property recently purchased. By this summer of 1863 Thaddeus Bobrowski's estate of Nowofastow included limitless miles of grain fields spread out "as big as a world," streams dammed into long and placid lakes, acres of oak forests threaded with birches, stables where servants wore the livery of tailless dark blue coats and full Cossack trousers, peasant villages of white thatched huts that lay tucked into folds of the plain "like clusters of boats hidden in the hollows of a running sea."

On a rise overlooking lands that had been in the Bobrowski family for more than a hundred years stood the main house with its eight columns supporting the long front veranda. Conrad shared that part given over to the women and the single child of the family, to the maids, nurses, and the governess who looked after her. Off the stone-paved hall with its high stove of white tiles was the big drawing room where guests gathered during sunny days and candlelit evenings. Beyond it was the game room with its massive English billiard table. On the further side of the sweet-smelling orangery were the private apartments of the widowed Thaddeus, his study-bedroom and library where he kept his pipe stand and Turkish *chibouk*.

His only child Josephine was a few months younger than Conrad. She was a quick-tempered little girl whose mother had died at the time of her birth and, cared for since like a royal princess, had a household of three personal attendants of her own. Francesca, a tender-hearted and round-figured woman who had been in the service of the Bobrowski family for thirty years, was the head *gouvernante*. A peasant woman, the former wet nurse, took charge of Josephine outdoors. Mlle. Durand, a Frenchwoman with homely features and a complexion "like pale-brown paper," was the governess. Conrad shared the same care as his cousin, his constant playmate. He took his lessons with Josephine in the upstairs schoolroom and learned both to speak and read French when he was less than six during the three months Mlle. Durand concocted games for him and the frisking little girl in her red tartan skirt.

It was a whole world within itself at Nowofastow, off in the wide country on the road between Berdichev and Kiev, an eight hours' drive from the nearest town and that town far from any railroad. Carriages brought a continuing traffic of visitors and with a boy's eagerness Conrad hung about the stables. His grandmother's coachman Joseph allowed him to hold the reins of the four horses harnessed in double tandem, and outside the coach house let him play with the long four-in-hand whip he flicked them with while driving. With Joseph at the pony's head and his mother watching from the colonnade beyond the dining-room windows, he took his first ride on horseback in a careful walk through the grounds.

As the nephew of the master and the only boy of the family, Conrad was treated like a young lord, coming to know by sight all the peasants of the village, "the grave faces with long mustaches of the heads of families, the downy faces of the young men, the faces of the little fair-haired children, the handsome, tanned, wide-browed faces of the mothers seen at the doors of the huts." The peasants were then buying the plots they had lived on for generations, paying Thaddeus Bobrowski as Tolstoy and other landlords were being paid a quit-rent at the rate of thirty rubles a year.

For the first time in his life Conrad's days were merry and active and he ate with a boy's hunger in the large dining room where servants passed steaming dishes, ate his fill of freshly baked bread, yellow butter, meat pies, radishes, all the greens of the garden, the milk and cheese of the dairy, the meat of beef, pigs and sheep raised on the estate.

Nowofastow was a boy's paradise. The summer days sped by under a warm sun and ran into the crisp days of fall. One evening at dusk when the drawing room was still unlighted the police captain of the district drove his troika along the road from the village and through the great gates of the drive. The dust cloud of his coming signaled the end of the only carefree time the boy was to know.

Because of ill health Conrad's mother had been allowed to leave Chernigov in August, to take Conrad with her to her brother's estate in Volhynia. Doctors had frequently called to see her there; they held out little hope of her recovery.

Toward the end of her exile-leave she became too ill to travel the 250 miles back to Chernigov. Thaddeus petitioned Governor-General Bezak in Kiev to permit her, a desperately ailing woman under no charge and no sentence, to remain with him another two weeks. The petition was refused. The police captain's orders from Bezak instructed him to ignore any plea of her illness "and if she has not left her brother's house on the morning of the day specified on her permit, you are to dispatch her at once under escort, direct to the prison-hospital in Kiev, where she will be treated as her case demands."

On the November morning her permit expired Evelina, concealing her illness from her son, walked to the waiting carriage with its four post-horses and drove with Conrad back to exile in Chernigov. She died a few months later, on April 6, 1865, at the age of thirty-four. Conrad, at seven, took care of his melancholy and brooding father whose health and spirits were shattered by his wife's death.

For a year father and son lived a hermit existence in a small house at the edge of town. It was a year made more bleak by famine. On Tolstoy's estate somewhat north the crops were withering in the drought where, he wrote, "that evil hunger-devil is already at work, covering the fields with goose-weed, chafing the hard heels of the peasants and their wives, and cracking the hoofs of the cattle."

In the old tenth-century river port of Chernigov bordering the Pripet Marshes, Conrad was shut away from the wide fields, knowing only the back yard he and his father shared with their landlord. When Apollo was well enough he spent full days in silence, translating French and English literature into Polish, work which brought him so little he was forced to rely on relatives for financial support.

When his father was ill in bed Conrad read aloud to him. At eight he read the proofs of his father's translation of Victor Hugo's *Toilers of the Sea,* his first introduction to the life he was to follow. Reading those proofs from beginning to end, he performed to his exacting father's satisfaction. At the same age, a small boy still in the black blouse of heavy mourning, he made his first contact with English literature through his father's translation of Shakespeare's *The Two Gentlemen of Verona.* On an afternoon when he should have been out playing he stopped in the room where Apollo did his writing.

"What emboldened me to clamber into his chair I am sure I don't know, but a couple of hours afterward he discovered me kneeling in it with my elbows on the table and my head held in both hands over the MS. of loose pages," Conrad wrote in *A Personal Record* forty-six years later. "I was greatly confused, expecting to get into trouble. He stood in the doorway looking at me with some surprise, but the only thing he said after a moment of silence was:

" 'Read the page aloud.'

"Luckily the page lying before me was not overblotted with erasures and corrections, and my father's handwriting was otherwise extremely legible. When I got to the end he nodded, and I flew out-of-doors, thinking myself lucky to

47

have escaped reproof for that piece of impulsive audacity."

Apollo translated other plays and verse which Conrad as a small boy saw in proof, among them Alfred de Vigny's *Chatterton,* Shakepeare's *Much Ado About Nothing, As You Like It, A Comedy of Errors, Othello.*

At forty-five Apollo thought of himself as a man in his old age. Saddened by a grief for his wife that never lessened, he tried to bring himself to send his son away from the gloomy house where the sight of his despair might "freeze and wither" Conrad's young heart. But a year passed before he could brace himself to the loneliness a separation from his son would bring. Finally, in May, 1866, he sent Conrad for a five months' stay with his Uncle Thaddeus on the estate that had the only permanence and warmth of a home the boy ever knew. When his grandmother took him back to Chernigov in September to the house where his father sat for hours in brooding silence, Conrad became so ill as to require weeks of medical care in Kiev. Convalescing from that illness, he went again to Nowofastow, to the white land of winter where the great lawn was "as pure and smooth as an alpine snowfield."

On a cold morning there in January, 1867 Conrad slipped out of the schoolroom, the less daring Josephine staying behind, and crept through the house. With a nine-year-old boy's eagerness he was looking for the head forester, due at that hour to make his daily report, and to hear from him a new tale of the sensational wolf prowling the neighborhood. Instead of the forester Conrad bumped into his uncle and Prince Roman Sanguszko on their way through the billiard room. The Prince had come the night before and Conrad, his nose glued to the dark windowpane, had seen his big sleigh with its six horses arrive. Two stable boys with road torches—balls of tow and resin blazing in iron baskets at the end of long sticks—had earlier been sent out along the snow tracks to meet him and light his way back.

The Prince had been a comrade-in-arms of Theodor

Korzeniowski during the 1831 Polish insurrection. He had been captured and sentenced for life to the Siberian mines but after fourteen years, physically disabled and stone deaf, had been allowed to return to Poland. He had remained a close friend of Conrad's grandfather and of the family. From their stories of the romantic patriot Conrad was to write his "Prince Roman" forty-four years after meeting him on truant leave in the billiard room.

Throughout the spring and summer of 1867 Conrad stayed for the last time with his uncle, grandmother and cousin Josephine at Nowofastow. Leaving those lands in the Ukraine in September, when he was nearing ten, he was not to visit them again for twenty-three years. That fall he lived in Zhitomir with his grandmother Bobrowska who, ceaselessly using all the influence she could draw on to secure Apollo's release, finally succeeded. His six years of exile ended in January, 1868.

Though only forty-eight, Apollo was a shattered man too ill to travel far. He had been given a passport valid for one year to go to the warmer climate of Madeira, but he could not use it. Taking Conrad with him, he spent three weeks convalescing with relatives and friends in the Ukraine before settling down in a two-room apartment in Lwow, in Austrian Poland. There Poles had comparative liberty and were allowed to speak their own language. Conrad, at ten, went to his first school. He was a high-strung, nervous boy. After a few weeks he became too unwell to continue and Apollo kept him at home, tutoring the boy himself. The bitter hurt of exile, the wasted years and the disastrous cost of his political beliefs spilled over in a letter Apollo wrote to his friend Stefan Buszczynski.

"My main purpose is to bring up Conrad to be neither a democrat, aristocrat, demagogue, republican, monarchist—or a servant or lackey of any of those parties—but only to be a Pole."

In his short half-term at school Conrad had his first lessons in geography and became acquainted with the world maps which were to fascinate him all his life. Looking at a map with the blank space of the Belgian Congo which Dr. David Livingstone was then exploring, he put his finger on the unmarked heart of Africa and with a ten-year-old's daring told himself:

"When I grow up I shall go *there*."

Chapter VII

✧✧✧✧✧✧✧✧✧✧✧✧✧✧✧✧✧

Two candles shed a circle of wavering light on the small table where Conrad, his head propped in his hands, sat hunched in the tangled position of a boy reading. The high-ceilinged drawing room was bare and silent. On Cracow's narrow Poselska Street, the old house at number 136 was out of earshot of the hoofbeats of city traffic; inside, voices were lowered to funereal murmurs.

In the drawing room, dark beyond candle range, the tall white door facing Conrad was closed. At intervals nurses passed through it walking on tiptoe. They rarely spoke. Books lay about in the disarray of new tenants, Conrad and his father having but lately moved from Lwow.

The year in Lwow following his release from exile had been one of constant sickness for Apollo. Hoping to be well enough to work and intending to join the editorial staff of the newspaper *Cjaz* (the *Times*), he had brought his son to these rented rooms in Cracow. But, in an advanced stage of tuberculosis, his health had failed rapidly. Conrad, a boy of eleven spending solitary evenings after school in the house where his father lay dying, read to escape the terrifying hush.

"I don't know what would have become of me if I had not

been a reading boy," he wrote in *Notes on Life and Letters*. "My prep finished I would have had nothing to do but sit and watch the awful stillness of the sick room flow out through the closed door and coldly enfold my scared heart. I suppose that in a futile, childish way I would have gone crazy. But I was a reading boy. There were many books about, lying on consoles, on tables, and even on the floor, for we had not had time to settle down. I read! What did I not read! Sometimes the elder nun, gliding up and casting a mistrustful look on the open pages, would lay her hand lightly on my head and suggest in a doubtful whisper, 'Perhaps it is not very good for you to read these books.' I would raise my eyes to her face mutely, and with a vague gesture of giving it up she would glide away."

From his father's books strewn over the room the frightened and lonely boy who later in the evening would "go to bed, in a room at the end of the corridor, and often, not always, cry myself into a good sound sleep," opened a French edition of Captain McClintock's diary of a voyage into the Arctic begun in the year Conrad was born. The explorer had sailed up Baffin Bay along the coast of Greenland in the *Fox*, a small ship "of 170 tons burthen," in a new attempt to solve the mystery of the disappearance of Sir John Franklin.

Franklin had arrived in the Arctic seas north of Canada in 1846 with an exploring party of 129 men in two British ships, *Erebus* and *Terror*. They had never been heard of again, though for a decade British and American explorers in more than forty expeditions continuously hunted for some trace of them. McClintock solved that riddle of polar exploration's greatest tragedy and told of his two frozen-in winters of search in *The Voyage of the "Fox" in the Arctic Seas*. It was a grave report already ten years old to the world but in the 1869 evenings of early spring it was a new and exciting tale to the boy reading.

Blanking out the sight of the closed white door and

thoughts of his father lying beyond it in the stiff pose of fatal illness, Conrad read of men adventuring in a region of walruses, white whales and Eskimos within the Arctic Circle off the coast of Greenland. He read how the *Fox* on its way north in the winter of 1857 was caught in the pack ice of Melville Bay and drifted helplessly south for 1,385 miles, a backwards voyage lasting 242 days which McClintock despairingly recorded. When warm spring currents released his ship McClintock resailed the bay made dangerous by fog and prowling icebergs. More than two hundred ships had previously perished in those waters and in them the *Fox*, at the end of its long life many years later, was to be discarded, a crumbling relic other sailors were to see still on a Greenland beach in 1950. Off that coast, and on the route Robert E. Peary was to follow to discover the North Pole in 1909, McClintock wrote of the frequent sight of polar bears. Conrad, with a boy's racing imagination, buried himself in the explorer's story.

A native of Upernivik, one dark winter's day, was out visiting his seal-nets. He found a seal entangled, and, whilst kneeling down over it upon the ice to get it clear, he received a slap on the back—from his companion as he supposed; but a second and heavier blow made him look smartly round. He was horror-stricken to see a peculiarly grim old bear instead of his comrade! Without deigning further notice of the man, Bruin tore the seal out of the net and commenced his supper. He was not interrupted; nor did the man wait to see the meal finished.

Cracow and its confining world of sickness vanished for Conrad in the substituted world of a book. Reading McClintock's account of the prized Eskimo dish of young dog, he recalled the story often wheedled out of his grandmother, of the dinner of dog in a Lithuanian woods eaten by his great-uncle Nicholas Bobrowski during the Napoleonic retreat from Moscow. A story-hungry boy always, Conrad was held spellbound by McClintock's Arctic adventures—tales of seal hunts, of dogteam trips over the ice, of snow villages, of igloos hastily built when night fell on the white wasteland.

He read on to the last entry in the "Narrative of the Discovery of the Fate of Sir John Franklin and His Companions," a book the nursing nun had not thought suitable for a boy. McClintock, thawing ink with which to write his diary as he sat aboard the ice-embedded *Fox,* told of the end of the Franklin party. In a stone cairn on King William Island was the single sheet of paper that explained the fate of Franklin, the first discoverer of the Northwest Passage who had died on his ice-locked ship before he could make his discovery known. McClintock had come upon the discarded clothes, guns and food of the remaining 105 men of the expedition. He had found three of the skeletons, the animal-gnawed bones of men sickened by scurvy who "fell down and died as they walked" in their hopeless attempt to reach some settlement north of Hudson Bay.

Conrad, at a time when "almost each day of my schoolboy life had its hour given up to their company," read other books of explorers. With his father growing more terrifyingly ghostlike in his illness, he spent evenings poring over books that told of strong men walking through the deserts and the jungles, of canoeing on tropical rivers and the Great Lakes of Africa.

"It was only right that, grown to a boy's estate," he wrote in "Geography and Some Explorers," "I should have in the later 'sixties done my first bit of map-drawing and paid my first homage to the prestige of their first explorers. It consisted in entering laboriously in pencil the outline of Tanganyika on my beloved old atlas, which, having been published in 1852, knew nothing, of course, of the Great Lakes. The heart of its Africa was white and big."

He read of three Scottish explorers in Africa, James Bruce, who searched for the source of the Nile and traveled down that river from Gondar to Cairo in 1771; Mungo Park, who

was exploring the Niger River in 1805 when his party
attacked in their canoes by hostile natives and slain; D
Livingstone, who discovered the Zambesi River in 1851
in the 1869 year of Conrad's reading, was even then in
Congo, a man of fifty-six still searching for the source of
Nile.

From those boyhood impressions Mungo Park rema
for Conrad "a young, emaciated, fair-haired man, clad si
in a tattered shirt and worn-out breeches, gasping pair
for breath and lying on the ground in the shade of an
mous African tree (species unknown), while from a neigh
ing village of grass huts a charitable black-skinned won
approaching him with a calabash full of pure cold wa
simple draught which, according to himself, seems to
effected a miraculous cure."

David Livingstone, whose death in the Congo four
later was to make a lasting impression on him, always
to Conrad "an old man with a rugged, kind face
clipped, grey moustache, pacing wearily at the head of
black followers along the reed-fringed lakes towards th
native hut on the Congo head-waters in which he
clinging in his very last hour to his heart's unappeased
for the sources of the Nile. That passion had changed
his last days from a great explorer into a restless w
refusing to go home any more."

At bedtime Conrad, who was also to become a
wanderer refusing to go home, put away the book
ventures experienced by sturdy men older than hi
and leaving that vigorous story world returned to
one of sickness that had surrounded him for mos
eleven years of his life. In a nightly ritual he woul
into the sick-room to say good-night to the figure
the bed, which often could not acknowledge my pre
by a slow movement of the eyes, put my lips dutifu
nerveless hand lying on the coverlet, and tiptoe o

On an evening late in May Apollo had himself lifted from bed and propped up with cushions in an armchair while he supervised the burning of his manuscripts. The following day, May 23, 1869, he died at the age of forty-nine.

The city of Cracow turned out to honor the man who had won fame as a patriot. In the funeral procession eleven-year-old Conrad walked alone behind the hearse, followed by a long file of schoolchildren, delegates from the University, representatives of all classes of Polish society. Dry-eyed, with his face made more pale by the black suit of mourning, Conrad led the cortege to the tomb where a plaque bearing the signature "His Compatriots" was erected to his father, dedicated "to the man who loved his country, worked for it, and died for it."

Apollo had survived his wife four years, years of unrelieved mourning. More than half of that time Conrad had lived alone with him. The enduring imprint made upon him by that desolate period showed in Conrad's letter to Edward Garnett, written thirty years later, when he described his father as "a man of great sensibilities; with a terrible gift of irony and of gloomy disposition; withal, of strong religious feeling, degenerating after the loss of his wife into mysticism touched with despair."

Conrad, who, as his grandmother wrote, took care of his father up to the last moment "with most tender solicitude," was left an orphan in a strange city. His grandmother and Uncle Thaddeus placed him by his father's wish in a private boarding school, the Pension Georgeon, where his teachers praised him for his intelligence and application, describing him as a child easy to teach, with an exceptionally generous nature.

Still a nervous, fragile boy suffering from severe headaches and stomach ailments, he was taken by his grandmother to Bohemia for the summer. When school began again in the fall she moved to Cracow to watch over his health.

In 1870 a family council selected two legal guardians for the boy—his grandmother, Mme. Bobrowska, and Count Ladislas Mniszek, a cousin of the Count Georges Mniszek who twenty years before had become the son-in-law of Balzac. His Uncle Thaddeus, a practical, unromantic man "of clear thought and warm feeling," became Conrad's personal guardian, looking after his nephew with affectionate care. For twenty-five years, until his death at sixty-six in 1894, Thaddeus Bobrowski was a father to Conrad, becoming even more closely attached to the boy after the loss of his fifteen-year-old daughter Josephine in 1873.

Thaddeus was the favorite brother of Conrad's mother and, a sober-minded and earnest law student at the University of St. Petersburg, had dreamed of a great career. But in his early twenties, his father had died and he had returned to the Ukraine to look after his mother's large properties. A conscientious landowner respected for his sound judgment, he acted as guardian for many orphans of Polish landowning families in the neighborhood around him, commencing more than thirty years of foster-fatherhood in 1860. For Conrad he was "the wisest, the firmest, the most indulgent of guardians, extending over me a paternal care and affection, a moral support which I seemed to feel always near me in the most distant parts of the earth."

Conrad, who had had but a few scattered months of schooling when he entered the Pension Georgeon, was behind other students in Latin and German. To help him with his studies Thaddeus Bobrowski selected a tutor, a young student of philosophy at the University of Cracow, Adam Pulmann. He tutored the boy, a good student in mathematics and history but not in grammar, for the next four years.

In memory of his father the municipal council of Cracow gave Conrad, a boy of fifteen, the freedom of the city, a honor that exempted him from all taxes. The praise giv his patriot father in that ceremony on December 28, 1 found an echo in the Marquis's eulogy of Cosmo's father in the last book Conrad was to write, the unfinished *Suspense*.

"In the austerity of his convictions your father was more like a republican of ancient times . . . Your father understood every kind of fidelity . . . He was a scornful man . . . Yes. *Un grand dédaigneux*. He was that. But one accepted it from him as one would not from another man, because one felt that it was not the result of mean grievances or disappointed hopes."

The honor given Conrad by the city of Cracow carried with it his future naturalization as an Austrian subject. His grandmother and Uncle Thaddeus looked forward to that and to having him continue his studies in Vienna or at the University of Cracow, where Copernicus had studied astronomy in the fifteenth century.

But when he was fifteen Conrad told his family for the first time of his secret wish to go to sea, a dream that, fed by his reading, had been growing for two or three years. His announcement brought a storm.

"At first like those sounds that, ranging outside the scale to which men's ears are attuned, remain inaudible to our sense of hearing, this declaration passed unperceived," he recalled his boyhood crisis in *A Personal Record*. "It was as if it had not been. Later on, by trying various tones, I managed to arouse here and there a surprised momentary attention—the 'What was that funny noise?' sort of inquiry. Later on it was: 'Did you hear what that boy said? What an extraordinary outbreak!' "

His uncle made a special trip to Cracow from the Ukraine to talk the boy out of his notion and, after exhaustive, fruitless sessions, called a truce.

When spring came Conrad was sent south on the advice of his doctor and for three months in 1873 traveled with his tutor through Germany, Switzerland, Austria and Italy. Pulmann had been instructed to discourage the boy's insistence on a sailor's life, a romantic folly that "stirred up a mass of remonstrance, indignation, pitying wonder, bitter irony, and downright chaff" from his scandalized and astonished relatives.

His tutor relentlessly argued with Conrad against his odd choice, attacking it in railway trains, on lake steamboats, on the mountain paths of Switzerland as they hiked over the Furca Pass. Conrad "listened to him in despairing silence, feeling that ghostly, unrealized, and desired sea of my dreams escape from the unnerved grip of my will." But a hardy old Englishman passed the two climbers as they sat with their knapsacks resting on the mountain trail and the "unextinguishable and comic ardor of his striving-forward appearance" helped Conrad to take heart. Pulmann gave up the argument, calling his fifteen-year-old charge a hopeless Don Quixote, and Conrad's choice of the sea was partially won.

Late that summer they returned to Cracow and Conrad, spending September with cousins in Lwow, felt the tormenting pangs of first love for a girl who was able to make him suffer and "let herself go to her heart's content." He survived that agonizing teen-age love but felt "seamed, scarred, almost flayed," and told himself "if that's it then never, never again."

But the following September, a lanky schoolboy of sixteen again visiting relatives in Lwow, he fell in love with his eighteen-year-old cousin, Tekla Syroczynska. She was an austere girl, "an uncompromising Puritan of patriotism with no taint of the slightest worldliness in her thoughts." Conrad was only one of the boys who idolized her, a dedicated young patriot, one of the few left in a city that had become prudent and bourgeois. The political atmosphere had changed and Poles were reacting against revolutionary ideas.

Conrad passed his end-of-term examinations, completing five and a half years of formal schooling—all he was ever to have. Because of his father's tutoring he was more advanced in literature and history than other students his age, but he refused to go on with his studies. He was nearing seventeen and persisted in his determination to go to sea. He had caught sight of it but once, at Venice, when he and Pulmann saw it from the outer shore of the Lido on the previous school holiday of travel.

With the obstinate determination of a youth to be on his own, Conrad finally won consent to enter the "mysterious vocation" that seemed so out of place in the land-locked Polish provinces. Though he was unable then, at sixteen, to explain the pull of the sea and the open, unimprisoned contest it offered, when he was sixty-six he defined it in "Geography and Some Explorers."

"How much preferable a region of storms where man and ship can at least put up a fight and remain defiant almost to the last."

His Uncle Thaddeus bought Conrad a railroad ticket to Marseilles and on October 26, 1874 he left Cracow, never returning to live again in Poland. His grandmother and uncle, still lamenting his going, saw him off at the station. He also parted with the girl, his second love, to whom he had never confessed his feelings.

"That afternoon when I came in, a shrinking yet defiant sinner, to say the final good-bye, I received a hand-squeeze that made my heart leap and saw a tear that took my breath away. She was softened at the last as though she had suddenly perceived (we were such children still!) that I was really going away for good, going very far away."

In an old city washed by the first sea ever traveled, Conrad was not only to find his seaway to the world but to know a stormy love. From that love affair he went away, very far away, and in the mood of "never, never again" became a wanderer of the sea for nearly twenty years.

Chapter VIII

◇◇◇◇◇◇◇◇◇◇◇◇◇◇◇◇◇◇◇

The whole recollection of that time of my life has such a peculiar quality that the beginning and the end of it are merged in one sensation of profound emotion, continuous and overpowering.

The Arrow of Gold

The mistral, the hard dry wind from the mountains, charged down the Rhône Valley. Unblunted by the hills it swept the streets of Marseilles, strummed the closed shutters of the Cannebière, scoured the cobblestone alleys of the Old Town, blasted through the wide and fashionable Prado, rasping the bare branches of the sycamore trees. It came, an imperious and relentless wind of hurricane force which old heads maintained would stand in its habitual sequence, blowing for three days, or six, or nine.

With the mistral howling the night was cold even for December. Carriage horses, pulling victorias along the Cannebière, leaned against the wind, their tails spreading in stiff fans as seaweed feathers when sucked by the tide. Broughams and fiacres rolled to a stop before the gaslit cafés crowded with women in long ruffled and bustled skirts, with men in the high-buttoned jackets, tight trousers and fashionable beards of 1874. New arrivals held their hats, their coat-tails flying, as they walked against the furious gale. Gay with the excitement of the wind, shivering in the harshness of it, they crossed the wide avenue through whirls of scuttling dust. Occasionally a lady's hat, clawed free by the wind, soared and tumbled down the street, its plumes flouncing in the nervous movements of a bird uncertainly settling.

Conrad left the café evening crowds and walked down the Cannebière toward the Vieux Port. Gas lamps gave a pale glow to the streets. Some were noisy beacons jangling in darkness, their flames extinguished by the wind. As he reached the Quai du Port, his head down bunting the wind, he passed the file of sailing ships moored in the harbor.

The deserted quays looked very white and dry in the moonlight, and as if frost-bound in the sharp air of that December night. A prowler or two slunk by noiselessly; a custom-house guard, soldier-like, a sword by his side, paced close under the bowsprits of the long row of ships moored bows on opposite the long, slightly curved, continuous flat wall of the tall houses that seemed to be one immense abandoned building with innumerable windows shuttered closely. Only here and there a small, dingy café for sailors cast a yellow gleam on the bluish sheen of the flagstones. Passing by, one heard a deep murmur of voices inside—nothing more.

Scenting the wide quay was the pungent smell of cargoes brought in bales and bags and casks from remote harbors—copra from New Caledonia, wild rubber from the Amazon, coffee from the Red Sea, licorice from Turkey, palm oil from West Africa, rice from Java, wines from Algeria, grain from Odessa. There was the tang of cinnamon bark, of peanuts, and the musty smell of hemp, a dry aroma the harbor had known when Greek mariners from Phocaea settled the town in 600 B.C., naming it Massalia, giving their word for hemp, *cannabis*, to the Cannebière.

In the Vieux Port, shaped like a teardrop squeezed from the Mediterranean, clippers, schooners and brigantines crowded the quays, emitting the subdued rumble of never-resting ships fidgeting like migrating wild geese bedding for the night. Hawsers tightened under the strain of tethered ships and creaked in the stuttering cry of ropes gripping. Waves spanked against the black-painted hulls, shouldering them high. The tap of rigging, passed like a signal from one moored ship to another, reiterated along the wharf. The rocking masts of ships lunging with the swell pointed skyward in staccato gestures, now to this cold star, now that.

Rising above the basin was the weatherbeaten brow of the Old Town, a rabbit warren of twisting canyons ten feet wide, a labyrinth more ancient than the kasbah of Algiers. Stone steps, built on climbing paths already worn when eleventh-century Crusading knights embarked there for the Holy Land, made furrows in the rocky hillside. Stray cats crept through the dark well-like alleys in search of fish refuse tossed from upstairs windows. In the tight stone honeycomb of the Old Town fishermen were asleep.

Conrad lived in a modest hotel near the quays of the Vieux Port, the Hôtel de Genève. In the two months since arriving from Cracow he had often gone out, as on this night, with the Marseilles pilots who boarded incoming ships beyond the breakwater. As a guest of the Corporation of Pilots, who manned the clock round in five companies covering pilot stations off the islets of Monte Cristo and Château d'If, he was free to go on any of their boats, in any weather, day or night. It was his first experience of the sea.

The twelve-hour turn of duty for the Third Company began at midnight. The big half-decked pilot boat waited for its crew in the little canal behind old Fort St. Jean, the Moorish-looking 1660 fort guarding the entrance to the harbor.

Conrad walked toward the canal along the Quai du Port in the night's stillness.

Not a footstep, except my own, not a sigh, not a whispering echo of the usual revelry going on in the narrow, unspeakable lanes of the Old Town reached my ear—and suddenly, with a terrific jingling rattle of iron and glass, the omnibus of the Jolliette on its last journey swung round the corner of the dead wall which faces across the paved road the characteristic angular mass of the Fort St. Jean. Three horses trotted abreast, with the clatter of hoofs on the granite setts, and the yellow, uproarious machine jolted violently behind them, fantastic, lighted up, perfectly empty, and with the driver apparently asleep on his swaying perch above that amazing racket. . . . I saw the tiny light of a lantern standing on the quay, and became aware of muffled figures making toward it from various directions. Pilots of the Third Company hastening to embark. Too sleepy to be talkative, they step on board in silence. But a few low grunts and an enormous yawn are heard.

The *patron* of the boat was the broad-shouldered brother-in-law of Baptistin Solary, a new friend of Conrad's and a jovial young Frenchman who had been a seaman before giving up that life for a better one ashore. In letters to Thaddeus Bobrowski before Conrad had left Cracow, Solary had promised to look after the boy and help him find a ship since he was bent on that *métier de chien*. But Solary had only managed to secure guest passage for Conrad on the pilot boats that sailed back and forth a few miles from shore, searching the horizon with long brass telescopes for the smoke or sails of ships needing conduct to the harbor. On the pilot boat of the Third Company Conrad was given the tiller, surrendered to him by the *patron* "in the same spirit in which the family coachman lets a boy hold the reins on an easy bit of road."

This night the pilot boat sailed within the usual bearings of its station, a mile or two west of Château d'If, whose white stone battlements had been built in 1524 to defend Marseilles against the Spaniards. For a century it had been famous for its dungeons, having had among its celebrated occupants the stormy Count Mirabeau and the Orléans prince, Philippe Égalité, imprisoned during the French Revolution. A new coloring of romance had been given the cells thirty years before when Alexandre Dumas *père* published *The Count of*

Monte Cristo, locking his Abbot Faria and Edmond Dantès in that dark prison.

At daybreak the pilots of the Third Company spotted the smoke of a far-off ship. They sailed toward it, a big, powerfully rigged cargo steamer. Conrad volunteered to pull bow in the dinghy to put the pilot on board and as the boat bumped against the steamer he touched the *James Westoll,* "the first English ship on whose side I ever laid my hand," and heard the first English ever addressed to him—a deckhand's call of "Look out there!" as he threw down a rope for Conrad to catch. As the *James Westoll* steamed off for Marseilles he watched her break out her flag, the "Red Ensign—the symbolic, protecting, warm bit of bunting flung wide upon the seas, and destined for so many years to be the only roof over my head."

For two months, off and on, Conrad went out with the pilots. Unable to secure a job and anxious to be at sea, he embarked as a passenger on the 22-year-old *Mont-Blanc* on December 11, bound for Martinique. Although his first Christmas night at sea was spent in a Gulf of Lyons gale, he made an otherwise unremembered crossing and returned to Marseilles on May 23, 1875. A month later, on June 25, he sailed on his first ship as a member of the crew, an apprentice on the *Mont-Blanc,* a three-masted sailing ship of 394 tons, again bound for the West Indies. The "old, weary, disenchanted sugar-wagon" was a leaky ship "extremely disposed to open out and swallow up as much salt water as she could hold." Aboard her, Conrad's initiation to a life at sea occurred in the stormy year, 1875, that saw 593 lives lost in three major shipwrecks. Only a month before the *Mont-Blanc* left Marseilles in June, the *Schiller* went down near the Scilly Islands with 200 aboard.

In the battered old ship Conrad learned the force of a gale, listened to "the song of the wind in a ship's rigging." The *Mont-Blanc* lumbered across the Atlantic, taking thirty-six days to reach Martinique. During two hot and rainy summer months Conrad saw something of the tropics—ravines dense with shoulder-high ferns, Negro girls in bright sarongs, their gold earrings flashing in the sun as they carried baskets of linen on their heads to a stream "overhung by the starry fronds of palm-trees."

From St. Pierre the *Mont-Blanc* put in at Guadeloupe, at St. Thomas in the Virgin Islands, at Haiti's north shore port of Cap Haitien, crossed the Gulf of Mexico to New Orleans —Conrad's first, short glimpse of a United States harbor. From Haiti the *Mont-Blanc* returned to France with a cargo of logwood, a heavy red wood giving the black, brown and blue dyes used in calico printing. She reached Le Havre on December 23, 1875 badly damaged by storms she had come through, storms which took the lives of 157 passengers in the sinking of the *Deutschland* at the mouth of the Thames. With his ship laid up in Le Havre for repairs, Conrad boarded the train for Marseilles, his enthusiasm for the sea unchilled by the heavy weather of his six-month voyage.

From the islands where he had seen a "multitude of humming-birds, whose delicate wings wreathed with the mist of their vibration the tops of flowering bushes," he came back to a land where humming-birds—40,000 arriving from the tropics in a single shipment—were *de rigeur* for ladies' hats. He reached Marseilles in the first days of 1876, a time when the "Aesthetic Movement" was taking hold in France, inducing women to abandon both monochromes and restraint. In gowns of reds, sea greens, ink-blues, women appeared in hues as vivid as those of the Impressionists who were the talk of Paris. They wore, in flagrant sex attraction, small ornamental aprons they unabashedly called "fig leaves," wore "mermaid tail" trains, donned peignoirs for the afternoon tea hour, appeared in the cuirass bodice with its corset-like suggestion of the unfinished toilette of the bedroom.

Conrad, an impressionable eighteen, came by chance into that fashionable world.

Chapter IX

◇◇◇◇◇◇◇◇◇◇◇◇◇◇◇◇◇◇◇

IT WAS the year in which the title of Empress of India was conferred on the 57-year-old Queen Victoria, halfway through her long reign; it was the year of the first world's fair in America, the Philadelphia Centennial Exposition where ten million people celebrated the hundredth anniversary of the Declaration of Independence and, in a British exhibit, saw bicycles for the first time. It was the year of the famous last stand of General Custer in the Montana battle of the Little Big Horn, with Custer's command annihilated by twelve hundred Sioux warriors under Chief Crazy Horse. Finally, 1876 brought the end of four years of civil war in Spain and exile for "the King."

The exile of "the King" overshadowed all other events in Marseilles and led Conrad to the most romantic adventure of his life.

Through his regular calls at the offices of C. Delestang & Son, bankers and shipowners, to collect the monthly allowance sent by his Uncle Thaddeus, Conrad made the acquaintance of a sober, provincial couple, Monsieur and Madame Delestang. The banking office was on the ground floor of the Delestang residence, on a shady side street at 3 rue d'Arcole, and like the living quarters upstairs, was permeated with an atmosphere of Royalism.

To Conrad, Monsieur Delestang was "such a frozen-up, mummified Royalist that he used in current conversation turns of speech contemporary, I should say, with the good Henri Quatre; and when talking of money matters, reckoned not in francs, like the common, godless herd of post-Revolutionary Frenchmen, but in obsolete and forgotten écus—écus of all money units in the world!—as though Louis Quatorze were still promenading in royal splendor the gardens of Versailles, and Monsieur de Colbert busy with the direction of maritime affairs."

M. Delestang was an influential banker and the owner of two sailing ships, one, the *Mont-Blanc,* on which Conrad had made his voyages to the West Indies. A bloodless man who was "born about fifty years old, all complete, with his iron-grey whiskers and his bilious eyes, which he had the habit of frequently closing during a conversation," he found it hard to believe in Conrad's youth, or to forgive it. Impeccable banker that he was, he yet financed unlawful gunrunning in the interests of "the King."

Madame Delestang came of an old aristocratic family of the Midi, a lineage giving her a social status higher than her husband and one furnishing her with the rank of hostess to a certain social set. She held a *salon* in her home where the name of Louis XIV was frequently mentioned, all it shared with that first *salon* of the Marquise de Rambouillet to whose home had come such eminent guests as Corneille, Mme. de Sévigné, La Rochefoucauld. The one attendant at Madame Delestang's *salon* whose name carried through time was a youth, Conrad, whom she condescendingly advised not to fritter away his life with the wrong people, in his wrong vocation of the sea.

Madame Delestang had the imperious quality of the arrogantly scornful Lady Honoria Dedlock of Dickens' *Bleak House.* Toward Conrad, who had chosen the less than aristocratic career of becoming a seaman, she was aloof, receiving him in the *grande dame* manner of haughty boredom. Yet when socially prominent guests gathered for her *salon* she fluttered from one to another, dropping crumbs of scandal with the lowered eyes and hushed voice of discretion. She drove in her carriage along the Prado at the correct hour for promenading, drives she occasionally invited Conrad to share. Since his social credentials were satisfactory, she conferred upon him the benevolence of her *salon,* exposing him to the talk of Royalists. To Monsieur Delestang the Royalist cause bore the aspect of a Crusade, but to his wife it was a roster of significant names, titled personages working for "the King."

Madame Delestang's *salon* was held in what Marseilles called "the company room," which, in the provinces, was an austere reception room reserved for formal affairs. Ornate and airless, the typical "company room" in 1876 Marseilles was furnished in the cold and ugly style of Napoleon I. Long, heavy drapes of dark red tapestry hung in rigid canopies around the windows, subduing the strong Mediterranean sunshine to a dusky light. Leather-upholstered mahogany seats of Pompeiian style and discomfort formed martial lines against the walls, where guests stiffly sat on winter days unthawed by two warming stoves that flanked the unlit fireplace and shed a tepid heat. On the white marble mantelpiece a towering symbolic figure eternally gamboled in a bower of artificial flowers eternally fresh under glass domes. A marble-topped table holding the coffee service, an upright piano never opened, gold-framed engravings on the walls of standard scenes—"Hippocrates Refusing Gifts from Artaxerxes," "The Awakening of the Sabines," "Cornelia, Mother of the Greeks," "The Oath of the Horatii" —showed in the gloomy light thrown by the gas lamp chandelier. A widow's veil of metal mesh drooped from the lampshade, effectively blocking out the light.

In other Marseilles *salons* bustled women, corseted in basque gowns of the fashionable tones of *cendre de rose* grey, Mexico blue or Grenat burgundy, sipped coffee from gold-rimmed porcelain cups as they listened to poetry readings or talked of art or of politics with men whose beards bore the modish Dundreary or "mutton chop" trim. But in Madame Delestang's *salon* a sedate and elderly group talked only of politics, the politics of Royalists who nostalgically harkened back to the more elegant days of kings. At eighteen, Conrad was by far the youngest of her guests, young enough to be excited by a lost cause when, on February 27, 1876, "the King" crossed the frontier into France, a defeated claimant to a throne.

"The King," as he was unfailingly called in Legitimist circles, was Don Carlos, Duke of Madrid, Pretender to the Spanish throne. A direct descendant of Louis XIV, he had a large following among Bourbon supporters in France, a following which grew vociferous in 1883 when his uncle, the Count de Chambord died, making Don Carlos—geneologically—the legitimate heir to the thrones of both France and Spain.

Don Carlos was Europe's last Royal Prince to fight for a crown and in that uneasy role was an explosive force for thirty years. From 1868 to 1898 he was an actual or potential challenger to the government of Spain and an exile so thorny as to be repeatedly expelled from France. His last opportunity to reach for the so-elusive crown came in 1898 when the fear that the Carlists might rise if Spain bowed to America without a struggle prompted the government of the Queen Regent to embark upon the Spanish-American War, a war Spain had little hope of winning.

Long as his prominence lasted, when Don Carlos died in Italy on July 18, 1909 the news of the end of Europe's uncrowned "King" was eclipsed by an occurrence that inspired the new century with awe. A young man of twenty-eight named Orville Wright won the headlines then by remaining aloft in his airplane for 80 minutes, doing 86 turns of the field at Fort Meyer, cutting figure eights and zig-zagging at the incredible height of 100 feet.

Democracy was new to France—the Third Republic was but a year old and the country's future form of government was still in challenge—when the second Carlist War began in Spain in 1872. It was still in full swing when Conrad reached Marseilles in 1874 and ended only after the last Carlist stronghold of Tolosa fell in 1876. Marseilles all that time was the shipping center for Carlist arms. For a year and a half, through the Delestangs and acquaintances he made there, Conrad heard the cause of Legitimacy, as Carlism was referred to on both sides of the Spanish frontier, fervently endorsed. Carlist supporters were numerous not only in the north of Spain, in the Basque provinces, Catalonia and Navarre, but across the south of France from Bayonne to Nice.

The Carlist cause was an old one in Spain, having become an issue in 1833 when Ferdinand VII died, leaving no male heir. By the Salic Law's stipulation forbidding succession to females, the throne should have descended to the King's brother, Carlos. But Ferdinand on his deathbed set aside the Salic Law and named his three-year-old daughter, Isabella II, as his heir. Carlos immediately challenged the succession of his infant niece and for six years, until 1839, fought the first and unsuccessful Carlist War. His grandson, Don Carlos, took up the challenge in 1868 when Isabella was deposed, and in 1872 began the second Carlist War against his fifteen-year-old cousin Alfonso XII, Isabella's son.

Entering Spain in July, 1873 to take personal command of his troops, Don Carlos established Royal Headquarters, his *Quartel Real,* at Tolosa and with the battle cry of "God, Fatherland and King!" directed his army of 38,000 through three more years of civil war against the 85,000 forces of Alfonso.

In France, and especially in Marseilles where Conrad heard awed reports of the *Quartel Real* in Madame Delestang's *salon,* a romantic aura encircled Don Carlos, a handsome young man of twenty-seven, a Royal Prince rapturously referred to as "the hero of a hundred battles." So glamorous was the descendant of a long line of monarchs—tracing back through Spanish rulers from his great-grandfather Charles IV to Charles III, to Philip V, the grandson of Louis XIV and the first of the Spanish Bourbons—that few artists in France failed to solicit the honor of painting him and for two or three successive years the Salon in Paris was deluged with his portraits.

A big man of rugged health, with a Jove-like beard and an Olympian carriage, Don Carlos was less of a god than his adoring public knew. Far from being a Caesar in Spain, he demanded ceaseless entertainment. Hardly a day passed at Tolosa without its festivities of state dinners, banquets and balls at the *Quartel Real* while battles were being fought in fields safely far away. A surfeited Prince with few illusions, he had a royal scorn for all mankind, regardless of position.

Much of his time at Tolosa was spent playing with his pet wolf cubs and monkeys, it being his caprice to tame wild animals and train them to command. While conducting his campaign in Spain he received a gift of a wolf, a tame and toothless beast named Ferdinand which Don Carlos trained to run after peasant girls, snapping at their petticoats. One evening after a banquet at Tolosa he had the wolf let into the dining hall. Ladies fainted, generals and colonels ran in search of their arms as it jumped on the tables and ran wild among the dishes. Don Carlos particularly enjoyed, by his own telling, the screams of his principal supporter, a wealthy marchioness who had given two sons and large contributions to his "cause."

Another of his amusements at Tolosa while the war was going on was one he termed his "tallow banquet." Cubing a tallow candle into potato soup, he invited some innocent to join him at the meal. No one refused so great an honor as dining with "the King." Serving himself first and taking the potato, he watched with delight while others swallowed the candle bits and turned ill on the diet.

These were the traits which led the London *Times* to say of

Don Carlos that "his personal habits, which he did not think necessary to keep private, appeared to be gross," and for *The New York Times* to call him "a worthless Pretender."

But at the time Don Carlos crossed the border into France to take up exile he was greeted everywhere with adulation. He settled down in Paris in the spring of 1876, taking a Pavilion in Passy at 49 rue de la Pompe, a house famous in society and a gathering place for Carlists, aristocrats and artists who flocked around the man who bore the titles of Charles VII of Spain and Philippe V of France, though he never ruled.

Around that Pavilion, where he lived with his wife and five children, Don Carlos gathered his supporters. As a direct descendant of Louis XIV, he reminded French aristocrats, dissatisfied with the new Republic, of the days of "Le Grand Monarque" when Versailles and the Invalides were built, when the gardens of the Tuileries and the Champs Élysées were laid out, when such figures as Corneille, Molière, Racine, Descartes, Saint-Simon, La Fontaine and Pascal gave Paris one of the most brilliant intellectual periods in its history. Monarchists were also drawn to the Pavilion through the wife of Don Carlos, Margaret de Bourbon, niece of the Count de Chambord, whom Don Carlos had married when he was nineteen, and through whom he acquired an enormous fortune.

The religious supporters of Don Carlos supplied his most potent force, the clerical party of extreme Right-wing Catholics sustaining Carlism because, in their eyes, it was the incarnation of the pure traditions of Spanish monarchy, putting religion first, enemy of all concessions to liberalism, insuring above all else the interests of the faith. Those followers, more dominant in Spain than France, more numerous in the Basque provinces than in the cities, sought a return to the days before Martin Luther when there was but one Church and that one loyal to the Pope.

The Carlists, with their reactionary program and international intrigue, were allowed to live unhindered in republican

France through the toleration shown them by Marshal Mac-Mahon, President of France, whose family sympathies were Legitimist. In Marseilles, particularly, they operated openly, with arms and supplies leaving that port for the Carlist groups that held out in Spain until 1882, when the last of them disbanded. Though the end of Carlist hopes for the throne came in 1936 with the death of Don Jaime, only son of Don Carlos, the Carlist movement did not die even then in Spain. In the Spanish civil war of 1936-39 Carlists formed a strong wing of Franco's forces, though not all Carlists fought on his side.

It was not so much his motto of "God, Fatherland and King!" which won Don Carlos his support in the north of Spain and the south of France, nor even his religious crusade. He championed the Home Rule aspirations of the Basque provinces and that regionalism was as strong a unifying force as the states-righters had made it a decade earlier in America's Civil War. In such an atmosphere in Marseilles Conrad found that "most of my acquaintances were legitimists and intensely interested in the events of the frontier of Spain, for political, religious, or romantic reasons. But I was not interested. Apparently I was not romantic enough. Or was it that I was even more romantic than all those good people? The affair seemed to me commonplace. The man was attending to his business of a Pretender."

Yet he went to homes other than the Delestangs where Don Carlos, entering France as a defeated Pretender, was the topic of the day. He was at the *salon* of a wealthy Marseilles hide-and-tallow merchant when "the possibility of raising Catalonia in the interest of the *Rey netto,* who had just then crossed the Pyrenees, was much discussed."

Though the Carlist campaign ended in the first months of 1876, it had come close to success. After overrunning Catalonia, Aragon and Valencia and winning the important Navarre battle of Estella in 1874, Don Carlos's failure to march on to Madrid was a result of his chronic indecision. With his fiery Basque fighters undaunted, his supporters expected another and not-far-distant try for the crown. The excitement of this future sally spread through Marseilles, catching up adventurers like young Conrad. In the heat of the 1876 flurry around him he thought of joining the Carlist forces, for the thrill of it, but his Uncle Thaddeus threatened to stop his allowance if he made such a move and Conrad dropped that plan.

Meanwhile other friends with other interests turned his attention to excitement in another field. As the young dandy which he was in part, he had a corner table always reserved at the Café Bodoul, a de luxe restaurant at 18 rue St. Ferréol known for its *paté de tuna*, ices, and *déjeuners à la fourchette*. It was on the corner of the rue Pavillon, a street filled with the warehouses of orange importers and foreign consulates. A clientele composed of consuls and the carriage trade of Marseilles, a large part of whom were Legitimists, came to this sedate and sumptuous restaurant in the downtown heart of the city. There Conrad, "the Count" as his sailor friends called him, handed over his hat and stick, deferentially greeted by the *maître d'hôtel*, Baptiste.

In addition to the supporters of Don Carlos, Conrad made friends in two other circles, all three groups having an important effect upon his life. Never out of touch with the sea, he kept in contact with the people of the Old Town, pilots and seamen, but spent a large part of his time with Marseilles' painters and poets. His own talent as an artist drew him to a Bohemian circle, "not very wide—half a dozen of us led by a sculptor whom we called Prax for short. My own nick-name was 'Young Ulysses.' I liked it."

Chapter X

◇◇◇◇◇◇◇◇◇◇◇◇◇◇◇

THE meeting place of the Bohemian set in Marseilles was the Café de l'Univers, a restaurant and café at 19 rue Cannebière, opposite the Place de la Bourse. Conrad ate his midday meals there or at the Café Bodoul, at lunch having "the choice of two places, one Bohemian, the other select, even aristocratic, where I had still my reserved table in the *petit salon,* up the white staircase."

Painters, journalists, poets, sculptors, writers and musicians gathered at the Café de l'Univers which was frequently "riotous with more than one 'infernal' supper" in the dining room upstairs. To the clink of beer and wine glasses and through a never-ending fog of tobacco smoke arguments rang out on art, politics, life, women, and the new perfect world ahead. Dean of the group by age and prestige was Adolphe Monticelli, painter of voluptuous Decameron scenes, of landscapes reminiscent of Watteau, whom critics named "the richest colorist of the 19th century."

Monticelli had achieved a promising start in Paris but when the Franco-Prussian War broke out he left the city in 1870 and walked to his birthplace, Marseilles, painting landscapes along the route during his thirty-six day trek. His 500-mile walk was still talked about six years later in the town where, a man of fifty-two with a luxuriant, grey-streaked, rusted beard, he was seen daily on the Cannebière and the quays of the Vieux Port. Although a thorough Bohemian and the least conventional of all, he had the manners of a grand seigneur, striking in his musketeer's salute as he greeted friends with a majestic lifting of his wide-brimmed hat, bringing it with a deep sweep to the ground. In his youth called *"beau* Adolphe," he was fastidious in his dress, wearing a velvet coat as a mark of the elegance he admired.

His love of elegance led him to clothe his models in satin dresses, with their caught lights reflected in his rich oils; it led him to crowd his studio with rare *objets d'art,* with fine stuffs opulent in texture and tone; it came out in the composition of work called "as infallibly decorative as a Persian crock or a Japanese brocade," in landscapes hailed as "magic countrysides full of musical vibrations and penetrating perfumes."

By 1876 Monticelli, a heavy man, had grown more careless in his dress. His famous velvet coat was splotched with paint, for the great artist, whose *Court Ladies* and *The Court of the Princess* were one day to hang in New York's Metropolitan Museum, had begun the decline into the fantastic though august vagabond, the half-mad, poor and neglected artist he was at the end of his life.

During his last sixteen years, Monticelli made the Café de l'Univers his headquarters, appearing there each day. The café owner, Monsieur Boyer, supplied him with meals and money, accepting in exchange such a large number of paintings as to acquire one of the great Monticelli collections.

Undoubtedly it was Monticelli whom Conrad described in *The Arrow of Gold* as taking his defence in 1877 against the young artists in the café who chaffed him for his mysterious disappearances at sea, showing "a certain amused tolerance" for his Royalist adventures.

I owed this tolerance to the most careless, the most confirmed of those Bohemians (his beard had streaks of grey amongst its many other tints) who, once bringing his heavy hand down on my shoulder, took my defence against the charge of being disloyal and even foreign to that milieu of earnest visions taking beautiful and revolutionary shapes in the smoke of pipes, in the jingle of glasses.

The dean of the Bohemians whose own work was called "painted music" gave his defence of young Conrad in words the novelist was to recall forty years later.

That fellow (*ce garçon*) is a primitive nature, but he may be an artist in a sense. He has broken away from his conventions. He is trying to put a special vibration and his own notion of colour into his life; and perhaps even to give it a modelling according to his own ideas. And for all you know he may be on the track of a masterpiece; but observe: if it happens to be one nobody will see it. It can be only for himself. And even he won't be able to see it in its completeness except on his death-bed. There is something fine in that.

Along the quays, where Conrad, too, spent so much of his time, Monticelli walked and painted, singing and joking in the artless, good-hearted fashion which caused the waterfront to give him the affectionate nickname of "Fada," "the innocent one" or "fool."

Another Marseilles artist in the Bohemian set Conrad knew was Raymond Allègre. The same age as Conrad, he was a student at the Marseilles École des Beaux-Arts. Allègre was born in Marseilles, in the Old Town, on the narrow, noisy street of the rue Longue-des-Capucins where his family had lived for generations. A small, slender man with wavy dark brown hair and lively dark brown eyes, Allègre had the swarthy look of a Saracen or Berber, an appearance inherited from an old Moorish strain. In his older years he wore the same pointed beard as Conrad and bore some resemblance to him. They left Marseilles in the same year but Allègre's rise to fame was more rapid. He won the Raigecourt-Goyon Prize in Paris in 1893, the year in which Conrad was working on *Almayer's Folly*.

Allègre had the same love of the sea as Conrad and made his name from such Marseilles seascapes as *Entrance to the Port* and views of Venice canals. His portraits of women included *The Huntress Diana* and *The Samaritaine*. He had an atelier on the Place Boiëldieu, near the Bourse in Paris, well known for years. In that atelier filled with rare bibelots, priceless tapestries and antiques, Allègre received an elite Parisian society like a patrician. Exhibiting in Paris from 1881 to 1932, Allègre knew all the good fortune and the recognition that passed Monticelli by. Like Monticelli, Allègre returned to Marseilles in his last years, living in the old house on the narrow alley of the Old Town where he was born. He died there in 1933 at the age of 76. Although his paintings were still bringing high prices in Paris in 1939, the popularity of his Venice scenes dwindled and his fame may last longest through a book, *The Arrow of Gold,* in which Conrad borrowed his name.

Another of the Bohemians whom Conrad at eighteen knew in Marseilles was a young poet and journalist, Clovis Hugues. He was one of the earnest minds at the Café de l'Univers taking "revolutionary shapes in the smoke of pipes." Although Conrad found himself linked with a Royalist circle through a *coup de coeur,* he heard the views of the Delestang *salon* counteracted at the café by such radicals as Hugues. Following the precept of his father to be "neither a democrat, aristocrat, demagogue, republican, monarchist—or a servant or lackey of any of those parties," Conrad listened to all shades of political opinion in Marseilles, developing into the judicious observer who could dismiss "the vociferations of idle fanatics extolling this path or that." His adult freedom from prejudice had its roots in the days when, exploring among men, he knew equally well sailors, Royalists and Bohemians. Like an actor taking three parts he went from one group to another, fitted with a hat and stick for the *"petit salon,* up the white staircase," with the red pompon cap and rough woolen shirt of a sailor. From that mingling, begun in Marseilles, came his final creed: "Class for me is by definition a hateful thing. The only class really worth consideration is the class of honest and able men to whatever sphere of human activity they may belong—that is, the class of workers throughout the nation."

Among the Bohemians in Marseilles the broad-faced Clovis Hugues was to have a career most spiked with drama. Six years older than Conrad, Hugues was born in Castellet, near the Vaucluse town of Ménerbes, a few miles from Marseilles. Son of a miller, Hugues had gone to Marseilles in his late teens to become a journalist, had written a revolutionary leaflet in defence of the Paris Commune in 1871 and, then twenty, was sentenced to four years in prison.

When Conrad met him in the early months of 1876 he was on the Marseilles socialist paper *L'Égalité,* in November becoming chief editor of *La Jeune République* and in the same month marrying a beautiful young sculptress in a civil ceremony. The following year Joseph Daime of the Bonapartist paper *L'Aigle* printed a slur on women married by civil ceremony. The slur was intended for Hugues's wife and Hugues challenged Daime to a duel with swords. The duel was fought in Marseilles on December 3, 1877. Daime was killed, a death for which Hugues was tried and acquitted on February 21, 1878.

Conrad was in Marseilles at the time of the duel, fought so shortly before his own. But he had left France when Hugues entered politics, elected to the French Chamber of Deputies as a socialist in 1881, continuing to serve with little interruption until 1906. Although Hugues was strongly socialist he was an independent, attached to no organization, who advocated "one world," a world of humanity and peace. Both politician and poet, Hugues wrote verse—*Les Soirs de Bataille, Les Jours de Combat, Le Temps des Cerises*—praised by Victor Hugo.

In 1883, when Hugues was a member of the Chamber of

Deputies, he was involved through his wife in *L'Affaire Morin,* a sensational case widely published in the Paris press. An unscrupulous lawyer, Morin, had attempted to extort blackmail from Mme. Hugues on a trumped-up scandal. He was brought to trial and convicted. As he was being led out of the courtroom under sentence Mme. Hugues shot and killed him. Public opinion was in sympathy with her; in her own trial she was exonerated.

Conrad was then in India, having arrived there as second mate aboard the sailing ship *Riversdale.* Long before that he had lost touch with Clovis Hugues, though he long remembered his poetry. In *The Arrow of Gold,* Conrad alluded to Hugues in a passage describing himself as a youth in Marseilles —"a young gentleman who had arrived furnished with proper credentials and who apparently was doing his best to waste his life in an eccentric fashion, with a bohemian set (one poet, at least, emerged out of it later)."

In the Marseilles of 1876 Hugues was a rising young poet, poets then starring in the intellectual life of the town, with poetry readings the favored form of evening entertainment. So highly was verse regarded in Marseilles that two squares owe their names to poets of that time—the Place Victor Hugo and the Place Victor Gelu, the latter a sailors' square named for Marseilles' folk-singing bard and "man of the people." Esteem for two politicians of the period caused two other thoroughfares—the Allées Léon Gambetta and the Place Jules Guesde—to be named for Gambetta, founder of the Third Republic, and Guesde, member of the Chamber of Deputies and the son-in-law of Karl Marx.

Conrad, with a poet father who had early instilled in him the feeling for cadence that was to mark all his writing, was drawn to the literary groups. Leading figures in them were Frédéric Mistral and Alphonse Daudet, both born in Provence, both then reaching the height of their fame.

Conrad, too young and unknown to be in the inner circle

of such a set, was an ardent admirer on the rim of it. "You know my worship of Daudet," he wrote to Mme. Poradowska in 1895 following the publication of *Almayer's Folly*. "Do you think it would be silly of me to send him my book—I, who have read all of his, under all skies? Not asking him to read it—just as an act of homage. For, after all, he is one of my youthful enthusiasms that has survived—even grown."

So much did the happy-hearted author of *Lettres de mon moulin* appeal to Conrad that in his warm essay in 1898 he wrote of Daudet as "a man as naïvely clear, honest, and vibrating as the sunshine of his native land. . . . Daudet did not whisper; he spoke loudly, with animation, with a clear felicity of tone—as a bird sings. He saw life around him with extreme clearness, and he felt it as it is—thinner than air and more elusive than a flash of lightning . . . the only thing he distinctly would not forgive was hardness of heart. . . . His creations are *seen;* you can look into their very eyes."

Although Daudet lived in Paris, he often came back to Marseilles during the years Conrad was there, finding it as hard as Monticelli and Allégre to break from his native Provence. On his homecomings he took part in boyish carousals with his friend Mistral. In an effervescence of high spirits, Daudet, whom everyone adored and whom Zola called "a charmer," teased the girls of the countryside and indulged in light-hearted pranks.

Daudet and Mistral were both members of the two art societies in Marseilles, as was Clovis Hugues. The older of the two, the Art Circle, had rooms on the rue St. Ferréol near the Café Bodoul where its members met to talk, give readings, exchange views and criticism on art and the politics of the day. As the majority of its members were painters—Monticelli and Allégre among them—it held an art show every year.

Mistral, awarded the Nobel prize for literature in 1904, was the leading poet of the Art Circle in 1876. The following year he was one of seven poets who founded the second cultural society in Marseilles, the *Félebres de la Mer,* a Provençal name meaning "the learned men of the sea." The group's aim was to revive Provençal as a literary language, to re-instate Provençal customs dating back to the troubadours, to encourage the wearing of the Provençal costume, painted by Van Gogh in *Arlesienne.*

Every seven years—the society placed a mystic value on the number seven—the *Félebres de la Mer* elected some Provençal beauty as Queen of the Floral Games, a fete in May inaugurating the Season of Roses. The first year the Queen was chosen, 1877, was a great event in Marseilles. For Conrad, linked as it was with his own love affair, the Season of Roses was the memorable time used in the ending of *The Arrow of Gold.*

Mistral was the leader of the *Félebres* and its greatest artist, first winning recognition in 1859 for his long Provençal poem *Mireio* upon which Gounod based his opera *Mireille.* During the three and a half years Conrad spent in Marseilles the tall, handsome Mistral with his Byronic appearance was the town's celebrity. Everyone read his poems—he gave repeated readings himself—and the infection of that time Conrad remembered when writing *The Mirror of the Sea* where he joined Mistral's name with august company, "Virgil, Homer, or Mistral."

Eighteen-year-old Conrad spent six months in Marseilles in one of the most glittering periods of its history, when any day on the Cannebière, two blocks from his hotel, he could meet men time would list as famous. Absorbing it all, he lived life fully—and expensively. By April, 1876, he had spent 1,200 francs, the whole of his allowance for eight months gone in three. He borrowed. By July another 1,569 francs were gone. In six months he had run through an allowance due to carry him for sixteen. With a room in the finest hotel costing but two francs a day, his flinging away of 2,769 francs was a sizable sum. His Uncle Thaddeus paid his debts and sent the sums Conrad desperately wired for, but he prepared a meticulously itemized account of the 6,219 francs squandered within two years by his free-spending nephew. In a letter written October 26, 1876—three months after the last of Conrad's July debts were settled, with the taste of them still rankling—he lectured Conrad on the high toll of his two years away from Poland.

Two years have gone by since the moment when, with a sobbing heart, Grandmother with tears, both of us with a blessing, we satisfied your wishes and let you go out into the world to fly on your own strength, though with our counsel and assistance. When you read this letter you will be nineteen years old, an age when one is already quite a youth, often earning one's own living and sometimes even that of one's family—at any rate an age when one is entirely responsible before God and men and before oneself for one's deeds!

At the time of our separation I took upon myself the duty of furnishing you with the means of support until such time as you would be able to provide them yourself, means which are modest but adequate and correspond to my income. . . . You, on the other hand, promised to use those funds carefully for the purpose of study, your own good and the good of your future! Well now, after two years let us see how each of us has responded to his duties. Answering this question will give us the opportunity to correct our mistakes, which we will find in our behavior, and will lead each of us to think about means of improvement in order to avoid them in the future!

The sum of 150 francs a month has been set aside for you; that is, 1800 francs allowance and 200 francs for extraordinary expenses —2000 francs a year; for two years—4000 francs . . .

I don't know whether you have ever, pencil in hand, added up what you have received from me in the last two years, on demand or without demand. I suppose you have not gone into these accounts too much, for if that were the case, what occurred would never have happened. . . . Briefly speaking: in the course of two years you have used up the maintenance *of the whole third year* with your mistakes!!!

Here is the naked truth, based on figures, which you will certainly not deny, since each of these expenses was caused either for you or through you. And now, my dear fellow, let us consider whether these expenses incurred by you are and were necessary, righteous and worthwhile??? As for the means? Perhaps you think that I can afford such extraordinary expenses for the love of my "dearest nephew"? But that is not the case. I have about 5000 rubles a year income, I pay 500 a year in taxes. Giving you 2000 francs I give you approximately 700 rubles, also 1000 rubles a year to your Uncle; so I give approximately one third of my income away. If I were to give you 300 rubles more a year (for two years ate up the third) I would have to deny myself underwear, shoes, suits—cut my personal expenses in half. Because for all this I have set aside 600 rubles a year in my budget, for the very important reason, namely, that I cannot have more, there is not enough for more.

Conrad knew a severe reprimand was in the wind, though he did not receive the above letter until his return to Marseilles from the Caribbean. Avoiding explanations of his vanished funds, he saved himself from deeper financial trouble by getting back to the sea.

On July 10, 1876 he sailed for the West Indies on M. Delestang's second and newer schooner, the *Saint-Antoine*, embarking on a ship that ran the risk of seizure.

Chapter XI

◇◇◇◇◇◇◇◇◇◇◇◇◇◇◇◇◇◇

Conrad's voyage on the *Saint-Antoine* was as flamboyantly romantic as a Dumas novel. On a sailing ship carrying illicit cargo he rode the old seaway of pirates. His schooner slipped into dark ports on surreptitious calls with hidden guns in her hold and dropped anchor off a fiery land crackling with revolution. It was a satisfyingly cloak-and-dagger adventure for an eighteen-year-old "Young Ulysses."

From that view of revolt in the tropics, where mine silver had replaced pirate gold as the violent metal, came *Nostromo* whose theme Conrad defined in a letter of March 7, 1923, to the Swedish professor Ernst Bendz.

Silver is the pivot of the moral and material events, affecting the lives of everybody in the tale. That this was my deliberate purpose there can be no doubt. . . . The word "silver" occurs almost at the very beginning of the story proper, and I took care to introduce it in the very last paragraph, which would perhaps have been better without the phrase which contains that key-word.

Silver was also the key-word in 1876 in the port of Cartagena.

When M. Delestang's small, six-year-old *Saint-Antoine* left Marseilles with Conrad aboard she was, ostensibly, outward bound for Martinique and Haiti, due to return loaded with logwood and sugar. But when she left France she was on a lawless mission.

After crossing the Atlantic in thirty-nine days and reaching St. Pierre, Martinique, on August 18, 1876, she sailed over the Caribbean, in an earlier time the home waters of pirates. For five weeks, before taking up her scheduled route again to St. Thomas and Port-au-Prince, she made secret stops along the coast of South America. In contacts with land which Conrad remembered were "short, few, and fleeting," she crept into several Venezuela harbors, including Puerto Cabello and La Guaira, and dropped anchor in Colombia's ancient port of Cartagena. Her concealed purpose was to carry contraband arms to the rebel side in a country exchanging its first shots in a bloody but short-lived uprising.

Cartagena, Queen City of the Spanish Main, was receiving smuggled arms for the revolution that broke out in Colombia the summer Conrad was there and the picturesque old city that had known a swashbuckling life in its more than three hundred years was living up to its buccaneering past. Lush tropical growth and high Cordillera mountains framed it in a setting unchanged since Spanish galleons left its harbor with gold. If the sound of fighting no longer rang out in the steel clash of cutlass duels, the whip of rifle shots carried their thrill for Conrad, a youth to whom everything in the fantastic Caribbean was "so fresh, so surprising, so venturesome, so interesting; bits of strange coasts under the stars, shadows of hills in the sunshine, men's passions in the dusk . . ."

The "passions in the dusk" were real in 1876. A decade of political contest in Colombia between Royalists and Republicans, between Tories and Liberals, exploded that year over a religious issue. Sixteen years before, the Liberals had secured the separation of church and state, had built non-religious public schools, had instituted civil marriages. Against those changes the Church had fought for, and won, concessions. In 1876, in a transatlantic echo of the Carlist War then ending in the former mother country of Spain, the clerical parties pressed their religious claims on a key issue. They demanded that the Church be given full control over education. The government refused. A tightly contested national election followed and the losing Right-wing parties took up arms.

Cartagena was a city dominated by wealthy Tories, according to U. S. Minister to Colombia William Scruggs, who were either secretly or openly Royalist. Unable to tolerate the free Negro, many of them left Colombia after 1863, moving to France where Royalists found life under Napoleon III more congenial. Others remained in Cartagena and fought the change to New World ways. When the national election of February, 1876, put in a Liberal again as President of Colombia—Dr. Aquileo Parra—the Right-wing parties attempted a forceful overthrow of the government. They sought French help, as thirteen years earlier the Conservatives in Mexico, losing ground to the Liberals, had maintained a temporary hold through the presence of French troops sent by Napoleon III. The empire of Maximilian, even so, had fallen in three years. With France a republic, the Tories of Colombia in 1876 were forced to rely on such aid as Royalist groups in France could give.

When the revolution broke out in the spring organized fighting centered in the more heavily populated part of the Republic, in Antioquia, south of Cartagena and near Medellín, spreading from there to the Cauca Valley. Two main battles were fought, Los Chances at Cauca—where three thousand government soldiers defeated four thousand rebels on August 31, 1876—and the final battle of Garrapata at Tolima. In the two-day battle of Garrapata, fought on November 20-22, 1876, the government's forces numbered five thousand against rebel troops of seven thousand. Although the revolution was quelled within six months, the government found itself moving ahead faster than its people were ready for and, adjusting to a slower pace, watered down its liberalism.

Conrad could have known little of the causes of the revolution, nor, in his short stay in the harbor of Cartagena, did he see much of it. What he learned at that time he drew from French-speaking sailors, for he knew neither Spanish nor English. But in the silver and gold mining center of Cartagena, where American and British interests were competing for concessions for mines and railways, where the French engineer de Lesseps was negotiating for the proposed Panama Canal, Conrad caught the tone of revolution and an insight into imperialism.

Added to his gunrunning experiences, which he recalled "had startled me a little and had amused me considerably," he also carried away from the Caribbean a story he heard "of some man who was supposed to have stolen single-handed a whole lighter-full of silver, somewhere on the Tierra Firme seaboard during the troubles of a revolution."

His story of modern sea theft along the Tierra Firme—the old map name for the Spanish Main, or mainland, of South America's northern coast—fitted the tradition of Cartagena, a city of adobe houses completely encircled by a stone wall thirty feet high and forty feet thick, built to protect it from buccaneers and pirates who during two centuries had raided it for bounty.

Ancestor stories of that capture of a lighterful of silver were common sea baggage in the Caribbean. Conrad could have heard then, or learned of it in later reading, of one that gained the widest world audience in its day—the exploit of Woodes Rogers, "he that took the Acapulco Ship." It dated back to a time one hundred and sixty-five years before Conrad sailed into Cartagena where Spain's great Plate Fleet had gathered. Of all the ports seen during those impressionable days of his youth Cartagena, redolent with a fantastic past, was least forgettable.

The harbor of Cartagena where Conrad anchored had natural defenses which had made it a key port in Spain's New World empire. It was seen by Columbus, settled by Spaniards in 1533. Impenetrable mangrove swamps, open shelterless beaches and the closed neck of the harbor made it a natural fortress and Cartagena was chosen as the vault for Spanish booty.

In spite of its hard defensive shell the attraction of Spanish gold caused it to be subjected to repeated siege. Sir Francis Drake plundered it in 1585; French buccaneers captured it in 1697, taking five million dollars' worth of gold in the raid. Each time its fortifications were rebuilt and strengthened, for it was a treasure house worth breaching when the gold of the New World was hoarded there to await the annual arrival of the Spanish Plate Fleet. No harbor in the Americas held as much wealth at one time as Cartagena when the Plate Fleet lay there, heavy with gold bullion.

All the galleons, those from Vera Cruz with Mexican and Philippine gold and those from Cartagena with South American bullion, met in rendezvous at Havana and sailed in convoy up the Gulf Stream between Florida and the Bahamas for the return to Spain. During those weeks pirates had been on the prowl and striking. Jamaica was a pirate's nest and on the island of Nassau a pirate republic flourished. Many pirates were rich but none made as large a single haul as Woodes Rogers, an English merchant seaman from Bristol who fitted out two private men-of-war, the 320-ton *Duke* and the 260-ton *Duchess,* and with their combined crews of 225 men set off in 1708 after Spanish gold.

Rogers sailed south from England, turned Cape Horn, sacked the fortified Spanish city of Guayaquil in Ecuador, and captured the annual "Acapulco Ship" on its way from Manila to Mexico. He brought the Spanish galleon and its immense treasure of £800,000 back to England in 1711. He brought back too a Scottish seaman, Alexander Selkirk, a castaway clothed in goatskins he had picked up on the uninhabited island of Juan Fernandez, 400 miles off the coast of Chile. Selkirk had been chief mate of the *Cinque Ports* and following a quarrel with Captain Stradling, master of the English ship, had been put ashore on the island where he had been marooned for four years and four months when Woodes Rogers found him.

"Immediately our Pinnace return'd from the shore and brought abundance of Craw-fish, with a Man cloth'd in Goat-Skins, who look'd wilder than the first Owners of them," Rogers told of Selkirk's rescue and his castaway's life in *A Cruising Voyage Around the World.* From that 1712 account of the marooned Scottish seaman Daniel Defoe wrote *Robinson Crusoe* in 1719. A year later Defoe published *Captain Singleton,* which may have given Conrad the name for the old seaman, Singleton, of *The Nigger of the Narcissus.*

When Conrad wrote *Nostromo* he was living at Hythe, one of the Cinque Ports of England. The group of maritime towns of Sussex and Kent—the original five ports being Hastings, Romney, Hythe, Dover and Sandwich—dated back to a time before 1066. The Cinque Ports had been chartered by Edward the Confessor, and before England had a permanent navy provided her with what naval protection she had.

In his dispirited days before beginning *Nostromo* Conrad felt "there was nothing more in the world to write about," and read widely, picking up old volumes in second-hand bookstores. One may have been Woodes Rogers's account, a well-known book repeatedly reissued. The name of Selkirk's ship indicating she was from the historic Cinque Ports region where he lived may have fused in Conrad's mind, joining the early days of sea highwaymen with his own Spanish Main adventures.

One seaman with Conrad in Cartagena, whom he was to draw as Dominic in *The Arrow of Gold,* as Peyrol in *The Rover,* as Nostromo in *Nostromo,* as Attilio in *Suspense,* and under his full name in *The Mirror of the Sea,* was Dominic

Cervoni, a Corsican of forty-two, one of the four officers of the *Saint-Antoine*. He had gone to sea at seventeen and had served on ships for twenty-five years when Conrad met him.

Dominic was a rugged, broad-chested, strong-hearted man "superior to all scruples and terrors." There was little he held sacred, least of all Custom-house laws. When Dominic, as Conrad wrote in *The Mirror of the Sea,* was "wrapped up in a black *caban,* the picturesque cloak of Mediterranean seamen, with those massive moustaches and his remorseless eyes set off by the shadow of the deep hood, he looked piratical and monkish and darkly initiated into the most awful mysteries of the sea."

Dominic spoke Catalan Spanish, Italian and the French of Provence, and in them volubly dismissed grandiose subjects and poses with characteristic irony. Sound and quick in judgment, he was taken in by nothing. Luck, he thought, was even better than courage, for it was "surer than wisdom and stronger than justice." He was a man ready for challenge with a "great experience of all unlawful things that can be done on the seas."

He took Conrad, his signorino, under his wing during the long months of the *Saint-Antoine* voyage. Dominic had been a smuggler when a youth no older than Conrad, and the *Saint-Antoine*'s smuggling of contraband guns appealed to his robust satisfaction in the challenging of law. Like Nostromo, he was a Man of the People. An untamed Corsican sailor whose independence was still crisp after a quarter of a century of seagoing, he had a "general scorn for the beliefs, and activities, and abilities of upper-class people."

What Conrad learned of the revolution in Colombia—where more than three-fourths of the population were Negro, Indian, and mestizo and where the men in battle on both sides were peons impressed into service—he heard mostly from the hardheaded Dominic, a man with a warm heart but few illusions. He, more than any man, had the greatest influence on Conrad's life though the contact between them lasted less than two years.

In contrast to that brawny man was Dominic's nephew, César Cervoni, a Corsican youth a month younger than Conrad, one of the three apprentices on board the *Saint-Antoine*. César was an extremely pale and lean boy who "seemed to have no more blood in him than a snail." His temperament fitted his anemic appearance, for he lied, he stole, he was impudent and lazy. A youth with an "utterly, hopelessly depraved nature," he was to bring both Conrad and Dominic to grief a year and a half later.

When Conrad sailed out of Cartagena in the summer of 1876 it was the last he ever saw of the steamy tropical town with its green backdrop of mountains, its red-tiled roofs and starch-white churches, its Negro children playing naked in the square, its markets of vivid tropical fruits and gaudy flowers, its charcoal cooking fires glowing outside palm-roofed huts, its people lazily moving in the stifling heat, talking a soft and curious jargon mixed from many tongues. Yet from that one short view of a city and a country whose wealth had drawn Spaniards, pirates, and the concession-hunting men of foreign business, he was to write one of his greatest books twenty-seven years later.

Nostromo not only told the story of a revolution in a fictional South American republic. It was Conrad's attack on imperialism, focused on the enormously valuable foreign property, Gould's San Tomé silver mine, which destroyed Nostromo and all who shared in making it the consuming giant it became.

Mrs. Gould saw it "hanging over the Campo, over the whole land, feared, hated, wealthy; more soulless than any tyrant, more pitiless and autocratic than the worst Government; ready to crush innumerable lives in the expansion of its greatness."

The mine became one of the financial enterprises of the San Francisco millionaire who could say of the republic of Costaguana that it was a "bottomless pit of 10 per cent loans and other fool investments. European capital has been flung into it with both hands for years. Not ours, though. We in this country know just about enough to keep indoors when it rains. We can sit and watch. Of course, some day we shall step in. We are bound to. But there's no hurry. Time itself has got to wait on the greatest country in the whole of God's Universe. We shall be giving the word for everything: industry, trade, law, journalism, art, politics, and religion from Cape Horn clear over to Smith's Sound, and beyond, too, if anything worth taking hold of turns up at the North Pole. And then we shall have the leisure to take in hand the outlying islands and continents of the earth. We shall run the world's business whether the world likes it or not. The world can't help it—and neither can we, I guess."

Conrad wrote his great novel in 1903-04 at a time of empire-building, when within five years occurred the Spanish-American War, the Boer War, the Russo-Japanese War, and the severance of Panama from Colombia. Like a morality play, the theme running through *Nostromo* was the poison of silver. Against the force of greed there was only one combatant, love —but "love was only a short moment of forgetfulness, a short intoxication, whose delight one remembered with a sense of sadness, as if it had been a deep grief lived through."

At the time of writing *Nostromo* Conrad was an established author, a man of forty-seven. Nearly thirty years had intervened between then and the summer when he sailed the Caribbean in the *Saint-Antoine,* meeting other men along the way whom he was to bring into other books.

He recalled meeting one on "an extremely small and extremely dirty little schooner during a four days' passage between two places in the Gulf of Mexico whose names don't matter." The little schooner could only have been the *Saint-Antoine* and the two places minor Colombian ports of call of the region, "in the Gulf of Mexico . . . off the Colombian coast" described in *Victory.*

94

On the schooner was a man traveling as the companion of an aged, well-off Spanish invalid who died the last night of the passage and was buried at sea. When not answering a summons from the "rich man," the cat-like attendant talked to Conrad, telling him some of the more shocking episodes in his scoundrel's life.

"For the most part he lay on deck aft as it were at my feet, and raising himself from time to time on his elbow would talk about himself and go on talking, not exactly to me or even at me (he would not even look up but kept his eyes fixed on the deck) but more as if communing in a low voice with his familiar devil. Now and then he would give me a glance and make the hairs of his stiff little moustache stir quaintly. His eyes were green and to this day every cat I see reminds me of the exact contour of his face."

When the schooner reached port the sinister storyteller left the ship with the dead man's many trunks and disappeared. Thirty-eight years later Conrad wrote him into the unsavory "connoisseur in gentlemen," Ricardo, in *Victory*.

The gaunt and satanic Mr. Jones of *Victory* was a character developed around a man Conrad also saw during the 1876 voyage of the *Saint-Antoine*. The little schooner left St. Pierre, Martinique, on September 23 and sailed to the Virgin Islands. There in a waterfront hotel on the island of St. Thomas, Conrad caught a glimpse of a professional gambler. He was a cadaverous-looking man, stretched out on three chairs having an afternoon nap while flies buzzed around him in the burning heat of the day. He was pointed out to Conrad as a desperate gambler traveling about the islands on mail boats, taking part in card games in which "up to a certain point" he would play fair. Conrad's only sight of him was when, his nap interrupted, "he got off the chairs brusquely and walked out leaving with me an indelibly weird impression of his thin shanks."

The third man in that evil trio in *Victory* was the Pedro

whom Conrad based on a man he saw for a short and explosive two minutes just after the *Saint-Antoine* arrived in St. Pierre from Marseilles. Conrad had walked into a wayside shack to buy a bottle of lemonade when the man who was to become the Pedro of fiction took an instant and venomous dislike to him. Conrad beat a hasty retreat but that exhibition of fury, and a similar one shown by a Negro in Haiti two months later, "fixed my conception of blind, furious, unreasoning rage, as manifested in the human animal, to the end of my days."

The hero of *Victory*, Axel Heyst, also grew from the *Saint-Antoine* voyage. In an unpublished letter of June 3, 1917 Conrad revealed that Heyst dated back to "my visual impression of the man in 1876; a couple of hours in a hotel in St. Thomas (West Indies). There was some talk of him after he left our party; but all I heard of him might have been written down on a cigarette paper. Except for these hints he's altogether 'invented.' "

While in the West Indies Conrad received from his Uncle Thaddeus the first of the long letters which were to reach him in a variety of ports during his twenty years of sea roving. They came from the man who took the place of his father, a man rigorously strict, with deep affection, but a constant scold. The tone of their reproofs carried in the September 27, 1876 letter delivered to Conrad while on his secret contraband adventure on the *Saint-Antoine*.

My dear boy,
Your letter, the second from Marseilles dated September 8-10, I received yesterday and although I answered the first not so long ago, just taking a chance, I write again although I have nothing new to say, but only to calm you in case my first letter missed you. I am in good health and you should get rid of all anxiety in that matter. I had not seen any merit in showering you with letters without having an exact address, or to write without being certain my letters would reach you. That is the whole secret of my silence; there is no anger in it at all. The question still remains whether my silence would constitute a

punishment for you. From what I read in your last letters I feel it could be. But that is not what I had been thinking of, quite the contrary. I believe it my duty to lead you by way of advice and reprimand on the right path, which is the path of reason and duty. That is what I am doing and will continue to do whenever the need arises. And if I should ever turn silent from "*anger*," which would depend entirely on you, then it would probably be forever. However, I do not even admit such a possibility. . . .

My dear, you have always made me impatient, and you did it with your carelessness and off-hand treatment of things, reminding me of the Korzeniowski family who always wasted everything, and not my dear sister, your mother, who always cared for everything. Last year you lost your trunk. What else was there to think about on your journey but yourself and your belongings? Do you need a governess, and why should I be one? Now you have again lost the family photographs and Polish books and you ask me to replace them! What for? So that you can lose them at the first opportunity? He who values an object also needs it. To this day I have a *paper picture* given me by my mother in 1829 when I left home for school for the first time. It has always been with me and I still have it as it was then. Why? Because I watched over this souvenir with my heart.

Conrad watched over his uncle's letters, carrying them with him everywhere, retaining them all his life, the only ones he consistently saved. He feared his uncle's disapproval enough to hide from him the Marseilles episode of his life and to the heroes of his future books he gave fathers equally stern who "could not be told."

On the *Saint-Antoine* Conrad left Port-au-Prince, Haiti and sailed back to Marseilles, arriving on February 15, 1877. His seven months' voyage to the West Indies and the Caribbean coast of South America gave him the settings and characters for future books, men sharply focused during the days of his youth, the key time of his life. His lasting fondness for Marseilles, and its importance to him, came out in a 1905 letter to John Galsworthy in which he referred to his 1874 arrival in the port—"in Marseilles I did begin life 31 years ago! It's the place where the puppy opened his eyes."

For Conrad his youth was a "care-free and fervent" time. "It is the privilege of early youth," he wrote in *The Shadow Line*, "to live in advance of its days in all the beautiful continuity of hope which knows no pauses and no introspection. One closes behind one the little gate of mere boyishness—and enters an enchanted garden."

Chapter XII

◇◇◇◇◇◇◇◇◇◇◇◇◇◇◇◇

Woman and the sea revealed themselves to me together, as it were: two mistresses of life's values.

The Arrow of Gold

THE Mardi Gras carnival was over. It ended two days before Conrad returned to Marseilles and on the Thursday of his arrival the city had settled down to the subdued observance of Lent. But with three carnivals to remember of that circus celebration spreading over twelve days each year, the festive and riotous time was one that never ceased to color Conrad's thoughts of the town.

It retained for him a youthful ring. Mardi Gras: when Marseilles took on the painted air of pantomime from Pierrots and Pierrettes, Fausts in plumed velvet toques, Nights in black gowns sewn with golden moons, anonymous faces behind cardboard noses and black velvet eye masks; when the shrill cries of masqueraders jingled through the streets, the harsh winds of February nights making them run more quickly, yell more loudly, as they snake-danced with linked arms down the Cannebière, the chain breaking as masks dashed into one after another of the five big cafés flanking the Bourse to carry their revelry indoors, winding in and out among the tables.

Each year the Bohemians of Marseilles made the most of Mardi Gras. For three seasons Conrad had a part in that bedlam. Its atmosphere of cloaked identity was a stage drop aptly framing the unreal year that, more as Pierrot than "Young Ulysses," he was to spend in Marseilles.

Too lately arrived for the fete, though such Bohemians as his sculptor friend "Prax" Frétigny were loath to let it end, Conrad adjusted to the carefree circles he had left seven months before. His ambition for a life at sea had grown stronger as a result of the Caribbean voyage and he had signed on with the *Saint-Antoine*, due to sail again in less than six weeks.

In the restlessness of a sailor on shore leave, he strolled into the Grand Café on the Cannebière on an evening more than a week after his return to Marseilles. He sat in the big gilded café bright under the clustered lights of hanging gas lamps. It was almost deserted at that hour, early for customers of its featured specialties of Neapolitan ices and Vienna beer.

With three voyages behind him, Conrad, at nineteen, could call himself a seaman and in that worldly and contenting knowledge he sat idly smoking. He was still filled with the memory of the *Saint-Antoine* voyage, a transatlantic journey carrying cargo both "lawful and lawless." To him, a ship's steward earning thirty-five francs a month, those gunrunning exploits were "other men's adventures, not mine." The remembered sights of green tropics, of torrid, starlit nights, of thrashing storms that in this February saw 192 vessels of all flags lost at sea, were sharp in his mind. The cold mistral blowing outside, the ring of hoofbeats on the Cannebière, café newspapers reporting fresh troubles for the twenty-year-old Alfonso XII in Spain, were activities of a world tastelessly dry for a youth as romantic as the Don Quixote he never ceased to admire.

Like the still air between charges of the mistral's fury, the sudden Lenten quiet following the hilarity of carnival expressed the volatile mood of Marseilles. Always a seaman's town, it was rough, rowdy and raffish, with a hardy spirit as rocky as its hills. Burly independence had been a mark of the port as far back as Roman times when it underwent Julius Caesar's long siege, outlived its rival Carthage. Through 2,400 years of seafaring it had become a melting pot of races and nationalities—Algerians, Moroccans, Greeks, Italians, Senegalese, Spaniards, Corsicans—seamen and traders who came into the Vieux Port and gave up ships for shore life. A town of rebels throughout those years, France's oldest city remained as fiery as Rouget de Lisle's *Marseillaise* battle song sung by Marseilles soldiers as they marched into Paris to attack the Tuileries during the French Revolution.

It was a tempestuous city at any time but in this year of 1877, in a France fatefully groping, Marseilles hummed with intrigue. Drives for power and position came from all quarters in gusts no more temperate than the mistral. The Third French Republic was struggling to its feet in a country shedding monarchy. Claimants to thrones were maneuvering for crowns that sat loosely on royal heads. The Victorian frame of the times dictated decorous behavior, but behind the mask of propriety the mistresses of Kings, of Pretenders, of statesmen, held shares in the power of the men who loved them. Out of *drames d'amour*, out of political challenge, men met with swords or pistols in walled gardens, in isolated clearings. It was a time of duels.

Conrad was young, "inconceivably young," when he returned from the West Indies. Yet within twelve months he was to be initiated into "the life of passion," to fight a duel of his own, to carry away the "incurable wound" of a love that forty-two years later could still bring anguish to a man past sixty.

Two men came up to his table in the café. One was a tall, serious, bookish Englishman of thirty whom Conrad had met some days before in a Royalist *salon*. The other was a stranger, an American of thirty who frequently asserted in haughty pride, "I live by my sword." Both men were supporters of Don Carlos.

Don Carlos, who had entered exile in France the year before, decided in the early months of 1877 to make a new try for the Spanish crown. The time seemed suited for it.

The Carlist War had divided Spain; it was divided still. In an attempt to cement the disturbed country, to win its allegiance to a new and young ruler whom few of his subjects had ever seen, Alfonso XII made a royal tour of Spain in February and March of 1877. The Spanish fleet escorted him, coming into the harbor of Rosas on March 6. The King and his court landed at Barcelona, conducted a royal procession on horseback through the city, attended the opera, made frequent public appearances. They were watched by curious crowds, but there were no cheers for the King. A hostile population looked on coldly, in pointed rebuff, during his stay.

In a salute to Alfonso during his Barcelona visit the French fleet came out to meet the Spanish fleet near the border in a Mediterranean display of ironclads. One ship in the Spanish fleet was the *Numancia,* a warship having enough association with his exciting twelve months in Marseilles for Conrad to remember it for forty years. It may well have chased a gunrunning steamer ashore on the Mediterranean coast, as Conrad wrote in a first, and later altered, version of *The Arrow of Gold.*

The antipathy shown by Barcelona toward Spain's crowned King encouraged Spain's Pretender. He was further heartened when, on March 16, the Basque provinces announced their refusal to give up the Carlist cause and assimilate with the rest of the country. Don Carlos sent the rebel provinces a letter commending their decision and hastened his plans for a new civil war. While he negotiated in Paris for financial aid, his supporters in Marseilles undertook to keep the seceding Basques supplied with arms.

Into that whirlpool Conrad was to be caught like Odysseus

by another siren song, becoming embroiled in Carlism through the spell of a beautiful girl with "blue eyes like melted sapphires," whose lips "that almost without moving could breathe enchanting sounds into the world," a girl with seductive inflections in her voice "that no matter in what mood she spoke seemed only fit for tenderness and love."

When the Englishman and the American approached Conrad in the Cannebière café they had a proposal fantastically daring enough to lure him. As spokesmen for the Carlists in Marseilles, they were looking for a gunrunner to transport arms to the Basque rebels in Spain. M. Delestang would finance the ship to be used, for "in these operations," Conrad wrote in *The Mirror of the Sea*, "a banking-house, too, was concerned—a very respectable banking-house."

When the Englishman met Conrad at what was probably the Delestang *salon* and heard of his part in the *Saint-Antoine*'s contraband venture, it occurred to him "that this eccentric youngster was the very person for what the legitimist sympathizers had very much at heart just then; to organize a supply by sea of arms and ammunition to the Carlist detachments in the South."

Conrad spent the whole night talking with the two men, learning something of them. The American was John M. K. Blunt—or Blount as Conrad originally spelled it—who described himself as *"Américain, catholique et gentilhomme."* He had grown up on a plantation in the Carolinas, had been educated in an aristocratic school in Paris, had fought in the American Civil War, entering the Confederate Army when he was eighteen and for a few months fighting under General Lee until its end. After Lee's surrender, and following the death of his father, Key Blunt, he had gone to live in France with his mother. They had joined the emigration of a large number of Southerners who, embittered by the defeat of the Confederacy, chose France as their permanent home. Along with the wealthy

Tories of Colombia who abandoned their country when the liberal government freed the Negroes there in 1863, the former plantation owners of both North and South America congregated in Paris. There, where Napoleon III lived in the Tuileries surrounded by a brilliant court, self-exiled Americans could mingle with princes, dukes and counts. It was a time when *"grandes dames* in their splendid toilets promenaded in their gilded phaetons on the Champs Élysées and in the Bois de Boulogne," wrote American ambassador E. B. Washburne in his *Recollections of a Minister to France*; a time when Paris was filled with Americans from the Confederate states "who were flattered and feted not only at the Tuileries but by the people generally of the city."

Madame Key Blunt and her son John were among them. Their fortune had been drastically diminished by the Civil War and Madame Blunt, a widow of fifty, sought a career in the French theater. She appealed to Théophile Gautier, the dramatic critic, poet and novelist so prominent in the Second Empire's "art for art's sake" movement.

Madame Blunt's appearance at the critic's door was described by Judith Gautier in *Le Second Rang du Collier* published thirty-two years after her father's death:

> From all parts of the world people came to Théophile Gautier to ask for aid and protection. His advice, his influence, and the support of his pen were all he had to give but he gave royally.
>
> Among these unknown solicitors, who came without introduction or references, was a certain Madame Key Blunt who was particularly tenacious and pestered us for a long time. She came from America and had been the wife, so she said, of a President of the United States, who had recently died.

Her husband, Madame Blunt claimed, had left her with children and without resources, but she hoped to regain her fortune in the theater. "She was a pretty enough woman," Judith Gautier described her, "of medium height, who was always draped in mourning crepe: 'My husband is always dead,' she would reply to those who pointed out to her that the period for mourning had passed."

Gautier was touched by the "exotic unfortunate" and the widow won her plea—to play in an act of *Macbeth* in English before a Paris audience. It was something of a fiasco, for few Parisians understood English and Madame Blunt—whose husband had never been a President of the United States, nor held any position in North Carolina prominent enough to be recorded—had "exceedingly little talent." She turned from that stifled career to seeking a rich marriage for her son.

John Blunt was a handsome, debonair young American, more French than the French, who seemed to have been excessively schooled in the 1661 precepts of Thomas Blount's *The Compleat Gentleman*. Conrad described him in *The Arrow of Gold* as appearing "in all the elegance of his slimness and affirming in every line of his face and body, in the correct set of his shoulders and the careless freedom of his movements, the superiority, the inexpressible superiority, the unconscious, the unmarked, the not-to-be-described, and even not-to-be-caught, superiority of the naturally born and the perfectly finished man of the world."

Blunt was a soldier of fortune who had fought for France in the short seven-month Franco-Prussian War of 1870 and two years later, continuing to live by his sword, became a cavalry officer in Don Carlos' army fighting in Spain. He had been a Captain attached to the *Quartel Real* in Tolosa and in the year since that war's end had lived in Paris, coming down to Marseilles on a liaison assignment for the Carlists.

The Englishman was a man whom Conrad never identified, giving him the fictional name of Mills in *The Arrow of Gold* and the obscure cut name of London-born Henry C—— in *The Mirror of the Sea*. Freed by the deaths of important actors in his illegal international episode, he could be more factual in the later of his two accounts, the 1919 *The Arrow of Gold*, in which the burly Englishman in ill-fitting clothes,

Mills, was presented as a cousin of the very wealthy English Lord X, " 'A good friend of the King.' Meaning Don Carlos of course."

It is unlikely that the identity of Mills will ever be proved—the sensitivities of international intrigue, even after eighty years, being what they are—but he may have been either a cousin of the wealthiest and strongest friend Don Carlos had in England, or the man himself—Henry Fitzalan Howard, the 15th Duke of Norfolk. Born in London, the Duke was immensely wealthy, and in March, 1877 was a tall, serious, bookish young bachelor of twenty-nine. He was a heavily built man "like a bourgeois figure out of Dickens," so careless of his appearance, the Paris edition of the New York *Herald* reported after his death on February 11, 1917, that "it was often said he was the worst dressed man in London."

An ardent Catholic, two of his sisters nuns, the Duke undertook his lifelong religious work at twenty-one. Maintaining close relations with the Vatican throughout his life, he gave extensive financial aid to Catholic churches and schools, and abroad, said the London *Times*, "was looked upon as the representative of Roman Catholicism in England."

It was this religious tie which bound him to Don Carlos, whose strongest supporters in France were defined by *Le Figaro* as "the clerical party of intransigeant Catholics," adherents similar to those in Spain.

The Duke of Norfolk threw the weight of his name and position behind Don Carlos when the Spanish Pretender arrived in London on August 1, 1880, expelled from France. On that occasion, when Don Carlos' expulsion was made permanent, the Duke of Norfolk was among the first to call upon him at Brown's Hotel. Two years later at the first communion of Don Jaime—a ceremony taking place in Old Windsor for the only son and heir of Don Carlos, who in 1909 was to become in his turn Pretender to the Spanish throne—the list of guests selected for a service of such significance that leading Carlists were called from Europe to attend it was given as "Don Carlos, Doña Marguerita, Don Jaime, the Duke and Duchess of Norfolk and the visitors attending the ceremonial."

The Duke of Norfolk was a man of "ardent seriousness," the London *Times* said of him, of "intense loyalty to causes and individuals," who was both "courageous and cautious in public affairs," and who preferred to use his great influence behind the scenes.

Possibly in March, 1877 the serious-minded young Duke, passionately devoted to his religious faith, expending his great fortune in behind-the-scenes ways, an unfailing supporter of Don Carlos, was the "Lord X" of Conrad's adventure who financed the chartering of a small steamer despatched from the Clyde with arms for the Basque rebels in Spain. But if the Duke came into Marseilles himself, to pose in part for the portrait of Mills—"a solitary man of books but with a secret taste for adventure which somehow came out; surprising even me" —he could only have done so incognito. With his great name, with his uncle then the British ambassador to France, he could not have taken an open part in the political disturbance of a foreign country.

The Mills who introduced Conrad to "Rita," the highly placed Englishman who came into Marseilles on a short visit and selected young Conrad as a gunrunner for the Carlists was a man with a mission, dedicated to Carlism, that austere crusade which Conrad in *The Arrow of Gold* labeled "the Principle of Legitimacy," a dry and unpeopled Cause.

"It sounded to my positive mind the most fantastic thing in the world, this elimination of personalities from what seemed but the merest political, dynastic adventure. So . . . it wasn't the Pretender with his big infectious laugh, it wasn't all that lot of politicians, archbishops, and generals, of monks, guerrilleros, and smugglers by sea and land, of dubious agents and shady speculators and undoubted swindlers, who were pushing their fortunes at the risk of their precious skins. No. It was the

Legitimist Principle asserting itself! Well, I would accept the view but with one reservation. All the others might have been merged into the idea, but I, the latest recruit, I would not be merged in the Legitimist Principle. Mine was an act of independent assertion."

Toward Mills, Conrad could write after the mellowing of forty years, he had "never harboured a single reproachful thought" for the dangers to which he was exposed as "the latest recruit."

Yet it was not Mills nor Carlism—"There was indeed nothing great there worthy of anybody's passionate devotion"— that enticed Conrad into "a very dull if dangerous business." It was the girl "Rita." In his "product of my private garden," *The Arrow of Gold,* Conrad told his own love story.

Chapter XIII

◇◇◇◇◇◇◇◇◇◇◇◇◇◇◇◇◇

"THE subject of this book I have been carrying about with me for many years, not so much a possession of my memory as an inherent part of myself," Conrad wrote of *The Arrow of Gold*.

In a handwritten note attached to the original typescript of the novel he further explained its personal tie. "The subject belongs to my early life. I was conscious of it through all the years of my writing life but I was reluctant to take it up, not seeing my way and not feeling this mood, though I thought of it more than once."

He held back from writing it largely out of mistrust of his own ability to handle so personal a story and out of concern for her whom he referred to as La Señora. She, the third woman of his experience, who "might well be called the first" since the earlier two were young girls he had known as a schoolboy in Poland, was one Conrad feared the public would censure. In deleted allusions to her in the manuscript progressing tentatively as "The Laugh" and "Rita Lastaola" before finally emerging as *The Arrow of Gold* Conrad wrote of her as "a Mancini," referring to Maria Mancini, court favorite of Louis XIV whose life was one of amorous escapades, and as posing for an artist's conception of the Byzantine Empress Theodora, the courtesan Justinian married.

It was only after Edward Garnett—who years before had persuaded Conrad to abandon the same subject in *The Sisters*—gave his approval to the first parts of *The Arrow of Gold* that Conrad went on to complete the novel which puzzled critics by its "facts concealed."

To that story of his Marseilles days, "so much of a portraiture of vanished years, of feelings, that had once their actuating power, and of people who probably are all at rest by now," he had wanted to give the title *L'Amie du Roi*. But "as in English (The Friend of the King) the gender is not indicated by the termination, I can't very well do that," he told his American publisher before the book appeared.

Had the book been titled *L'Amie du Roi*, perhaps the real name of Conrad's youthful love would have been discovered years ago instead of remaining the puzzling key to the mystery surrounding his personal life, perhaps the key to the troubled theme heard in all his writing. For what he defined as "the Study of a Woman" was not only his own love story but was equally the story of a particular Friend of a particular King—or of the man whose followers in Marseilles, Paris and Spain referred to as "the King": Don Carlos.

Conrad's description of her and the history of her life as he gave it in *The Arrow of Gold* were close to reality. Again he had the problem of the earliest days of his writing: "What bothers me most is that my figures are so real. I know them so well that they fetter my imagination." Most of all was that true of the girl around whom his thoughts so long revolved. His memory of her was so vitally accurate it permitted little deception.

Rita was tall—"but then I was always a long thing"—blonde, with "rust-coloured" hair which "abundant and misty, unearthly and adorable," formed around her face "a mass of tawny hair that seemed to have hot sparks tangled in it." She had blue eyes so magnificent that Conrad repeatedly returned to the one simile he found right to describe them—"melted sapphires," "the still, deep sapphire gleam in those long eyes," "her glance of melted sapphire level and motionless."

She had an appealing and provocative trait which enchanted him, an "almost imperceptible play of her lips," an image reverberating over and over in his remembered picture of her: "at any time her lips moved very little"; "the stillness of her lips was so perfect directly she ceased speaking that I wondered whether all this had come through them or only had formed itself in my mind"; "the words seemed to form themselves, fiery or pathetic, in the air, outside her lips. Their design was hardly disturbed; a design of sweetness, gravity, and force as if born from the inspiration of some artist; for I had never seen anything to come up to it in nature before or since."

She was a peasant girl and as a child had been a barefooted goatherd in her native hills, a devil's imp, a scantily dressed bag of bones who chased her goats over the crags, clothed in little more than "rain and wind." She was an orphan—"I never knew my mother. I don't even know how she looked. There are no paintings or photographs in our farmhouses amongst the hills. I haven't even heard her described to me. I believe I was never good enough to be told these things."

Rita had been raised in that hilly region by her uncle, the brother of her mother, a parish priest. He was a cold, stern man "too holy to take notice of anything," a gaunt ascetic with a terror-instilling voice who thundered "the road to Heaven is repentance!"

The priest put her "at the age of thirteen or thereabouts," in the care of another uncle and his wife. She attended school for a time, then was set to keeping the books of her uncle's orange business.

One morning Rita, "an ignorant girl of seventeen, a most

uninviting creature with a tousled head, in an old black frock and shabby boots," entered a private garden enclosing a very wealthy man's famous Pavilion.

Conrad gave him the name of Henry Allègre. Henry Allègre caught Rita "very early one morning in his own garden full of thrushes and other small birds. She was sitting on a stone, a fragment of some old balustrade, with her feet in the damp grass, and reading a tattered book of some kind. . . . She raised her eyes and saw him looking down at her thoughtfully over that ambrosian beard of his, like Jove at a mortal."

With his "princely airs," he made "the fact of his notice appear as a sort of favour dropped from Olympus." Into his "mysterious Pavilion hidden away in Passy somewhere," the man of great wealth took Rita as his mistress. He was a collector of fine things, a man without real friends, difficult of access, "like a severe prince with the face of a tombstone Crusader," who looked down on others as if "from a balcony." To his exclusive Pavilion in Passy came "the privileged personalities great in art, in letters, in politics or simply in the world."

To fit into her new world Rita was advised by Henry Allègre's man of business that she required "a name," one suited to the elegant sphere of "the heiress of Henry Allègre." The adolescent girl adopted the title of Doña Rita de Lastaola, drawing it from the region of her childhood, "just a bit of the earth's surface" where she had tended her goats "from after my uncle had said his Mass till the ringing of the evening bell." That assumed name, recalling the wooded, stony slopes, the streams and hamlets of her own country, was the only one she retained, her family name being taken from her "like all the rest of what I had been once."

"To this day," Conrad wrote of that land of Lastaola in *The Arrow of Gold*, "I am not quite certain whether it was the name of any human habitation, a lonely *caserio* with a half-effaced carving of a coat of arms over its door, or of some hamlet at the dead end of a ravine with a stony slope at the back. It might have been a hill for all I know or perhaps a stream. A wood, or perhaps a combination of all these. . . . Once I asked her where exactly it was situated and she answered, waving her hand cavalierly at the dead wall of the room: 'Oh, over there.' "

Allègre undertook the schooling of the girl he had captured in his garden, "in the precincts of some temple . . . in the mountains," preparing her for the fashionable world in which it pleased him to have her appear. He trained her for it, first showing her to that select, Parisian world of high society who began their day with a ride each morning in the Bois de Boulogne.

In something less than a year and a half from the time he found her sitting on a broken fragment of stone work buried in the grass of his wild garden, full of thrushes, starlings, and other innocent creatures of the air, he had given her amongst other accomplishments the art of sitting admirably on a horse, and directly they returned to Paris he took her out with him for their first morning ride.

Allègre's blatant flaunting of his mistress created a stir in the *beau monde*. "Many of those men on that great morning had some of their womenkind with them. But their hats had to go off all the same, especially the hats of the fellows who were under some sort of obligation" to the leader of their world.

Some, to cover the impropriety of her presence among them, hastily circulated a story that Rita was the great man's "adopted" daughter. It was a pretence soon dropped as she continued to ride with him in the Bois each morning "through three successive Parisian springtimes," joined by many of the most distinguished men in Paris.

Rita had "what some Frenchman has called the 'terrible gift of familiarity.' " All who came in contact with her felt "the seduction of her native intelligence and of her splendid physique." She was compared to Louise de La Vallière, the lovable, tall girl with blue eyes, fair hair and an intriguing mouth who, also at seventeen, became the mistress of that ancestor of Don Carlos, Louis XIV.

Like La Vallière in her first years as the King's mistress before he publicly established her as his favorite, Rita too knew only the society of men, and lacked the guidance of "some woman soul that would have known, in which perhaps I could have seen my own reflection." From that isolation in which "the only woman I had anything to do with was myself," came her cry: "A lady! Women seem such mysterious creatures to me. I don't know them."

For five or six years Rita lived in that rarefied air of the ultra-fashionable world. Imaginative, with a "young, virgin intelligence," an unusual mind which caused her to be called both a "marvellous child" and "as old as the world," she was steeped in the world of "great clever men" who circulated about the Pavilion in Passy. There she had a constant "sensation of plotting and intriguing" around her as those men, like "a lot of intellectual dogs," demolished the world in their talk at the famous house "where every hard truth had been cracked and every belief had been worried into shreds."

The ruler of that "aviary," who loomed up "three sizes bigger than any of them," spoke little at the sessions, expressing by his silence his "complete, equable, and impartial contempt for all mankind." Guests were admitted only to "feed and amuse" his scorn of the world, "which was insatiable."

He, who "if any man, might have been certain of his own power," dominated all sorts of people, including Rita.

"For six years he seemed to carry all the world and me with it in his hand." He masked the world for her; he was big enough for that.

Then, as Conrad wrote the story, that great man died. His death had in it "the character of a heartless desertion," "something lofty and sinister like an Olympian's caprice."

Rita, whose life "might have been described as looking at

mankind from a fourth-floor window for years," was dropped into a world she knew little of, with no protecting arm about her. "When the end came it was like falling out of a balcony into the street. It was as sudden as that . . . all I know is that I didn't break anything—not even my heart." She recalled that "when he was gone I found myself down there unhurt, but dazed, bewildered, not sufficiently stunned."

It was the last time that she "surveyed the world of men and women from the saddle." She had to dismount "right into the middle of it. Down to the very ground, you understand. I suppose you can guess what that would mean. She didn't know what to do with herself. She had never been on the ground."

Rita had known Don Carlos during those Pavilion days, having seen a great deal of him in Paris where "he used to ride with us nearly every morning" in the Bois. A man with a "big, irresistible laugh" who made the whole house ring with it, he was not then an active Pretender.

Because of the well-known laugh of the playboy Pretender, Conrad gave the title of "The Laugh" to the first draft of *The Arrow of Gold*. Portraying Don Carlos there under the name of Alegre, the Spanish word for "merry," he changed the spelling to Allègre in the final version of the novel. For a deeper disguise of factual history he created two characters, Henry Allègre and Don Carlos, for the role filled in real life by only one—Don Carlos. Yet the true history was so strong in his mind that he repeatedly drew actual occurrences in *The Arrow of Gold*.

One day—in the novel—Don Carlos' aide, Don Rafael de Villarel (in an early draft it was Tristany, a real aide) visited Rita in Paris, saying that His Majesty wished to call. The "Venetian episode" followed. A Parisian journalist saw Don Carlos and Rita together on the Lido and wrote a vignette about it, describing "how the Prince on landing from the gondola emptied his purse into the hands of a picturesque old beggar, while the lady, a little way off, stood gazing back at

Venice with the dog romantically stretched at her feet." Other Paris papers reported the Venetian affair of "the King."

Rita as *l'amie du Roi* was soon the topic of royalist gossip. She was called "the guardian angel of Legitimacy," was credited with being the inspiration for moves being made in Spain, became devoted to his "cause."

She took a furnished house in Marseilles, on the Prado, "for the good of the cause—*Por el Rey!* She was always taking little houses for somebody's good," Conrad wrote in *The Mirror of the Sea,* "for the sick or the sorry, for broken-down artists, cleaned-out gamblers, temporarily unlucky speculators—*vieux amis*—old friends, as she used to explain apologetically, with a shrug of her fine shoulders. Whether Don Carlos was one of the 'old friends', too, it's hard to say. More unlikely things have been heard of in smoking-rooms."

She was constantly rushing off to Paris "in the interests of the cause—*Por el Rey!* For she was a Carlist . . . with something of a lioness in the expression of her courageous face (especially when she let her hair down), and with the volatile little soul of a sparrow dressed in fine Parisian feathers, which had the trick of coming off disconcertingly at unexpected moments."

In her villa on the Prado she smoked cigarettes "of the same pattern as those made specially for the King," she received Carlist emissaries, made the plans, gave the instructions which centered on "the King's" campaign in Spain.

Because she had in her "something of the women of all time"—her "genius" or "ancient spells" as Mills called it—she could accomplish extraordinary things. Doors flew open to her: "She could get a whole army over the frontier if she liked . . . And why? Because every bald head in this Republican Government gets pink at the top whenever her dress rustles outside the door."

Blunt was in love with her, "like two hundred others, or two thousand, all around." He was in Marseilles because of her, as was Mills. Don Carlos never came to Marseilles but he, to whom she was trying to give a crown, was reported to have offered her his love.

"There was a time that they thought I could carry him off, away from them all—beyond them all. Verily I am not very proud of their fears. There was nothing reckless there worthy of a great passion. There was nothing sad there worthy of a great tenderness."

Yet she wore, and clung to, a significant jeweled ornament, "an arrow of gold feathered with brilliants and with ruby gleams all along its shaft," an ornament of a "very Philistinish conception" which Conrad—who gave himself the name of Monsieur George in *The Arrow of Gold*—wished to have from her. For Monsieur George was also in love with Rita.

From the day when Mills had taken him to her villa on the Prado, proposing him as the gunrunner the Carlists sought, Monsieur George had felt the "intolerable weight" of that love. He soon "acquired the conviction that there was nothing more lovable in the world than that woman; nothing more life-giving, inspiring, and illuminating than the emanation of her charm. I meant it absolutely—not excepting the light of the sun."

Before long he was "at that stage when all her words, all her gestures, all her silences were a heavy trial to me, put a stress on my resolution, on that fidelity to myself and to her which lay like a leaden weight on my untried heart."

In the course of the twelve months of "his first great adventure," his initiation "into the life of passion," he experienced all the stages of ecstasy and torment.

Love for Rita . . . if it was love, I asked myself despairingly, while I brushed my hair before a glass. It did not seem to have any sort of beginning as far as I could remember. A thing the origin of which you cannot trace cannot be seriously considered. It is an illusion. Or perhaps mine was a physical state, some sort of disease akin to melancholia which is a form of insanity? The only moments of relief I could remember were when she and I would start squabbling like two passionate infants in a nursery, over anything under heaven, over a phrase, a word sometimes, in the great light of the glass rotunda, disregarding the quiet entrances and exits of the ever-active Rose, in great bursts of voices and peals of laughter.

That love grew. From the early days of nursery squabbling it gathered the momentum of a storm. For some months Monsieur George, carrying on his gunrunning as the recruit of the woman he loved, saw her in the villa on the Prado between his expeditions to the Spanish coast. A crisis came; they quarreled; she left for Paris and her work there for "the King." In loyalty to her he continued his illicit voyages three months longer, until one day his vessel, "broken and gone like the only toy of a lonely child," was destroyed in a shipwreck that left in him "the memory of a suicide." The shipwreck had come close to taking his own life. He returned, heartsore, to Marseilles and with Rita went to a "retreat in the region of the Maritime Alps," to a "small house built of dry stones and embowered with roses," where they appeared to be "less like released lovers than as companions who had found out each other's fitness in a specially intense way."

Conrad wrote that moving love story of his youth, *The Arrow of Gold*, when he was a man of sixty, when the real people he drew upon for it were truthfully "all at rest," as he knew. Out of a close feeling of privacy he guarded throughout his life the identity of her whom he called Doña Rita. Yet the girl he wrote of so tenderly, described so accurately, could only have been one, whose name a certain world at that time knew.

Chapter XIV

◇◇◇◇◇◇◇◇◇◇◇◇◇◇◇◇

WHEN Don Carlos entered exile in France he sought escape from the recriminations, charges and counter-charges that followed the collapse of the Carlist War, and, then twenty-eight, led a Don Juan life in the demi-monde of Paris. Later in the year he went to Austria.

He was a restless man always, perpetually on the move. For the next twelve years, until he settled down permanently in the Loredan Palace in Venice in 1888, he traveled widely, to England, Switzerland, Egypt, the United States, Mexico, Greece, Rumania, Bulgaria, India, and South America. He took houses everywhere. One he lived in longer than most during the first years after the Carlist War was the Pavilion in Passy.

The Pretender was "not a sympathetic character," according to a New York *Times* comment upon him in 1880. His once faithful General Böet charged him with being a coward during a lawsuit between them in Milan in 1880 and the London *Times,* with more temperance, noted that "he showed no inclination to engage in hazardous adventures." Described by *The New York Times* as having a "coarse, sensual face which more resembled the type of an *extra-muros* Don Juan than the descendant of a long line of monarchs," there was "nothing reckless there worthy of a great passion," and "nothing sad there worthy of a great tenderness." Wholly directed by whim, he was so wavering in interest, even in his own cause, that his supporters sought for years, without success, to induce him to abdicate his Pretender's claims to his son Don Jaime.

Yet it was ennui that drove Don Carlos, rather than fear. Of towering height and with superlative health, the monarch-trained king without a kingdom constantly sought diversion, amusement. His one regular activity was to spend two hours each morning in the saddle. He was an excellent horseman and often took his own string of horses about with him when he traveled.

Every year he invariably spent a part of the summer in Austria, staying at the Count de Chambord's castle, Frohsdorf, the Villa Nieves at Gratz, or at the Hotel Kaiserin Elizabeth in Vienna. The court of Emperor Franz Josef was then the most outstanding in Europe and in Vienna Don Carlos had family ties. His uncle, the Count de Chambord—Pretender to the throne of France and known to Legitimists as "King Henry V"—was childless and unusually close to the nephew of an age to be his son, to whom he left the bulk of his vast fortune when he died in 1883. At Frohsdorf the Count de Chambord held informal court, directing from there the political course of the Legitimists in France and Spain.

Set in the mountains near Vienna, with immense grounds around it, Frohsdorf was to Legitimists something of a shrine, a temple. As the residence of the last male representative of the elder branch of the Bourbon family, who in his 1866 manifesto welded the Pope's cause into the Principle of Legitimacy, it was both a political and religious fount to followers who disowned the growing democratic and free-thinking spirit of the times.

In the late months of 1876 Don Carlos arrived at Frohsdorf. The Turks had invaded Bulgaria in October and the first skirmishes of the Russo-Turkish War of 1877-78 were taking place. In that war, fought over control of the Balkans and the Black Sea and concluded by the Treaty of San Stefano, King Carol I of Rumania sided with Russia. To demonstrate his support of King Carol, Don Carlos made a short stay at the Bulgarian battlefront, arriving at Rustchuk (Ruse) in January, 1877 and returning within a few days to Vienna.

But more important than his war trip was an event recorded by the Count de Melgar, a Spanish aristocrat who left Madrid toward the close of the Carlist War to join "the King" at his *Quartel Real* in Tolosa, moved with the Carlist emigration in March, 1876 to Paris, where he received his appointment as secretary to Don Carlos. For twenty years, until 1900, he filled that role, being with Don Carlos in Paris, London, and Venice, and on his various travels about the world. Before the Count de Melgar died in 1926 he wrote his memoirs of those years, *Veinte Años con don Carlos,* which his son, Count Francisco de Melgar, edited and published in Madrid in 1940.

In his memoirs the Count de Melgar gave the history and the name of *l'amie du Roi:*

At the end of 1876 or the beginning of 1877 when Don Carlos returned from the Russo-Turkish War, during which he took sides with King Carol I of Rumania who honored him with the Military Bravery Cross for his brilliant conduct in the field of battle, he stopped in Vienna to see his relatives.

He was accompanied by his aide, Don José de Suelves, who later became the Marquis de Tamarit. During his stay in the capital of Austria Don Carlos met a young and very beautiful Hungarian actress with whom he fell madly in love, becoming intimate with her and taking her to Paris.

Her name was Paula de Somoggy. She was scarcely eighteen years old and a proud young miss who brought out admiration from those passing her in the street; blonde, with magnificent blue eyes, tall and with a majestic bearing, she possessed at the same time an extraordinary intelligence.

When Don Carlos met her she spoke only Hungarian and a few words of German; after two years she could speak almost every European language: French, Spanish, Italian, German, and

English, although the first of those was the language she favored until her death.

"Actress" being a term loosely used in the 1870's, it was more than likely that Paula, then barely eighteen, met Don Carlos in the grounds of Frohsdorf Castle—"in the precincts of some temple . . . in the mountains"—in the manner in which Rita and Blunt told her story in *The Arrow of Gold*. She was Hungarian, not a Basque, as Conrad disguised her history in his "imaginative rendering" of *The Mirror of the Sea*.

Paula, like Conrad's "Rita," was a peasant girl, an orphan raised in her native hills by her uncle, the brother of her mother and a parish priest. When Don Carlos decided in Vienna to take her with him to Paris his "man of business," his aide Don José de Suelves whose later title was Marquis de Tamarit, suggested that she required "a name" suited to the aristocratic circle she would enter.

It was under the assumed name she kept until her marriage, Baroness Paula de Somoggy—or Somogyi as it was more correctly spelled by *Le Figaro*—that she was presented in Paris as the favorite of "the King," *l'amie du Roi*. It was a name she adopted from the hills of her childhood, the woods and stony slopes, the sparsely settled land of poor peasants and large landowners, of hamlets with houses of thatched roofs and whitewashed walls, a farming country of fruit and grain, of pigs and sheep and goats—that pastoral region of Hungary south of Balaton Lake and near Kaposvar, the district of Somogyi.

Paula was not only tall and blonde, she was not only an intriguingly beautiful girl so captivating as to call out wonder from passers-by in the street, she had magnificent sapphire-blue eyes and a personal trait so alluring it furnished Don Carlos with the pet name he gave her and always retained. When she spoke her lips scarcely moved, giving an impression of traceless speech. The charm of that conspicuous feature caused Don

Carlos to nickname her "Nyul," the Hungarian word for hare.

Don Carlos immediately set about training the peasant girl he was madly in love with, "the most admirable find of his amongst all the priceless items" surrounding "the King" in his sumptuous home. Paula's career became a true story in the vein of *Pygmalion* which George Bernard Shaw was to write thirty-five years later.

El Rey, who had passed the time training wild animals at his *Quartel Real* in Tolosa while the Carlist War was on in Spain, organized Paula's instruction to the end of having her appear in Paris society as the creditable choice of a royal Prince of Bourbon. Her amazing intelligence made the teaching easy.

"It's a fact that a woman like Rita has never been put on the stage," Conrad wrote to Eric Pinker in 1922. Still vivid to him after forty-four years, Conrad was then eager to write a play about her, with facts of her story he had not previously given, and "would sign an agreement with the Devil himself for the chance" of seeing it staged.

Within a year and a half of the time Don Carlos met Paula in Vienna he had taught her among other accomplishments to sit well on a horse. In her long-skirted riding habit and tall silk hat she rode side-saddle beside him at the fashionable morning hour in the Bois during the three Parisian spring-times of 1878, 1879, and 1880. Within those first two years she not only learned to speak five languages but she dressed and acted with a grace sufficiently royal as to be included in His Majesty's parties at the theater, at the seaside, at any social function where he chose to show her.

He established Paula in her own house in Paris, on the rue Pauquet, a short street later named rue Jean-Giraudoux near the Étoile, in the ultra-exclusive quarter off the Avenue d'Iéna. There, less than a dozen blocks from Don Carlos's Pavilion on the rue de la Pompe, Paula, but a few months before an un-tutored peasant girl, entertained a world of "great clever men."

Princes, prominent Carlists, politicians, distinguished men in art, letters and the whole range of Paris society dined at her house.

Don Carlos showed off his "find" everywhere. He took her with him to Italy, to Venice, accompanied by his favorite pets, his two Great Dane dogs. He took her with him to Vienna, to London.

For almost six years, until May, 1882, Paula lived the life of an heiress. She lived it with splendor. Surrounded with luxury, dressed in the latest mode and wearing the jewels an enthralled Prince gave her, she was also unstintingly generous to "the sick or the sorry," to artists broken-down or coming-up.

During the years of her fame Paula knew only the society of men, never of women, and her cry of isolation, of longing for "some woman soul that would have known" was one the Count de Melgar frequently heard her give.

Paula's extraordinary seductive quality, her "genius," was very much as Conrad described it, for the "woman of all time" was a sensation in both Paris and London. Reports of her provocative charm spread quickly, even at the beginning of her career. Conrad learned something of it the night before he met her: "I had never heard before a woman spoken about in that way, a real live woman that is, not a woman in a book. For this was no poetry and yet it seemed to put her in the category of visions."

Toward Paula Don Carlos acted with an air of jealous possession. When the end of the affair came it was not "an Olympian's caprice" but was forced by a threatened break in his ranks, by powerful supporters who were hostile to her influence, disdainful of her peasant birth, angered by her lack of interest in religion.

Paula's devotion to Don Carlos came, not out of love, but from loyalty. "With me it is *pun d'onor*," Conrad had Rita describe that tie. When her reign as *l'amie du Roi* ended, however much the suddenness of her changed fortunes was "like falling out of a balcony into the street," Paula received that blow sturdily, and with no broken heart.

However, that day when she found herself "dazed, bewildered, not sufficiently stunned," was to come much later, more than five years after Conrad met her in Marseilles.

In the early months of 1877 when Don Carlos decided on a new attempt at the Spanish throne—or to make a "gesture" of a new attempt at the throne, as Count de Melgar phrased it— Marseilles was to continue as the shipping center for the arms Carlist forces would need. Paula was eager to serve in his "cause" and through an agent took a furnished house on the Prado, to act as the link between Don Carlos and Legitimist circles in Marseilles. She shuttled back and forth to Paris at a time which seemed favorable for a Carlist campaign.

In February King Alfonso, finding his turbulent country difficult to rule, dissolved the Spanish Senate and called for new elections, hoping to win more popular support. But the Basque provinces openly rejected his sovereignty, broadcasting their allegiance to Don Carlos in a stand newspapers reported on March 16, 1877.

To supply the Basques with arms, to slip by the Spanish coast guard and land rifles for which Arragonese muleteers would be waiting in the neighborhood of the Gulf of Rosas, a gunrunner was needed.

Conrad, at nineteen, took on that hazardous adventure. It was not from interest in a dynastic quarrel, since Alfonso or Carlos "if they were both to vanish from the earth together or separately it would make no difference to my feelings," he told Dominic. He defied "a whole big country for the sake of—what is it exactly?—the blue eyes, or the white arms of the Señora."

Chapter XV

❖❖❖❖❖❖❖❖❖❖❖❖❖❖❖❖❖

THE sharp end-of-winter days whipped into Marseilles when the "mistral howled in the sunshine, shaking the bare bushes quite furiously." The whole of the night before Conrad had listened, fascinated, as Mills and Blunt talked of *l'amie du Roi*. Paula had been in France less than two months when he drove out with Mills in a hired victoria for lunch at her house on the Prado.

He walked with Mills up the circular drive to her door in a stinging wind, when "everything was bright and hard, the air was hard, the light was hard, the ground under our feet was hard." Conrad was being presented as a candidate for the Carlist gunrunner she was seeking, since it was upon her wit and information that the scheme depended. His first view of her as he waited in the hall had the dramatic quality of a stage entrance.

The woman of whom I had heard so much, in a sort of way in which I had never heard a woman spoken of before, was coming down the stairs, and my first sensation was that of profound astonishment at this evidence that she did really exist. And even then the visual impression was more of colour in a picture than of the forms of actual life. She was wearing a wrapper, a sort of dressing-gown of pale blue silk embroidered with black and gold designs round the neck and down the front, lapped round her and held together by a broad belt of the same material. Her slippers were of the same colour, with black bows at the instep. The white stairs, the deep crimson of the carpet, and the light blue of the dress made an effective combination of colour to set off the delicate carnation of that face, which, after the first glance given to the whole person, drew irresistibly your gaze to itself by an indefinable quality of charm beyond all analysis and made you think of remote races, of strange generations, of the faces of women sculptured on immemorial monuments and of those lying unsung in their tombs. While she moved downwards from step to step with slightly lowered eyes there flashed upon me suddenly the recollection of words heard at night, of Allègre's words about her, of there being in her "something of the women of all time."

Four hours after meeting her Conrad left her house "committed to an enterprise that could not be talked about; which would have appeared to many senseless and perhaps ridiculous, but was certainly full of risks."

For the next ten months he led a double life. He stayed on for a time at the Hôtel de Genève, continuing to spend idle hours with the Bohemian set, guarding the secret that absorbed him. He called on Paula to talk of it on her trips down from Paris; he met with the other members of the "syndicate" at Madame Léonore's Café de la Colonne Trajane near the quays of the Vieux Port. Since the success of the gunrunning hinged on a seaman skilled in contraband maneuvers, Conrad talked Dominic Cervoni, the indomitable Corsican, into joining him.

It was Dominic who found the light, fast ship they needed, a sixty-ton balancelle, "with two short masts raking forward and two curved yards, each as long as her hull; a true child of the Latin Lake, with a spread of two enormous sails resembling the pointed wings on a sea-bird's slender body, and herself, like a bird indeed, skimming rather than sailing the seas." The ship had been built near Genoa and rigged in Corsica. In her new career of gunrunning she would pose as a fruit and cork-wood trader plying between Marseilles and Barcelona. In addition to Dominic as the Padrone, and Conrad, she would carry a crew of five, of whom one was Dominic's nephew, the untrustworthy César Cervoni. Delestang & Son would finance the ship with Carlist funds but nominally she would be owned by a syndicate of four young men—Conrad, Blunt, a Frenchman whom he identified as Roger P. de la S——, and an Englishman given the equally cryptic name of Henry C——.

With his new adventure underway, Conrad canceled his berth on the *Saint-Antoine* and it sailed without him and Dominic on March 31. If Dominic's record of service showed him in his usual position as second officer on board the *Saint-Antoine,* leaving Marseilles March 31 and returning on October 14, 1877, it may well have been adjusted to keep the illegal *Tremolino* enterprise from French officials. The pliability of service records was illustrated when Delestang & Son, owners of the Marseilles ships on which Conrad served, issued a certificate in 1880 stating that during three years of constant service, from February, 1874 to February, 1877, he had been on the *Mont-Blanc* and the *Saint-Antoine* in the West Indies and South American trade. Conrad, however, had not arrived in Marseilles from Poland until October, 1874 and he served only thirteen months on the two ships, not three years.

The *Tremolino,* the name he gave to the balancelle, was a quick and sturdy craft which he remembered with deep affection.

"I owe to her," he wrote nearly thirty years later in *The Mirror of the Sea,* "the awakened love for the sea that, with the quivering of her swift little body and the humming of the wind under the foot of her lateen sails, stole into my heart with a sort of gentle violence, and brought my imagination under its despotic sway. The *Tremolino!* To this day I cannot utter or even write that name without a strange tightening of the breast and the gasp of mingled delight and dread of one's first passionate experience."

Conrad set off on his first contraband voyage with "a certain gnawing emotion." His fear had solid grounds. To land rifles and ammunition on the Spanish coast the *Tremolino* needed to pass government ships on a sharp lookout for illegal traders, dodging in to shore when the way was clear; she had to enter a strange cove in any weather; wait for the night light signal of contact, of muleteers arriving for a cargo which, by the very secrecy surrounding it, aroused the countryside's suspicion. Bribes insured friends who were bought with the gold Conrad carried in a belt around his waist. Ashore, carabineers would fire without asking questions at figures slinking through the dark on a forlorn coast. At sea, the guns of a *guardacosta* might quickly end the *Tremolino* and all aboard her. Arrest itself offered a severe enough fate in the edgy country still roiled by the slowly-dying hatreds of its civil war.

There could be no mistakes, no delays. Conrad had to count on the intelligence, the boldness, of strangers, of Spaniards he had no way of knowing; to rely on the holding power of bribes. Yet, with layers of oranges covering the contraband arms in her hold, the *Tremolino* successfully made her first rendezvous in the Gulf of Rosas.

Meanwhile, in Paris, Don Carlos was winning support for his projected renewal of the civil war in Spain. He was "conspiring freely in France in the company of Cardinals, Bishops, Deputies and Senators," the London *Times* reported on April 9; attending a meeting of Catholics in Paris, becoming acquainted with the Count of Paris, with the Emperor of Brazil, Pedro II, with the Duke of Nemours, the influential son of France's earlier king, Louis Philippe.

Carlist activity in France mounted to a threatening peak. Spain, to halt the fast approaching outbreak, took exceptional action: the Spanish embassy in Paris requested that Don Carlos be expelled from France. On May 21 the French Government served him with a formal invitation to leave the country.

In a counterpart action in Marseilles the Spanish consul, the Marquis de Gonzalez, protested to Bouches-du-Rhône authorities against the sending of Carlist munitions to Spain, Conrad's ship being but a small part of the supply network operating from that port.

Don Carlos left Paris on May 22 for Austria, his wife and children following later. He had been warned that a demand for his departure was to be made by the Spanish government and had arranged to take his family, including his seven-year-old son Don Jaime, to visit his ailing mother, a married nun living in a convent near Gratz. The large group of Carlists in Paris who once before had shared their chief's sentence expected to be compelled to do so again. They made scurried preparations to close their houses and leave.

The Carlist debacle affecting many socialites at the height of the season drew lively comment from the Paris press, few republican journals being sympathetic either to Don Carlos or to the MacMahon-appointed ministry whose members had, with subsidies and protection, aided the Carlist cause. Gossip writers and political writers, peddling scandal sanctimoniously in a Victorian day with its rules of behavior immoderately strict, seized on the sudden change in Carlist fortunes.

Paula, with Don Carlos out of Paris, became an exposed target. It was a year when the limits of decorum were rigid enough to bring a hostess as prominent as the Comtesse de la Ferronays, "an ultra Legitimist, ultra Clerical lady" as the New York Daily *Tribune* described her, under reproof. The Comtesse gave a masked ball during Lent but the fete was considered so improperly timed that, though five hundred male guests responded, only thirty-five ladies dared attend.

Anticipating banishment as a Carlist, Paula had placards placed about Paris announcing the sale of her household furnishings, antiques and art treasures. That sale, glaringly in the limelight, brought acid treatment from the gossip columnist Pierre Véron of *Le Monde Illustré*. A self-styled moralist who fulminated against the "barbarous" paintings of Impressionists, the absurd new telephone gadget of Bell supposed to send the voice as much as twelve miles, and the shocking proposal to make divorce legal, Véron ran full tilt at Paula and her sale. Referring to her as "Mlle. X, less of a celebrity than a demi-mondaine," he alluded to the time in March when a desperately infatuated young man of eighteen shot himself in her house after firing his pistol at her (a drama which doubtless gave Conrad the material for the Ortega scene in *The Arrow of Gold*) and to the more recent scandal of Paula seen walking on the arm of Don Carlos.

"Don't you recall this person whose adventures, even more than those of other gay ladies, made France and England blush?" he asked his readers on May 26, 1877. "You remember that she walked only lately on the arm of a prince *déclassé*? You remember that because of her a young man shot himself with a pistol? Yes, you've guessed it, she's the one. Run then to her sale. You will probably be able to buy the souvenirs of the prince and the others. Perhaps even the pistol will be among the trinkets."

Within four months of her arrival in France Paula was, in Conrad's phrase, "a celebrity of a sort." To escape the sniping of too-attentive journalists she closed her house in Paris and took refuge in Marseilles.

Meanwhile Don Carlos, banned from France for what turned out to be six months, traveled from Vienna to Bucharest, arriving there on June 21. He was accompanied by a small escort which included General Böet and Viscount de Monserrat. He visited Carol I of Rumania, and went on to Ploesti to pay his respects to Czar Alexander II—the Czar who had exiled Conrad's father fifteen years earlier. Alexander II, described by the British diplomat Lord Frederic Hamilton as a man of freezing hauteur with "something in his voice and a look in his eye reminiscent of the Great Mogul addressing an earthworm," was to be assassinated on March 1, 1881 when two bombs painted white to resemble snowballs were hurled as he drove along Petrograd's Catherine Canal in a special steel-armored coach formerly owned by Napoleon III.

When Don Carlos paid his formal call the Czar was a man of fifty-nine directing Russian strategy in the Russo-Turkish War of 1877-78. The Spanish Pretender had taken a number of horses with him to Bucharest and Rumanian officials let it be known that "should he offer his services to the armies opposing the Turks they might be accepted."

But Don Carlos—or his supporters—were determined on his enthronement as King of Spain. The Basque provinces were still in revolt, their defiance of Alfonso's government flaring up again in December when officials of San Sebastian and other towns in the north of Spain resigned in protest against Madrid's tax and conscription levies. France, involved in her own political troubles following President MacMahon's monarchist *coup d'état,* overlooked the Carlists on French soil. Their plans for a military campaign in Spain had been halted but not abandoned.

Paula rented a second house in Marseilles, on the rue Sylvabelle, where Carlists on clandestine missions could stay without interference from the French police. Needing a trustworthy woman to run the boardinghouse, she sent to Hungary for her sister. Conrad gave her the name of Therese and described her as an unmarried woman from six to ten years older than her exotic sister, a peasant woman who arrived in Marseilles from her own country wearing a coarse nun-like habit, carrying a crooked stick, her belongings tied in a bundle.

His fictional portrait of her was undoubtedly a true one, for Conrad's landlady bore the Hungarian name of Fogas, a name of peasant families in the region of Somogyi. On her first trip away from her mountain village in 1877 Mme. Fogas, as she was referred to in landlady terms, more than likely did arrive in Marseilles in homespun clothes with bundle luggage.

Exactly which house she managed in Marseilles, the house

where Conrad lived, is still a question. The records of Marseilles show four lodginghouses existing on the rue Sylvabelle in 1877-78: Number 15, owned by Mme. Chabert; Number 32, owned by Jean Roses; Number 36, owned by Gustave Petilhon; Number 55, owned by Pierre Mayard. The four houses were around the corner from the offices of Delestang & Son on the rue d'Arcole where Conrad, arranging the missions of the *Tremolino,* called regularly. Since the list of lodgers on the rue Sylvabelle during those years has been lost, it has never been possible to identify which house Conrad used as the setting for *The Arrow of Gold.* But the accuracy of the account of his life in Marseilles as he gave it in that novel was verified by his friend and official biographer, Georges Jean-Aubry, and more recently by the French literary historian and Conrad scholar, Professor Marcel Clavel of the Faculté des Lettres in Aix-en-Provence.

"You ought to emphasize that there is more than 'a basis of fact' in *The Arrow of Gold,*" Professor Clavel wrote to the author on June 9, 1957. "Jean-Aubry told me that Conrad had assured him that practically everything was taken from life in his novel (as in most of the others). They [Jean-Aubry and Conrad] had started from Paris with the purpose of going together to all the places mentioned [in *The Arrow of Gold*] but, unfortunately, Jean-Aubry had to stop at Lyons, and the opportunity was lost for ever.

"You may say that I have investigated the police reports (for Carlist activities) and also the fashionable and somewhat scandalous weeklies of Marseilles (for accounts of brilliant receptions and balls, duels, etc.). All this to no avail. In Paris, perhaps, a search for the satirical 'vignettes' of a newspaper might give the name of the lady [Conrad's 'Rita'] staying with Don Carlos in Venice . . . Nothing came of my appeals to find elderly people who might have heard of the duel, of the salon of the Prado villa and of the honeymoon locality on the Riviera."

Since that incompleted French journey of Jean-Aubry and Conrad nearly thirty-five years ago little has, up to now, been learned of the eventful Marseilles years of Conrad's life. The answers given here to what has long been referred to as the "Conrad Enigma" may one day lead to a fuller telling of his life in Marseilles, of the house on the street to which he appropriately gave the fictional name "the street of the Consuls," where his great adventure began and—waking up "after an hour, or a day, or a month" in recovery from his nearly fatal wound—it was to end.

Chapter XVI

◇◇◇◇◇◇◇◇◇◇◇◇◇◇◇◇◇◇◇

THE last coupés were driving away from the Opera, their carriage lamps blinking like fireflies along the quieting night streets. Hoofbeats, fading, left a thin trail of sound. The encircling line of gas jets holding the Opera House in the basket of its own light were extinguished. The Place de l'Opéra became still, dark and empty.

Conrad sought the darkness. He walked across the silent square, avoiding lighted streets to lessen the risk of recognition. He was in his sailor's clothes returning from his third gunrunning expedition to the Spanish coast and had waited until a late hour in Madame Léonore's café for the streets to empty.

At his lodginghouse on the rue Sylvabelle his landlady greeted him with the harrowing account of a murder committed while he was away, one that had "affected the imagination of the whole town." She ended her gruesome tale with the severe warning "that's what carnal sin (*péché de chair*) leads to." The dark allusion to his own love affair, which was sending him stealthily over the Mediterranean and as stealthily over the deserted streets of the town, formed a time-tie in Conrad's mind with the most macabre event of the year in Marseilles.

That "peculiarly revolting case of murder," as the London *Times* on July 6, 1877 described a crime so sensational as to horrify newspaper readers on both sides of the Channel, became known during the Boyer trial. The victim was a widow, Madame Boyer, a Marseilles shopkeeper. The murderers were her seventeen-year-old daughter Marie, and Léon Vitalis, a young clerk.

The girl had been in a convent intending to become a nun but was dismissed following discovery of her correspondence with Vitalis. Although Vitalis proposed to marry her, he had formed an immoral relationship with her mother. The girl believed her mother to be preventing her marriage and instigated the crime; she supplied Vitalis with a cheese knife which he plunged in the widow's throat, the girl kicking her mother during the struggle to weaken her resistance. To ensure himself of the widow's shop and money Vitalis dissected the corpse, tying the human fragments in packages and depositing them near the old fortifications where they were found on March 21. Three and a half months later the trial ended with the girl sentenced to hard labor for life, her paramour Vitalis condemned to death.

Long years later in *The Arrow of Gold*, Conrad associated that murder and the stir it caused with the clandestine days of his youth when he lived on the street conspicuous for its "quantity of flag-poles." Opposite his room was the Consulate of Paraguay at 79 rue Sylvabelle. He could stand at his windows in the distraction of a nineteen-year-old youth in love "not knowing what I was looking at across the road—the Desert of Sahara or a wall of bricks, a landscape of rivers and forests or only the Consulate of Paraguay." A second flagpole from the same portico at Number 79 flew the standard of the Argentine Consulate. Jean Pianello for Paraguay and Spiridion Pianello for Argentina officiated as consuls for two of the South

American countries whose representatives clustered like cherries on a branch in that corner of Marseilles.

Three more flagpoles jutted from the nearby building at 89 rue Sylvabelle for the consulates of Ecuador, of Colombia, of Guatamala. From the house where Conrad lived his fellow lodger John Blunt could "survey the flags of all nations almost —except his own," the American Consulate being a dozen blocks away at 123 rue Dragon.

Conrad knew, at least by sight, the American consul, Frank W. Potter, who carried his miniature dog on his arm "in all places, at all hours, but mainly at the hour of the fashionable promenade on the Prado." From the American vice-consul and later consul, J. B. Gould, Conrad may have taken the name for his Charles Gould, the "Idealist-creator of Material Interests," of *Nostromo*. Having returned but four months before from the contraband-running voyage of the *Saint-Antoine,* he may have learned the background of Colombia's 1876 revolution from his neighbor across the street, the Colombian consul B. Chaix-Bryan, adapting that knowledge for use in *Nostromo* as he admittedly drew—in the character of Don José Avellanos —the personality of the 1903 Colombian Minister in London, Perez Triana.

"I am compunctious as to the use I've made of the impression produced upon me by the Ex. Sr. Don Perez Triana's personality," he wrote Robert Bontine Cunninghame Graham on October 31, 1904. "Do you think I have committed an unforgivable fault there? He'll never see or hear of the book probably."

Nostromo was so linked in Conrad's memory with his Marseilles days that he significantly gave to Gould, the administrator of the San Tomé silver mine, the title of Don Carlos, seeing in both the Spanish Pretender and the foreign owner of the silver mine parallel drives for power involving revolution.

Deserted at night, the rue Sylvabelle was an active center of commerce by day. Surrounding the five consulates were nineteen import and export firms located on the street. Near the Vieux Port, it was a center of the sea traffic of Marseilles, an industrial city of 318,000 shipping from its harbors many of the products of its soap factories, olive oil refineries, tanneries, textile mills, brick and chemical plants. Its two ports could contain 2,400 ships, sailing ships and steamers whose masts rose like a denuded forest from the crowded basins.

By day the rue Sylvabelle echoed to the clatter of drays and vans, the pawing of cart horses restlessly standing, the calls of teamsters, the jingle of harness. To the noisy dray traffic of firms handling bricks, wool, oils and grains were added the splashing of watering carts settling dust, the rumble of washerwomen's wagons trotting with heavy loads, women street sweepers with kerchiefs on their heads singing throaty southern songs as they loaded refuse into waiting carts.

A few blocks from the rue Sylvabelle's commercial din was the open Place de la Bourse facing the meeting ground of all Marseilles, the Cannebière's "five big cafés in a resplendent row." Long awnings shielded the sidewalk tables of the Café de Marseilles at 1 rue Cannebière; the Café du Commerce at 15 rue Cannebière where foreign newspapers attracted the port's multi-tongued arrivals; the cosmopolitan Café de l'Univers at Number 19, modestly priced for artists and commercial travelers; the gilded Grand Café at 23 rue Cannebière and 1 Place de la Bourse, most ornate of all.

Consulate officials as well as Legitimists made the nearby Café Bodoul their lunching place and there Conrad met one of his friends, Raymond de Campou, a businessman engaged in marine insurance who was also the vice-consul in charge of the Japanese Consulate at 27 rue Vacon. A few blocks away at 5 rue Noailles, an extension of the Cannebière, was the café-restaurant Maison Dorée. Conrad used its name in *The Arrow of Gold* and it may have been a café which he and the younger set favored. Two of the friends he made in Marseilles he was to see in later years—young Pascalis, whose family had an import business at 70 rue Montgrand and who in 1895 was a journalist on *Le Figaro* in Paris; and young Jullien, who became a banker in Paris.

The hotels of Marseilles, like its cafés, were in the downtown heart of the city, within carriage reach of the Vieux Port. Largest and most elegant was the Grand Hôtel Noailles, on the Cannebière and a few blocks from the harbor, where at the rate of two francs a day guests could benefit from the new innovation of a hydraulic lift taking them up to all floors. The Grand Hôtel de Genève had no such modern device but could advertise the rare convenience of baths in the hotel. The Grand Hôtel de Bordeaux et d'Orient relied on its sole appeal of being a haven for "commercial travelers and clergy."

Gas-lighted as it was—even Paris was not to see its first electric street lamps until a few were tentatively placed on the Avenue de l'Opéra in June, 1878 to the amazement of Parisians and their outspoken protests at the cost—Marseilles was a lively town and for Conrad, a youth adventure-bound, it was expensive. In June, 1877 he asked his Uncle Thaddeus for eight thousand francs, a four years' advance on his allowance. To conceal the high toll of his secret *Tremolino* venture, he offered a proposed voyage to India as the excuse for needing that large a sum of money.

When his uncle refused, Conrad borrowed. He quarreled with M. Delestang and transferred his banking arrangements from Delestang & Son to Richard Fecht, employed in the firm of Albert de Toussaint, commodity brokers with German connections having offices in Mannheim and Ludwigshafen. Richard Fecht repeatedly loaned Conrad money and, becoming a close friend, handled his financial affairs for five years.

In the fall Conrad appealed to his uncle again, giving as the excuse this time his plan of sailing with Captain Escarras, master of the *Saint-Antoine,* on a year-and-a-half to two-year voyage around the world. His uncle believed the tale enough to send 1,000 francs, also an additional 1,000 in December when

Conrad pressed for more. The *Tremolino* was consuming his funds at a fast pace. To prevent news of his risky venture from reaching his supremely cautious uncle, and to protect himself —a Pole with uncertain passport standing—from possible complication with the French police, Conrad adopted the name of Monsieur George.

"It served me then as it will serve for this story," he wrote in *The Arrow of Gold.* "In all sorts of strange places I was alluded to as 'that young gentleman they call Monsieur George.' Orders came from 'Monsieur George' to men who nodded knowingly. Events pivoted about 'Monsieur George.' I haven't the slightest doubt that in the dark and tortuous streets of the Old Town there were fingers pointed at my back: 'There goes Monsieur George.' I had been introduced discreetly to several considerable persons as 'Monsieur George.' I had learned to answer to the name quite naturally; and to simplify matters I was also 'Monsieur George' in the street of the Consuls and in the Villa on the Prado. I verily believe that at that time I had the feeling that the name of George really belonged to me."

Assumed names were not rare during a period in France particularly stormy, a year for Conrad of tumbled joy, exultation and sadness which had in retrospect the unreal quality of a daydream.

The times in France were chaotic, with the country undergoing a revolutionary change in politics and art.

The greatest event for many decades in the art world occurred in March, 1877 when the famous collection of Firmin Didot was sold in Paris. The sale of that tremendous collection, the largest of any private owner, lasted three weeks. Buyers from all over the world competed for the several hundred paintings, drawings, and engravings of the great masters Didot had spent a lifetime and a fortune collecting. Following that event focused on a past art was the Impressionist show in Paris where, almost for the first time, painters of lighter, gayer colors were receiving less than jeers. Paul Cézanne, a Provençal artist, exhibited with Edouard Manet, the originator of Impressionism who was to die, still receiving but stinted recognition, six years later.

Repercussions of the Impressionists' struggle in Paris reached Marseilles where the sale of the Didot collection and the swing toward a fresh form of painting divided the Bohemian set into defenders of old art and new. That Conrad strongly supported Impressionism then, as he was later to be an impressionist writer, came out in his one novel dealing with the world of art, *The Arrow of Gold,* where he centered the art of a past time on the dead Henry Allègre, an artist-connoisseur who had collected "brocades, old jewels, unframed pictures, bronzes, chinoiseries, japoneries" and whose great art collection when it was sold "made a noise enough in the world."

Painting with color words throughout the novel, Conrad used a vivid palette: Rita coming down the white stairs on the deep crimson carpet in a light blue dress; Therese a brown-clothed figure out of an old cracked and smoky painting whose weather-tanned complexion had an "extraordinary clayey aspect which reminded me of a strange head painted by El Greco"; Mrs. Blunt looking "a perfect picture in silver and grey, with touches of black here and there"; Blunt a man so correctly tailored he "might have been reproduced in marble on a monument."

Some twenty years after leaving Marseilles Conrad was to become an acknowledged master of impressionist story-telling, a painter in prose saying, "My task which I am trying to achieve is, by the power of the written word to make you hear, to make you feel—it is, before all, to make you *see*. That—and no more, and it is everything."

The steps toward that future time led from a period in France extraordinarily rich in both creators of prose and painting. What were to become some of the leading names in world literature were then men writing in the country where he lived.

Victor Hugo was a white-haired grandfather of seventy-five in Paris completing the last of his great novels *Ninety-Three*. He was the venerated dean of French letters but age had not weakened the man described by Sir Sidney Colvin as a "life-long fulminator against kings and priests and conquerors and oppressors, and all the cruelties and tyrannies and treacheries of the world."

Émile Zola, who had spent his boyhood near Marseilles, was a writer of thirty-seven at the beginning of his career, publishing his first great success *The Dram-Shop* in 1877. Alphonse Daudet, also thirty-seven, brought out *The Nabob* that year. Gustave Flaubert at fifty-six was ending his work, three years before his death, with the most famous of his short stories "A Simple Heart" in his new collection *Three Tales*.

Turgenev, a friend of Flaubert and three years older, was at his home near Paris, a voluntary exile from Russia who had left his country for France sixteen years before following criticism of *Fathers and Sons*. Guy de Maupassant, a young Norman of twenty-seven, was ending seven years of literary apprenticeship in Flaubert's circle, a group that included Turgenev, Daudet and Zola. Three years later his long study bore fruit in a masterpiece when he published his first short story *"Boule de Suif,"* the beginning of an incredible decade in which he produced three hundred stories and six novels.

Anatole France at thirty-four was writing poetry and criticism, settling down to work on his first novel, *The Crime of Sylvester Bonnard,* to be published in three years.

Whether it was the corruption of money exposed by Daudet in *The Nabob,* alcoholic decay bared by Zola in *The Dram-Shop* or political chicanery fired upon by Hugo in *The Story of a Crime,* the social and political upheaval in France supplied endless targets for its writers. The end of the Empire had left the country with a murky carry-over from an era whose decadence Daudet summed up in *The Nabob:* "All scandals, all turpitudes were there; consciences sold, or for sale; the vice of an epoch without greatness and without originality."

Out of the "deep rumbling of popular discontent" heard during those Empire days by Ambassador Washburne from his observer's post in the American Embassy, France was forging a new republic. It leaned in that violent time most of all on one man.

Chapter XVII

◇◇◇◇◇◇◇◇◇◇◇◇◇◇◇◇◇

"UNLESS you have chaos within you cannot give birth to a dancing star." The epigram of Friedrich Nietzsche applied equally to himself and to the country stretching beyond the border where he lived in 1877, Nietzsche then being a young professor of Greek at Basle, already the author, at thirty-three, of *The Birth of Tragedy* and *Untimely Opinions.* Across the frontier from Basle was a France knowing chaos and, in the comet blaze of a man of "incessant vibration," was discovering in Léon Gambetta a dancing star.

Gambetta had flashed into prominence in 1870 by means of a feat as phenomenal as any Jules Verne was to offer two years later in *Around the World in Eighty Days.*

With German troops surrounding its capital and pressing France toward defeat in the Franco-Prussian War, Gambetta, a thirty-three-year-old member of the Chamber of Deputies from Marseilles, escaped from Paris in a balloon in a sensational night ascent. With him in the swaying wicker basket were five passengers including two Americans who took off over the rooftops as released ropes and ejected ballast sand sent the hydrogen ball beyond the reach of German guns. Paris on that night of October 7, 1870 had been under siege for nineteen days. Defying starvation, reduced to eating the animals in the zoo, the city was to live behind its barricades for 132 days, in its fury publishing twenty-three daily newspapers all that time.

Gambetta's balloon disappeared into a black sky. A dense cheering crowd, tossing their caps in the air, stood by the high-leaping flames of bonfires and watched the soundless ball soar off like a toy. That night, three months before German shells were to bring devastation to its streets, Paris felt sure of rescue.

Gambetta reached Tours safely. As Minister of the Interior and of War, he took charge of the provisional government and organized an army for the relief of Paris. But time ran out; the holding armies in Metz and Orléans surrendered and France ignominiously fell to Prussian conquest in January, 1871.

With Napoleon III deposed and dying in exile, with his Luxembourg Palace throne room empty—the most fabulous *Salle du Trône* in all Europe lavishly hung with purple velvet studded with golden bees—France underwent six violent years. The political pendulum swung from the extreme Left of the Paris Commune to the extreme Right's efforts to restore monarchy. There were three contenders for the tantalizingly empty throne room. Legitimists backed the Count de Chambord as king; Orléanists sought a monarchy under the Count of Paris; Bonapartists championed as Emperor Napoleon IV the twenty-one-year-old son of Napoleon III, the Prince Imperial who was killed in 1879 fighting in the British campaign against the Zulus in South Africa.

Monarchists, struggling to stave off exit from the stage, gave France one year of disorder after another. Adolphe Thiers, an elderly historian from Marseilles, was made President of the Third Republic in 1871 but less than two years later the mildly progressive statesman of seventy-six was forced out of office when Orléanists, Legitimists, Clericals and Imperialists combined to unseat him and elect Marshal MacMahon in May, 1873. MacMahon, a General during the Franco-Prussian War and a Duke of Irish descent, aided the reactionary parties in their attempt to destroy the republic, to install a king in France, to prevent the elimination of the Church from state affairs.

When the general election of February, 1876 proved again to be a victory for the republicans and a check to the kingmakers, MacMahon defied the nation's vote. In his *coup d'état* of May 16, 1877 he dismissed the government and appointed a clerical-monarchist ministry.

Gambetta took up the challenge. A matchless orator and brilliant lawyer, he stood in the Chamber of Deputies, at that time meeting in Versailles, and gave his famous June, 1877 speech. "One man against a hundred," as the London *Times* described the unbalanced struggle, his was an exhibition of tremendous power.

In a last maneuver for the monarchists MacMahon dismissed the assembly and called for a new election. For four months Gambetta stumped the country. Victor Hugo threw in the weight of his widely circulated *The Story of a Crime,* as powerful a force in solidifying the republic as Gambetta's campaign. The elections of October, 1877 again went to the republicans and the monarchist threat gradually declined from then on to extinction.

For the next five years Gambetta was a power behind the ministries though he held no higher post than President of the Chamber and, for a few months in the last year of his life, the office of Premier. Yet his effect was lasting: he shaped the constitution of the Third Republic and, a firm anticlerical, his relentless agitation for the separation of Church and state led to that final achievement in 1905.

During his short and flaming career monarchists and clerical groups focused on Gambetta as a target. The hopes of republicans centered in the fiery, popular man with one eye; his left eye had been removed when he was sixteen, a handicap that failed to prevent him from becoming a lawyer at twenty-one.

His opponents, seeking to eliminate him, searched tirelessly for some means by which to bring him down. It was a time of scandal-mongering, the stakes of government were high. Not until many years after his death did they learn that Gambetta had been vulnerable.

A bachelor whose life seemed fully absorbed by devotion to his unsteady country, Gambetta had fallen in love when he was thirty-four. The girl, nine years younger, was Léonie Léon, intelligent, beautiful, accomplished, a sadly serious girl with an unhappy history. For nine years she refused to marry Gambetta because of the damage it might do to his career, the ammunition of slander her own life could furnish.

Mlle. Léon was the daughter of a Colonel in command of the post at Strasbourg who, committing suicide, left her and her sister penniless orphans when in their early teens. The sister was seduced and bore an illegitimate son whom Léonie Léon raised. To earn her own living and that of her sister's child, the young girl went to Paris as a governess, and was herself forced into relationship with a high official of the Imperial government. A temporary but crushing experience that had ended three years before she met Gambetta, she remained marked by it. Much as she loved Gambetta, she remained in the background totally out of sight, sustaining the man fighting at such great odds. No one but a few of Gambetta's closest friends knew of her existence.

By 1882 the republic was firmly established and Gambetta beyond the reach of petty scandal. The date of a marriage for which they had waited nine years was set. Three days before that ceremony Gambetta was repairing a dueling pistol when it exploded, wounding him in the hand. Though the wound was slight it bled profusely and he was taken to the hospital. There Gambetta became acutely ill, doctors treated him under a wrong diagnosis and he died of a ruptured appendix. Mlle. Léon, a grieving lonely woman, died, still unknown, in 1906.

Gambetta's death, untimely at forty-four, was widely reported as resulting from a duel, for it was a time when men as prominent as Gambetta or as unknown as young Conrad were prepared for challenge.

Duels were being fought with deadly regularity in Europe and America. More often they grew from political quarrels, as did an American one reported in the European press on February 1, 1878. That duel, fought with Colt revolvers, was between Walter S. Harley, a lawyer, and Robert Fishburne, county court clerk, who met on the field of honor at a railroad junction three miles from Savannah, Georgia. The two South Carolina men were brothers-in-law, married to sisters; both were Democrats. The insult was over an issue of local politics when Harley hurled the fiery words: "You and W. F. Fishburne are mean and cheap copies of the Rhetts, without their brains or courage." Harley was fatally wounded in the Colt combat.

In Paris, members of the Chamber of Deputies carried their debates to the dueling field. In Marseilles newspaper writers took their press battles to open-air sword meets, and in Rome journalists and politicians settled accounts with blades.

Fought less frequently but with more venom than political duels were those springing from insults involving women. On April 2, 1877 the Marquis de Compiègne and a Mr. Meyer fought a duel in which the Marquis was killed. The two men were strangers. At a masked ball they had a dispute over a lady during which the Marquis struck Meyer, resulting in the challenge.

Most savage of all was a duel at Linea outside Gibraltar between a Captain and a Lieutenant in the Spanish Army for an undisclosed cause. Fought with knives, the Spanish *navaja*, the two bleeding, still bodies of the men were found on the beach, the Captain dead of eighteen stab wounds.

In a country whipped by political fury, in a year crackling with the exchange of dueling shots, Conrad, far from "the orderly man" his prosaic uncle wished him to be, was whirled into crisis.

Chapter XVIII

◇◇◇◇◇◇◇◇◇◇◇◇◇◇◇◇

SPRING dropped on Marseilles suddenly, as if winter had ended like a play. With the swiftness of stage props hustled off to storage the inky skies were gone, the etched trees, the gaunt streets pruned to bleakness by the mistral. The new scene had the impromptu freshness of the drawing of a child.

Spinning discs of carriage wheels flickered in the sunlight, airy as the whirls of paper windmills children pushed through the breeze. Blue skies hanging flawlessly ironed crumpled under spasmodic bursts of rain. The washed air was as crisp as watercress and as peppery.

Spring came to Paris with the May Day opening of the Salon where crowds slowly moved along the yellow sanded walks under the great glass dome of the conservatory. Luxuriously dressed women wore the latest in extravagant trains, of ecru lace and bonnets, and strolled through the exhibits of sculpture and portraits in the indoor show that drew all Paris.

But Marseilles was an outdoor town, a southern town, demanding live color. There May brought the Floral Games that opened the season of roses. Flamboyant with blossoms, it bubbled with parties, parades, balls for the Beauty Queen, a festival pulsing with gaiety, vivid and spirited.

Spring and an unsettling love, an overpowering combination at nineteen, held Conrad like a kite in the wind, rising on hope, plunging in despair.

With Don Carlos banished from France for six months and June closing the Paris social season, Paula made frequent trips between her temporary Paris residence, the Hôtel Friedland, and Marseilles. Conrad had a standing invitation to lunch and coming away from her house on the Prado could think of nothing but the girl of quicksilver moods. She might swing him about in a dizzy waltz, receive him with her long hair loose and flying, or icily set him apart with unbridgeable distance, a "romantic resigned La Vallière." At eighteen she was trying on many roles.

To him there was always "something childlike in their relation," their "unreserved and instant sharing of all thoughts, all impressions, all sensations" having the "naïveness of a children's foolhardly adventure."

They quarreled and made up, argued and laughed in an "unmannerly, Arcadian state of affairs." Conrad had a keen wit, a lively sense of fun, and, as Galsworthy said of him, "an almost ferocious enjoyment of the absurd."

But the tension of a love at first unreturned gave him nightmare thoughts.

I felt tears come into my eyes at the memory of her laughter, the true memory of the senses almost more penetrating than the reality itself. It haunted me. All that appertained to her haunted me with the same awful intimacy, her whole form in the familiar pose, her very substance in its colour and texture, her eyes, her lips, the gleam of her teeth, the tawny mist of her hair, the smoothness of her forehead, the faint scent that she used, the very shape, feel, and warmth of her high-heeled slipper that would sometimes in the heat of the discussion drop on the floor with a crash, and which I would (always in the heat of the discussion) pick up and toss back on the couch without ceasing to argue. . . . I was haunted also by her waywardness, her gentleness and her flame.

Added to an emotional temperament equally shared, the two had much in common. They were of an age, each a foreigner in France, orphans without home ties finding a footing of their own. Both were reckless, severely honest, and outside society—Paula because her peasant origin barred her from any acceptable place in the only world she knew, a Royal Prince's circle conforming to the rules of Vienna's Hapsburg court where a lineage of "sixteen quarterings" was required for social recognition; Conrad deliberately repudiating every social box in his determination to be free.

Conrad explained the isolation they shared to Sir Sidney Colvin when in 1919 Colvin was preparing a review of *The Arrow of Gold* for which Conrad offered suggestions.

Perhaps you could also discover a "personal note of youth" both in the (so to speak) innocence and the completeness of this love affair—this emotional adventure fated to end as it ends in a world not meant for lovers and between these two beings both outside the organized scheme of society not because they are *déclassés* in any sense but because of the origin of one and the deliberate renunciation of the other.

Conrad's "deliberate renunciation," which was to mount with the years after Marseilles, reached a later peak of apartness when his fellow sea captains gave him, a gentleman sailor noticeably elegant in manners and dress, the hostile nickname of "the Russian Count." His idealistic determination to live without compromise—a rebel and alone—clashed with the human longing to be "one of us" and provided that conflict of loyalties in his own life which was to echo as a major theme in its writing. It was a conflict without solution for a sensitive man who, from childhood, carried an inner isolation which he was to tell of through many of his characters, among them Axel Heyst in *Victory*. Drawing much of himself in that man of fiction, he gave to Heyst a beckground similar to his own.

Heyst, never knowing his mother, was raised by his father, a writer who died an expatriate, "the most uneasy soul that civilization had ever fashioned to its ends of disillusion and regret. One could not refuse him a measure of greatness, for he was unhappy in a way unknown to mediocre souls."

Heyst lived with his father during the last three years of the older man's life. Although he kept his father's "pale, distinguished face in affectionate memory," the three years "of such companionship at that plastic and impressionable age were bound to leave in the boy a profound mistrust of life."

After his father's death Heyst determined to drift "altogether and literally, body and soul, like a detached leaf," believing that in restless wandering he could pass through life without suffering, "invulnerable because elusive."

Conrad, like Heyst, had had three years of the companionship of a despondent father. After his father's death he had set out as a wanderer but his scheme of making himself invulnerable as an "impermanent dweller amongst changing scenes" collapsed earlier than Heyst's. For him the barrier of detachment was broken, too, by a girl.

The fate Conrad created for Heyst, unendurably alone after the death of Lena, was suicide. Differing in that from Heyst—however much his reason-destroying romance in Marseilles may have suggested suicide to him then—Conrad's parting with the girl he loved resulted from an event less tragic than the ending of her life.

In November, 1877 Paula, summoned by Don Carlos, gave up her rented house on the Prado and left Marseilles. She joined the Pretender, then in Austria, for the Italian journey highlighted by what Conrad was to describe in *The Arrow of Gold* as "the Venetian episode." The Prince's Venice appearance with his mistress, an overt recognition of her as *l'amie du Roi,* was something of a debut for Paula. The first of the occasions on which he was to draw public attention to her, in defiance of Victorian etiquette, the "Venetian episode" was, as Conrad recalled, "talked about from a royalist point of view with a kind of respect" in Paris, where it also received veiled mention by gossip-writing journalists.

Unnamed by the Paris press then, the girl who accompanied Don Carlos to Venice—her identity being one of the major clues to Conrad's "Rita"—has remained unknown to the public since the mysteriously alluded-to trip of eighty years ago. Now, through unpublished Spanish letters of 1877 in Madrid, in the archives of a family at that time particularly close to Don Carlos, the presence of Paula on the journey causing a social flurry in the France of Conrad's youth has been established. The letters, concerned with the personal life of Don Carlos, were written when his affair with the Hungarian beauty was a closely guarded secret, before, as Conrad wrote, a Parisian journalist saw them together on the Lido and "shoved his nose into that business." From information given in these private records the Italian trip of Don Carlos—accompanied by Paula de Somoggy, as the letters tell—can be reconstructed. He was in Gratz (Austria) about the middle of November, 1877; he left Vienna around November 25th or 30th; he was in Venice until December 10, next in Milan, then in Turin, and from there to Paris, where he stayed for the Christmas festivities of this same year of 1877.

With Paula in Italy and becoming more of a celebrity than ever, Conrad had little hope of seeing her again. Before leaving Marseilles she had urged him to "take this fancy out and trample it in the dust," but he was powerless against an emotion that "was in me just like life was in me." For three months he continued to run guns to Spain, throwing himself into his unlawful trade "with a sort of desperation, dogged and hopeless, like a fairly decent fellow who takes deliberately to drink." His dangerous occupation was both his sole link with Paula and his excuse for remaining in Europe, "which somehow I had not the strength of mind to leave for the West Indies, or elsewhere."

He was tortured by visions of the girl: the tawny film of her hair, her warm contralto voice, the touch of her hand— "The very memory of it would go through me like a wave of heat. It was over that hand that we first got into the habit of quarreling, with the irritability of sufferers from some obscure pain and yet half unconscious of their disease."

Conrad carried away from his love affair a despondency cropping up in later years which his Uncle Thaddeus traced back to Marseilles.

"I may be mistaken, but I think this tendency to pessimism was already in you as long ago as the days when you were at Marseilles," he wrote to Conrad in 1891.

Misanthropic as his mood was in that December of 1877, Conrad persisted with his contraband voyages on the *Tremolino*. Meanwhile Paula, after the Italian journey, returned with "the King" to Paris, which became from then on her permanent home. A glimpse into her life there during the years before her break with Don Carlos was given by the Count de Melgar in his memoirs:

It should be known that I, until the time of the break, had not had the slightest contact with the señora, whom I knew by sight from having seen her so frequently at the theatre, sea bathing, and all the other places where we used to go.

Shortly after I received my official appointment as secretary to the King, he, who frequently spoke to me about her, told me that she greatly desired to meet me and invited me to come to her house; I declined the invitation with as much firmness as respect and answered Don Carlos thus:

"Forgive me, Sire, but it is impossible for me to accept this invitation. Being of all the people who surround Your Majesty the one who is privileged to be in closest touch with you, my position is such that I cannot sit alternately at the table of my Queen and at that of the lover of my King."

"But, man," Don Carlos exclaimed with amazement, "don't you know that almost all the Carlists who are my personal friends go to visit her and dine at her home?" And he cited a long list of names, among them Princes and close relatives. . . .

The following morning, when I appeared at the office, he hurried to tell me:

"Do you know that Nyul very much approves of your decision and told me that it increases the esteem she has for you." (Nyul was the pet name he had for her; that word means hare in Hungarian, and it suited her because of a certain way she had of contracting her lips.)

His banishment suspended, Don Carlos returned to Paris at the end of 1877, dining with Queen Isabella on December 30 at her residence, Basilewski Palace, very near his own Pavilion. After ending his long feud with Spain's Queen Mother, he was off again on New Year's Eve for London, there to spend a few days with his father before sailing on an American voyage. The Spanish press, angrily labeling him a rebel, "an enemy and stranger to Spain," denounced the Queen Mother for her contact with him. Because of writing a letter in his behalf, the Spanish government, said the London *Times,* was reported to have directed its ambassadors to break off all relations with her.

The New Year that brought such turmoil to Spain also brought tragedy for Conrad, and on Spanish soil.

His contraband game had become dangerous. The Basque bands were being closely hunted by Alfonso's troops; twice Conrad had narrow escapes. From an ambush on the Spanish coast carabineers fired on him and Dominic but their shots flew wild. Later the *Tremolino,* sailing without lights under the protection of the night, received a volley from a small coaster creeping up in the darkness, its own lights doused for pursuit. Conrad knew his trade had seen its best days.

The arrangements for the transport of supplies were going to pieces; our friends ashore were getting scared; and it was no joke to find after a day of skillful dodging that there was no one at the landing place and have to go out again with our compromising cargo, to slink and lurk about the coast for another week or so, unable to trust anybody and looking at every vessel we met with suspicion.

On her last voyage the *Tremolino,* with a big stake involved, moved cautiously. Conrad took her on a wide deceptive circuit and entered Barcelona for information about the location of patrol craft he needed to avoid. Bribed customs officials readily gave it. The only *guardacosta* in the neighborhood was safely twelve miles away, lying at anchor, undergoing painting repairs. The *Tremolino* made ready to sail but was delayed until dusk by her missing crew member César Cervoni, Dominic's nephew. When César returned, minus his coat, he refused to say where he had spent the day.

The ship sailed on a gusty breeze throughout the night but daybreak showed the *guardacosta* in chase. The pursuing ship, three times the size of the *Tremolino,* could overtake her. She had come out on information—César's—and had been lying in wait for Conrad's balancelle.

When a sudden gust of wind yanked the new mainsail out of its boltropes, its roping stitches showing César's knife cuts, the *Tremolino* lost way. Conrad watched the coastguard ship gain on them as his own swung along under one sail, a pursuit he told of in *The Mirror of the Sea.*

"They will get the poor barky," I stammered out, suddenly, almost on the verge of tears.

Dominic stirred no more than a carving. A sense of catastrophic loneliness overcame my inexperienced soul. The vision of my companions passed before me. The whole Royalist gang was in Monte Carlo now, I reckoned. And they appeared to me clear-cut and very small, with affected voices and stiff gestures, like a procession of rigid marionettes upon a toy stage.

To avoid capture and the penalties it would bring Dominic warned him that the ship must be driven ashore, wrecked. He turned to Conrad with that plan in mind.

"You love her well?"

"I do."

"Then you must find the heart for that work, too. You must steer her yourself, and I shall see to it that she dies quickly, without leaving as much as a chip behind."

Conrad took the tiller and at Dominic's command shot the *Tremolino* head on into a rock jutting off the Spanish shore near Cape San Sebastian.

Talk of splintered planks and smashed timbers! This shipwreck lies upon my soul with the dread and horror of a homicide, with the unforgettable remorse of having crushed a living, faithful heart at a single blow. At one moment the rush and the soaring swing of speed; the next a crash, and death, stillness—a moment of horrible immobility, with the song of the wind changed to a strident wail, and the heavy waters boiling up menacing and sluggish around the corpse. I saw in a distracting minute the foreyard fly fore and aft with a brutal swing, the men all in a heap, cursing with fear, and hauling frantically at the line of the boat.

The ship slid off the rock and sank swiftly. With it went César. The boy who had betrayed them—who, to carry treasonable news, had sold his jacket in Barcelona to pay for the hire of a horse—had been struck by Dominic in his "well-known, effective gesture, the horizontal sweep of his powerful arm." The stone weight of ten thousand francs in gold, contained in a money belt stolen from Conrad's locker, proved a death prize.

Conrad, knocked senseless by the swinging tiller, came to in the dinghy as it landed in a sheltered cove. Dominic left him in a familiar countryside to make his way back to Marseilles by any means he could. The man Conrad so affectionately remembered all his life parted with him for the last time, going off alone with his own particular burden.

That I, a confidential man and a Corsican, should have to ask your pardon for bringing on board your vessel, of which I was Padrone, a Cervoni, who has betrayed you—a traitor!—

that is too much. It is too much. Well, I beg your pardon; and you may spit in Dominic's face because a traitor of our blood taints us all. A theft may be made good between men, a lie may be set right, a death avenged, but what can one do to atone for a treachery like this? . . . Nothing.

Dominic returned to Marseilles but disappeared from there for more than a year, resuming his sea service out of that port in March, 1879. Twelve years after his farewell to Conrad on the Spanish coast above the wreck of the *Tremolino* Dominic died in his Corsican birthplace of Luri. On the last day of the fifty-six-year-old seaman's life, July 27, 1890, Conrad was undergoing a thirty-six-day trek through the scorching heat of the Belgian Congo, heading for the command of a small river steamer which, proving as much of a mirage as the hope that led him on, gave him both the experience for "Heart of Darkness" and the illness that turned him to writing it.

Conrad's narrow escapes tread one on the heels of another. The shots of carabineers and *guardacostas* had missed him, Dominic had saved him in the shipwreck of the *Tremolino,* but his next challenge was to come within a breath of being fatal.

Chapter XIX

AFTER the shipwreck of the *Tremolino* Conrad faced an ordeal getting out of Spain. Dodging arrest, penniless, he skulked across the country, walking many of the miles to the border, existing on handouts of food, repeatedly in trouble "with all sorts of people who looked upon me evidently more as a discreditable vagabond deserving the attention of gendarmes than a respectable (if crazy) young gentleman attended by a guardian angel of his own."

When he finally dropped off a train in Marseilles he was unshaven, with neither cap nor jacket to protect him from a cold winter wind, a grubby young man whom any passing stranger might have taken for the outcast he felt himself to be. Lacking even the fare for a fiacre, he walked across town from the Gare St. Charles to the rue Sylvabelle.

As he took stock of his disastrous days and his close brush with imprisonment in Spain he felt the full shock of their cost. "I had nearly lost my liberty and even my life, I had lost my ship, a money-belt full of gold, I had lost my companions, had parted from my friend; my occupation, my only link with life, my touch with the sea."

When news of his shipwreck reached Paris, which Don

Carlos had left for London, Paula came down to Marseilles. The Carlist adventure for the prize of a crown, in which she had involved him, was over. Don Carlos had signaled the end of the contest by the truce Queen Isabella announced. Regardless of the suspicious hostility with which it was received by Alfonso's Madrid mouthpiece *Cronista,* and despite new tremors in Catalonia in 1879, he was to make no further attempt to reach the throne by force.

Paula might have been "a little more at the mercy of contradictory impulses than other women" but she was supremely honest. Men, all men, found her attractive, tantalized by an elusive quality each sought to capture. Hers was a temperament provocative and wayward—"like all those on whom there is no peace I am not One"—but it was built on no deceit. For twelve months Conrad had shown a love for her so deeply ingrained that it would be there "on the day I die —when you won't be there." Because of the course her own life had taken, of "things that were neither correct nor playful and that had to be looked at steadily with all the best that was in me," she pleaded with him against it. But the strength of a passion which he felt would end either by killing him or driving him mad won over every defence of argument, time, separation.

A love that could draw from him the willing gamble of his life for the Carlist scheme, which he assessed in a later letter to J. C. Squire as "a very straightforward adventure conducted with inconceivable stupidity and a foredoomed failure from the start," brought from Paula such an answer as words he gave to Rita.

"Yes, my dear, I may be naturally wicked but I am not evil and I could die for you."

Love was as new to her as it was to him and in their retreat in the Maritime Alps she found as many ways of showing it. His might have been the greater self-surrender but "having once renounced her honourable scruples she took good care that he should taste no flavour of misgivings in the cup."

The weeks they had together were not many. It was winter, following the January 6 carnival of Twelfth Night. But the tenderness, the summer feeling of that perfect time led Conrad to dress it in fiction as six months spent in a rose-embowered hut. There, out of reach of everyone, they became "amazingly ingenuous in the practice of sentiment" and found in each other "in every phase of discovery and response, an exact accord."

But rent had to be paid for the stone house and groceries bought. Conrad returned for a few hours to Marseilles. He borrowed money and before boarding his train stopped for dinner in the station restaurant.

A Royalist acquaintance came upon him there and told him of the slander being circulated by John Blunt, the American who "lived by his sword," a rejected suitor made insanely jealous by his love for Paula. Blunt had, on three public occasions, "expressed his regret that she should have become the prey of a young adventurer who was exploiting her shamelessly." He named Conrad as the man. Conrad replied to the insult as the times required. He sent his challenge back by the messenger who brought the news. Blunt traveled down from Paris and on a day early in March the two met, with pistols, in a walled garden.

Conrad fired on the signal and wounded Blunt in the right hand. "Je lui ai fracassé la patte," Conrad told a relative many years later.

The duel should have ended with the first disablement but Blunt took his pistol from his injured right hand and with his left sent a bullet into Conrad's chest that nearly ended his life. With Blunt "taking careful aim to kill," as Conrad first wrote of that encounter, the shot entered—and he was to carry a reminding scar of it throughout his life—"on the left side of his breast bone."

Conrad's German friend and banker, Richard Fecht, sent his Uncle Thaddeus the urgent telegram: "Conrad wounded. Send money. Come." His uncle, believing Conrad to have sailed on a world voyage with Captain Escarras, received the alarming news of his nephew's gun wound while attending the Contract Fair in Kiev. Hurrying direct from Kiev, he arrived in Marseilles on March 11. During the days it took him to travel from the Ukraine to the south of France Conrad was nursed by Paula in his room on the rue Sylvabelle. A nearby doctor, the only one on the street being Dr. Pirondi at 80 rue Sylvabelle, was called in. Mills arrived, summoned by telegram.

For several days Conrad lived in a hazy nightmare, drifting from unconsciousness to a vague awareness of those around him. His life swayed like the flame of a draft-blown candle as he dreamed for "perhaps a year, or perhaps an hour" of events, of faces taking too much effort to identify, sinking into the region where all problems dissolved in the comfort of release. He was strong and young; he dropped into re-building sleep. When he woke, his life no longer in danger, Paula was gone.

Mills talked to him about the girl to ease his loss. She had told him, Mills said consolingly, "if this is any satisfaction to you to know, that till she met you she knew nothing of love. That you were to her in more senses than one a complete revelation."

From the knowledge, in 1917, of how her life did in fact turn out, Conrad wrote of her flight from Marseilles in *The Arrow of Gold*.

"She will be wasted," said Mills sadly. "She is a most unfortunate creature. Not even poverty could save her now. She cannot go back to her goats. Yet who can tell? She may find something in life. She may! It won't be love. She has sacrificed that chance to the integrity of your life—heroically. Do you remember telling her once that you meant to live your life integrally—oh, you lawless young pedant! Well, she is gone; but you may be sure that whatever she finds now in life it will not be peace. . . . Amid all the shames and shadows of that life there will always lie the ray of her perfect honesty."

However little Conrad in his desolation understood her flight during the days of his convalescence he was able to explain it forty-four years later in a letter to C. J. Fehbuts.

"A connection of that kind would have spelt ruin for a young fellow of 19 without fortune or position, or any young fellow for the matter of that. . . . By going away beyond his reach she gives him the supreme proof of her love, stronger than mere passion, stronger than the fear of her own and of his suffering."

Although referring to his love story as he told it in *The Arrow of Gold,* Conrad's memory unconsciously directed him to write the age of 19, his own age, one he failed to give to Monsieur George.

The jeweled arrow of gold pin, the "philistinish ornament" with brilliants and rubies gleaming along its shaft, had in actual life a fate other than that Conrad gave it in the book. In the novel when Rita disappeared from his life she left it for Monsieur George as a souvenir to end his troubling dreams, the relinquished dart of a huntress Diane. One day, years later, Monsieur George lost it during a storm at sea. He stood on the shore "looking at the seas raging over the very spot of his loss and thought that it was well."

The arrow of gold pin which Paula in real life wore—a gift of Don Carlos—was to Conrad during his youth in Marseilles a philistinish symbol of her alliance with the Royal Prince, a relationship which he no less than the marriage-proposing Blunt sought to have her end. But the strictures of Victorian society were rigid enough to make a man like Blunt, passionately in love as he might be, part from her "feeling tempted to brush the dust off his moral sleeve," and for such a woman as Paula there was no choice.

When she left Marseilles she returned to her house on the rue Pauquet in Paris, resuming her life with Don Carlos upon his return from his travels. In 1880, two years after Conrad parted from her, she was photographed in Paris wearing the arrow of gold pin.

Conrad was already able to walk when his Uncle Thaddeus reached Marseilles, but he was heavily in debt. His serious wound had entailed a high doctor's bill; back rent was due on his lodgings; he had loans to repay. He owed money to a M. Bonnard and to the brokerage firm of Albert de Toussaint. His thousand-franc allowance, plus the two thousand francs which his uncle had forwarded through a Polish cousin, Antoine Syroczynski, had disappeared with the *Tremolino*. Conrad's debts—at a time when $8 a week was a handsome wage, when his bill for room and board was but $25 a month—amounted to nearly four thousand francs, then $800.

His Uncle Thaddeus paid his debts during the two weeks he spent in Marseilles straightening out the finances and the tangled life of the nephew whose impetuous moves were to worry him for another sixteen years. Learning in Marseilles a disguised account of Conrad's gunrunning—but nothing of Paula—"Uncle Thaddeus B.," as he signed himself, attributed his nephew's troubles to a hunger for adventure and youthful imprudence. He accepted without inquiry Conrad's fable of a proposed world voyage with Captain Escarras, and the smuggling he laconically referred to as "speculation." But when he returned to the Ukraine, parsimonious man that he was, he tolled off each outlay made for his nephew in a notebook kept for that purpose, titled "For the information of my dear nephew Konrad Korzeniowski." In it—dating his entries according to the old style Russian calendar (twelve days behind the Gregorian)—he registered his still-burning anger over Conrad's duel, to which he gave a less romantic name.

In February, 1878 in Kiev I received from M. Bonnard a demand to pay your promissory note for 1000 francs and almost simultaneously news from M. Fecht that you were in a shooting. Therefore, at the end of February, [early in March by the Gregorian calendar] straight from Kiev, I hurried to Marseilles where, having found you already on your feet, I learned this: that you could not leave with M. Escarras for reasons beyond your control, that the 2000 francs sent you through A.S. [Antoine Syroczynski] were lost through speculation, as you confirmed and which I didn't see any reason to investigate; that you had contracted debts which I paid, namely: through Al. de Toussaint (Richard Fecht) 1706 francs—M. Bonnard 1000 francs—Mme. Fogas, your landlady, 233 francs—and to the doctor 700 francs. Which equals 3639 francs or 1228 rubles. In addition to that, my traveling expenses to Marseilles, also my stay there for two weeks—328 rubles.

Taking into consideration your needs, I have set aside for you, young man, 2400 francs a year. And so, for your first remittance covering April 15—October 15 of this year, I delivered 1200 francs to M. Fecht. Besides that I sent you 110 francs which were left over from the 1000 gulden banknote which belonged to you, and from which 2000 francs had been sent to you before. Those are now irretrievably lost and, what is worse, unproductively so. A fine state you have got yourself in! I suppose this will serve as a lesson to you but if I am mistaken, so much the worse for you.

A staid man of fifty, Thaddeus Bobrowski left Marseilles appalled by his young nephew's harum-scarum life. During his stay in the port he had learned little from seamen other than that Conrad went among them under the assumed name of Monsieur Georges. No one could tell him of Paula, nor did Conrad expose that sensitive area to the intolerant inspection of his uncle.

Called upon to explain his nephew's close-to-the-heart wound a year later in the Ukraine, Thaddeus Bobrowski wrote an account of it, "the yarn of Conrad's story," on March 24, 1879 to Stefan Buszczynski, an old friend of the family. His letter revealed the confused myth Conrad had woven to camouflage his romance. According to his uncle's report, Conrad had been unable to undertake his world voyage with Captain Escarras because of French passport regulations; failing in that, he had been talked into a smuggling affair by Captain Duteil of the *Mont-Blanc* [who, being off on a voyage could not be questioned]; losing financially in the smuggling escapade, Conrad had attempted, unsuccessfully, to join the American navy at Villefranche; disappointed there and without funds, he had borrowed 800 francs from Richard Fecht but gambled it away at Monte Carlo; in despair over his money problems, he had attempted suicide, shooting himself with a revolver.

"I never could invent an effective lie," Conrad was to write his friend, R. B. Cunninghame Graham, twenty years later. Yet the yarn he told his uncle, allied as it was with finances— the core of his uncle's interests—was convincing enough for Thaddeus Bobrowski to relate it. That he, even then, disbelieved Conrad's tale of a suicide attempt came out in his notebook entry—written for Conrad, alone, to read—where he referred to his nephew's being "in a shooting," his sarcastic term for the duel. "I have told everyone that he was wounded in a duel," he concluded the same perplexed letter to Buszczynski in which he recounted the overly romantic myth of Conrad's tea-hour, self-inflicted wound. He knew only too well how lightly his nephew took financial problems, the debts he had never been without during three and a half years of carefree living. But, lacking any hint of the true reason for the duel, the practical, accountant-minded Thaddeus could only ascribe money losses as the motive for the youth—a sympathetic "character" who was "ardent and original" in his imagination and talk, as he described Conrad to Buszczynski—guarding a private hurt far beyond the older man's understanding.

Once well enough to ship again and anxious to leave the town that so acutely reminded him of the girl he was to see in every face, "either by some profound resemblance or by the startling force of contrast," Conrad took the first sea berth available. An English coal-carrying freighter, the *Mavis,* put in at Marseilles on her way to Constantinople and when she sailed on April 24, 1878, Conrad was aboard, bound for the Sea of Azov. The end of her voyage on June 18, 1878, landed him in England at the east coast port of Lowestoft.

Even that voyage brought Conrad trouble. His Uncle Thaddeus, unaware of the cause of his nephew's turbulent behavior, chalked down the course of it in his notebook.

"Having received your allowance from M. Fecht, you set off on an English ship for Lowestoft and again you committed a new absurdity. For, having quarreled with the captain— and you could have been in the right—you went to London where you stupidly threw away the rest of your allowance. So, heeding your first call for help to M. Fecht, I sent 600 francs to M. Fecht through Warsaw."

The turmoil Conrad experienced during his tempestuous romance with Paula was caught in a paragraph of "The Laugh" which he deleted from the final draft of *The Arrow of Gold.*

"And over all there rests upon those days a mist of vague wonder, the sense of joy and pity, of smiles and anguish, of swiftness and fatigue . . . dreams one throws off . . . and which yet keep their place in one's past and influence one's future as much as any concrete experience that one ever plunged into or ran away from—both or either—for dear life."

Their two lives, Conrad's and Paula's, were to continue in strange attraction, each experiencing a series of crises to which the other simultaneously responded.

In Paris Paula's life, like Conrad's after his duel, came within a shade of ending. Count de Melgar told in his memoirs of the evening when Don Carlos came into his home on the rue de la Pompe looking so tragically unhappy his wife questioned him for the cause. She knew of and was undistressed by his relations with Paula, for whom she had great sympathy.

"I'm in despair," he told her. "Nyul is dying. She has a fatal throat infection and all the doctors say that nothing can save her."

Doña Marguerita knew a Dr. Raymond, a homeopathic doctor and throat specialist in Paris, and immediately sent her carriage for him. Through Dr. Raymond's treatment Paula recovered.

The extraordinary girl so appealing yet so ill-fated, who as Rita in *The Arrow of Gold* was characterized by the *Revue des Deux Mondes* as "a supernatural jewel, a pearl in the shadows" akin to Rembrandt's portrait of Saskia, was never to fade from Conrad's thoughts or to be untangled from the burden of his conscience. He was to form the heroines of his stories in large part on Paula. Freya of "Freya of the Seven Isles," Flora de Barral in *Chance,* Alice Jacobus in "A Smile of Fortune," Lena in *Victory,* Arlette in *The Rover* were, like Paula, seductive, childlike, enchanting girls. Mistreated by fate, all led tragic lives.

Chapter XX

❖❖❖❖❖❖❖❖❖❖❖❖❖❖❖❖

SEA.—WANTED, *respectable* YOUTHS, *for voyage or term in two splendid ships for Australia, and others for India, etc.— W. Sutherland, 11 Fenchurch-buildings, Fenchurch-street, near rail. Established 1851.*

CONRAD, at twenty, had been in England three months when he saw the advertisement in the London *Times* of September 25, 1878. He immediately sent off an answer, laboriously phrasing his first written English. Since arriving on the *Mavis* at Lowestoft in June he had made six trips as an ordinary seaman on *The Skimmer of the Seas,* a coaster plying between Lowestoft and Newcastle. He had picked up what English he knew from her crew of Norfolk sailors, from fishermen and shipwrights he met on the East coast run.

Back in Lowestoft after his last voyage on the barquentine, he made out the words of the *Times* advertisement and followed up his application letter with a train ride to London. He knew no one in England, had almost no funds, and the language he never succeeded in speaking without a heavy accent was new to him. More than ever he was on his own. His Uncle Thaddeus, dismayed by the tangle he had made of his life in Marseilles, his duel and his debts, had written "you have forfeited my confidence. Work now to regain it; you will win it back if you apply yourself steadily and pull yourself together."

Conrad set to work. With no schooling in the language, he taught himself English by reading newspapers. They told him of England's abnormal summer of tempests, of the new science of weather forecasting, of General Grant's world tour, of an eruption of Mount Vesuvius, of the surrender of Sitting Bull. His study took in advertisements of situations offered—for governesses, parlourmaids, footmen, pages, coachmen and grooms; covered letters to the editor protesting darkness caused by mischief-makers tinkering with London's street gas lamps, letters from doctors decrying the damaging effects of tobacco, of the poisonous alkaloids contained in that weed "whether chewed, snuffed, or smoked."

Conrad read of temperance meetings drawing crowds of seven thousand and more in London. In the face of strong temperance sentiment Gladstone, temporarily out of office as Prime Minister, wrote a cautious comment on a recent publication, "Clergyman's Sore Throat."

"When I have had very lengthened statements to make," Gladstone gave his nostrum for strained vocal cords in the London *Times* of September 28, 1878, "I have used what is called egg-flip—a glass of sherry beaten up with an egg. I think it excellent, but I have much more faith in the egg than in the alcohol."

Through his daily lessons in English Conrad acquired a newspaper view of life around the globe. A correspondent of the London *Times* told of one strange part of the world, the state of Colorado, over which he was journeying by railway and stagecoach. He rode on trains frequently stalled, their engines disabled by burst cylinders as they puffed up the mountains of Colorado, those magnified cliffs of Dover. He visited Alamosa in southern Colorado, a city then but six weeks old which already had a population of five hundred, two weekly journals, a hundred buildings mostly brought piecemeal from Garland, thirty miles away. At Pueblo he saw Mexican Indians and of them gave one of the reports of the Wild West—"It is common for both sexes to go to the river's bank and for the men to wash the women as if they were cattle"—accepted so credulously by readers in England.

Conrad's newspaper texts carried advertisements of the 109th performance at the Opera Comique of "H. M. S. Pinafore, or The Lass that Loved a Sailor, an original Nautical comic opera by W. S. Gilbert and Arthur Sullivan." Also being played was *Uncle Tom's Cabin* with a hundred Jubilee singers in its cast and "Real Freed Slaves."

In Lowestoft Conrad had studied the map of London. On the morning in late September when he arrived in the metropolitan heart of England he determined to find his way to Fenchurch Street without asking directions. From the railway station he walked miles across the city guided by a small map carried in the palm of his hand.

"No explorer could have been more lonely. I did not know a single soul of all these millions that all around me peopled the mysterious distances of the streets," he wrote in *Notes on Life and Letters*.

When he located Mr. Sutherland at 11 Fenchurch Buildings he found him to be a man with curly white hair and a full gray beard, an apostle of a man who looked through silver-rimmed spectacles as he talked, all the while eating his lunch. In the dark cobwebbed office in the City, a musty Dickens cubicle requiring a gas lamp's light in the middle of the day, Conrad learned that the advertisement for "respectable YOUTHS" was intended to draw premium-paying apprentices to be trained as future officers. He had no money for such a premium but something about him, his courage or his plight, induced the elderly agent to help him to a job as ordinary seaman on one of the "splendid ships" bound for

Australia. It was a wool clipper, the *Duke of Sutherland,* a thirteen-year-old ship of a thousand tons.

Within two weeks of his coming to London Conrad sailed on the clipper, on October 15, 1878, for Sydney. Eighteen years later he drew the opening scene of *The Nigger of the Narcissus* from the crew muster of the *Duke of Sutherland* as she prepared to leave Gravesend. A Negro member of her crew, James Wait, gave him the name for the central figure of his tale of the sea.

At Sydney, which the *Duke of Sutherland* reached at the end of January, 1879, Conrad was assigned the night watchman's job while his ship lay in port. In *The Mirror of the Sea* he recalled those nights when the burly chief mate would come rolling up the gangway after an evening spent drinking with his crony in some hotel parlor. An able officer who ended his life as a drifter, he lurched aboard and checked with Conrad on the state of the ship.

"Watchman!"
"Sir."
"Captain aboard?"
"Yes, sir."
Pause.
"Dog aboard?"
"Yes, sir."
Pause.
Our dog was a gaunt and unpleasant beast, more like a wolf in poor health than a dog, and I never noticed Mr. B— at any other time show the slightest interest in the doings of the animal. But that question never failed.
"Let's have your arm to steady me along."
I was always prepared for that request. He leaned on me heavily till near enough the cabin-door to catch hold of the handle. Then he would let go my arm at once.
"That'll do. I can manage now."
And he could manage. . . .

After a year's voyage Conrad was back in London, the *Duke of Sutherland* making port on October 19, 1879. He was in London when Don Carlos on November 1 came to Brown's Hotel for a stay of two months, probably, as he often was, accompanied by Paula. Don Carlos had again been requested to leave Paris, warned that the French government was "resolved not to tolerate political manifestations, for which his stay in France recently afforded a pretext." Monarchists were renewing their activity in France as were Carlists in Catalonia where a state of siege was threatened.

Conrad suddenly felt an overwhelming longing to see the Mediterranean. He shipped on the first vessel taking that route, leaving December 12, 1879, on the *Europa*. The steamer called at several Italian ports but in its seven-week voyage failed to stop at Marseilles.

Returning to London, he put in four restless months dallying with thoughts of other careers, tempted by the offer of a secretarial job in Canada. But the toss was decided early in June, 1880, when he passed his third mate's examination. Two years from the time of his arrival in England he had learned seamanship and English rapidly enough to become a ship's officer.

That summer of 1880 Conrad, twenty-two, proud of his new rank, was daily making the rounds from his furnished room in Stoke Newington to search for a ship. It was a summer that also saw Paula in London. She, whose fictional portrait in *The Arrow of Gold* the London *Times* likened to Helen of Troy, Mona Lisa and "Mother Eve herself," was a celebrated beauty enjoying Mayfair luxury.

At the end of July, 1880, Don Carlos was permanently expelled from France for allying himself with the Count de Chambord's partisans, so energetically trying to enthrone him as King of France. Don Carlos' expulsion was made final when the French Chamber passed a law forbidding princes belonging to dynasties which had reigned over France to reside in the country.

Sent in a special train to Boulogne, the Pretender reached

Dover on August 1. For the next three years he lived in England. In London, according to the Count de Melgar, he received a cordial welcome. "All of the high society, beginning with the Duke of Norfolk, the first peer of England and head of the Catholic church, came to see him at Brown's Hotel."

Paula lived in that circle, retaining her house in Paris, traveling back and forth between the two capitals. At twenty-one she was winning such eulogies as "the lovely, the inaccessible, the enigmatic, the half-fabulous" descriptive flights which critics used for Rita.

Conrad read the London *Times,* a main source of shipping news, and in its issues of early August read of the outcry caused by the abandonment of the *Jeddah.* The screw steamer of 1,500 tons, built at Dumbarton in 1872 and owned by the Singapore Steamship Company, had left Singapore bound for Jeddah with Moslem pilgrims on board. She was first reported as having foundered on August 8, 1880, off Cape Guardafui with all on board lost except her captain and his wife, the chief officer, the chief engineer, the assistant engineer and sixteen natives.

Lloyd's agent in Aden quickly telegraphed a correction: "The *Jeddah,* which was abandoned at sea with 953 pilgrims on board, did not founder, as reported by the master. She has just arrived here, all safe, in tow of the steamer *Antenor.*"

The desertion of their ship by the captain and his officers —they taking safely to boats, leaving the passengers on the unmanned steamer to perish—brought a deluge of outraged letters.

One master of pilgrim ships maintained that conditions on them were worse than those on slave ships. For the eighteen or twenty days of the voyage, he declared, a thousand "fanatics" were cooped up on the deck of a small vessel with no room to move, little or no fresh air, and no medical man on board. He believed the Bedouin and Turcoman pilgrims to be dangerous, coming aboard armed with daggers, swords and firearms, lighting open fires on the bare deck to prepare their tea.

A Member of Parliament, George Campbell, defended the pilgrims, asserting that they were not fanatics but frightened Easterners unaccustomed to sea voyaging. The shocking conditions on pilgrim ships, he insisted, were due to the avaricious Britishers who were making money from them.

"This is far from being the first case in which wrecks have been brought before the Indian Government where very large numbers of native passengers have been left to drown while the officers and crew escaped," Mr. Campbell wrote to the *Times*.

The desertion of the *Jeddah*, causing such a stir in London while Conrad was there, was the subject of a marine investigation held in Singapore. The ship, the inquiry showed, was heavily insured by her owners, the captain, J. L. Clark, and a Singapore Arab named Seyyid Muhammad Alsagoff, who wished to collect on her. She was abandoned at night during heavy weather 600 miles beyond Cape Guardafui near the mouth of the Red Sea by all her officers except one. The junior engineer who did not leave the ship, because he was not quick enough to get into the captain's lifeboat, was made a hero.

Conrad, reading the beginning of this sensational case in London, heard the end of it in Singapore. Twenty years later it served as a basis for *Lord Jim*.

He left London on August 21, 1880, sailing as third mate on the *Loch Etive* for Sydney. It was a Glasgow ship of 1,200 tons, three years old. Its master, Captain William Stuart, had made a reputation for speedy voyages.

On Christmas Day, 1880, the *Loch Etive* was on her way back from Sydney to London when she closed with a ship which, from the number of boats she carried, Conrad recognized as a whaler.

"She was the first whaler I had ever seen," he wrote in

"Christmas Day at Sea." "She had hoisted the Stars and Stripes at her peak, and her signal flags had told us already that her name was: 'Alaska—two years out from New York—east from Honolulu—two hundred and fifteen days on the cruising-ground.' "

Ending a voyage of eight months, the Loch Etive was back in London on April 25, 1881. Conrad had spent three years in the British merchant marine, had made two voyages to Australia, had sailed around Cape Horn. He was twenty-three, an officer, and riding high.

But in August he had his first experience of a serious disaster at sea. He was aboard the Anna Frost when she went down not far from England. Conrad was lucky to have escaped alive, though it required a hospital stay of several days to put him on his feet again. With his funds lost in the shipwreck, he asked his Uncle Thaddeus for ten pounds, which were promptly sent from the Ukraine, and as promptly recorded in his uncle's account book.

The sinking of the Anna Frost failed to dampen Conrad's high spirits. In little more than a month he embarked on the adventure related in "Youth." The gale that was to blow with such force upon his life was to give an equally dramatic twist to Paula's.

Chapter XXI

◇◇◇◇◇◇◇◇◇◇◇◇◇◇◇◇◇◇◇

UNLIKE Louis XIV's La Vallière, Nelson's Lady Hamilton or Napoleon's Countess Walewska, Paula de Somoggy had the handicap—insurmountable in the *beau monde*—of being peasant-born. For five and a half years she led a fabulous life as *l'amie du Roi* but her career as a Royal Prince's favorite, the target of jealousies flaming in the court Don Carlos gathered round him, was certain to be short. It was the more remarkable that she survived in such an atmosphere for a reign half the length of La Vallière's.

By 1882 the Carlist cause in Spain was flickering to its end. On March 19 the last revolutionary force in Catalonia disbanded. Don Carlos' partisans were splitting apart, circulating rumors which found him publicly denying on March 23 that he contemplated renouncing his claims to the Spanish throne in favor of his twelve-year-old son Don Jaime.

Carlist harmony was partly contingent upon the sacrifice of Paula. The Pretender's struggle in the middle of May, 1882, to bring himself to part with her was told by the Count de Melgar in his account of a ceremony conceived to reknit the warring factions.

One day it was decided that don Jaime, who was then a student at Belmont College, a religious school in Windsor, should receive his first communion with great ceremony and with the assistance of all the royal family, including his august grandfather, don Juan, who rarely visited his family, although he did not hesitate to come from Polo, where he had been hunting, to London to take part in the communion of his grandson.

Don Carlos suffered a great conflict of conscience. He would be unable to receive absolution unless he formally promised to break the illicit ties with his mistress, and his absence at this solemn ceremony would produce as much scandal as suffering for his son, his father, his wife, and for the whole Carlist movement.

The priest don Manuel Barrena, then don Jaime's tutor and with whom he lived at Beaumont College, being a very clever man, proposed a way around the impasse.

"The evening before the communion," he said, "we will all go to his bedroom and there make an appointment to meet the following morning at the foot of the altar, and, before the mass begins, he, I, and anyone else in whom you have absolute confidence will announce to the royal family that Don Carlos suffered a severe vomiting attack in the early hours of the morning which compelled him to take medicine and so interrupt the sacramental fast."

Don Carlos would not consent to participate in this subterfuge, since his profound horror of lying was even more overpowering when it involved doing it in church.

We had then been deliberating until midnight when Don Carlos, making a superhuman effort, decided to write to Señorita de Somoggy, who was also in London, telling her that having given the matter much serious thought he was forced to separate from her, that he would always be her best friend and that he would give her a settlement for life, a very generous one that would protect her from every need until the end of her days, but that it was essential that all intimate relations between the two of them should cease.

The girl, who had a very fine character and a great deal of integrity, and who had been brought up in the Christian faith by her uncle, a brother of her mother, a parish priest in a Hungarian village, accepted with resignation, and in order to avoid temptation left immediately for Paris, from which Don Carlos had been banished. . . .

At the time Nyul left for Paris Don Carlos, telling me she had gone, added:

"You see that our amorous relations have ceased and that we are not united by anything but an honest and close friendship. She has a strong desire to meet you and it seems to me that under present conditions you could have no objection to visiting her."

"None at all, Sire," I answered. So, on my first trip to Paris I went to her home on the rue Pauquet.

Her sudden drop from the luxurious world of royalty to ordinary life was for Paula, as it was for Rita, "like falling out of a balcony into the street." At twenty-three she had to dismount "down to the very ground." The balls were ended, the morning rides in the Bois, the summers at select spas, the grouse-shooting parties at Yorkshire estates, the whole exotic round of wealth and splendor.

With Paula dispatched to Paris, the Carlist reunion ceremony took place near London. Doña Marguerita left Italy with her four daughters and rejoined Don Carlos who had rented the Priory, a residence near Old Windsor, for his family. On June 9, 1882, the London *Times* reported the ceremony to which Carlists came from their estates in Europe.

The College of the Jesuit Fathers at Beaumont, Old Windsor, was yesterday the scene of the first communion of Don Jaime, the son of Don Carlos and Doña Marguerita, his wife. The ceremonial took place at the early hour of 7, in the chapel of St. Joseph, Low Mass being said by the Rector of the College. Among the congregation were the parents and sisters of the communicant and a few prominent Carlists. In the afternoon, it being the festival of Corpus Christi, there was a procession of the clergy with the Host, Don Carlos, Doña Marguerita, Don Jaime, the Duke and Duchess of Norfolk and the visitors attending the ceremonial.

By one of the strange twists of fate which were to fascinate him as a writer, Conrad was then in England involved in troubles of his own, clinging for a year to a ship that was due to leave England but could not be sailed.

On September 21, 1881 Conrad left London on a bark of 425 tons, the *Palestine,* an old and rusty ship, an ancient tramp of the sea. Her captain, Beard, was an aged man undertaking his first command. Conrad, almost twenty-four and for the first time sailing as second mate, felt his youth accented by the ark of a ship and its hoary command.

In the North Sea the *Palestine,* held up by a gale, spent three weeks reaching Newcastle where she was to load her cargo for Bangkok. She was so long delayed she missed her turn for loading. With her cargo finally on board, she put to sea, had a collision, returned. Ten weeks after her start from London, she sailed from Newcastle on November 29 with a crew of eight men and two cabin boys, and with five hundred tons of coal in her hold.

Three hundred miles out in the Atlantic she was buffeted by the storm Conrad described in *Youth.*

"It blew day after day: it blew with spite, without interval, without mercy, without rest. The world was nothing but an immensity of great foaming waves rushing at us, under a sky low enough to touch with the hand and dirty like a smoked ceiling. In the stormy space surrounding us there was as much flying spray as air. Day after day and night after night there was nothing round the ship but the howl of the wind, the tumult of the sea, the noise of water pouring over her deck. There was no rest for her and no rest for us. She tossed, she pitched, she stood on her head, she sat on her tail, she rolled, she groaned, and we had to hold on while on deck and cling to our bunks when below, in a constant effort of body and worry of mind."

The old ship leaked, she was being gutted by the storm. There was no easing in the weather.

"The sea was white like a sheet of foam, like a cauldron of boiling milk; there was not a break in the clouds, no—not the size of a man's hand—no, not for so much as ten seconds. There was for us no sky, there were for us no stars, no sun, no universe—nothing but angry clouds and an infuriated sea."

The ship was strained, the stores spoiled, the sails and deckhouse blown away. She put back to Falmouth, barely afloat. Repaired and reloaded, and with a new crew, she set off for Bangkok again. A week later, a leaking sieve, she returned. Her second crew quit.

During the next nine months Conrad lived aboard the forgotten bark in Falmouth. In stubborn allegiance, in spite of the uncommonly low pay of £4, or $20, a month, Conrad stayed with the unseaworthy ship his Uncle Thaddeus pleaded with him to abandon. Winter, spring and summer passed. His Uncle Casimir, writing in March from the Ukraine, looked forward to Conrad's return from his voyage by autumn. But autumn found him still in Falmouth.

The long delay ended with the *Palestine* being put in drydock, recaulked and new-coppered. On September 17, 1882—a year after leaving London—the decrepit vessel got underway for Bangkok. In those twelve months the "old thing," as she was jeeringly called in Falmouth, had traveled no more than three hundred miles from England. She had made four starts for the East, had put back three times. When she finally went to sea it was with a fourth crew, men sent down from Liverpool. South coast seamen, knowing her history, refused to risk their lives in her.

The ancient sailing ship that absorbed eighteen months of Conrad's life failed even then to reach Bangkok. At the weary pace of three miles an hour she crawled around the globe. Six months out from Falmouth, on the last lap of her interminable voyage but still 1,100 miles from Bangkok, the *Palestine* blew up. Her cargo of coal, too frequently handled during reloadings in England and too often soaked, caught fire on March 11, 1883. Captain Beard ordered the ship, then between Borneo and Sumatra, to be held to her course. Water was pumped into her hold in an attempt to stifle the blaze, four tons of coal were jettisoned. But three days after the first heavy paraffin smell gave warning of the fire the coal gas exploded. Conrad was thrown in the air and came down on the cargo. His face cut, his hair and eyebrows singed to the skin, his shirt in tatters, he scrambled up to the wrecked deck, "a wilderness of smashed timber, lying crosswise like trees in a wood after a hurricane."

The ship was abandoned, the three officers and crew taking off in three boats. Conrad was in command of the smallest, a fourteen-foot dinghy, with two seamen for his crew. The boats stayed by the flaming *Palestine* throughout the night watching her burn. Just before daybreak the masts fell with "a burst and turmoil of sparks that seemed to fill with flying fire the night patient and watchful, the vast night lying silent upon the sea."

The antique coal carrier, so reluctant to be pried from retirement in England, burned like a funeral pyre and sank on the morning of March 15, shooting down into the water with a great hiss of steam. Land was a hundred miles off, Singapore four hundred miles away. Conrad at twenty-five faced the empty sea with a youth's elated challenge. He would navigate the strange waters on his own, beat the other boats, be the first to land.

He made a jury rig with a spare oar for a mast and a boat awning for a sail. Some days after leaving the spot where the *Palestine* had gone down, he sighted a small island harbor. That landfall was his first view of the East, of the Malay archipelago he was to use for the settings of six of his novels, eight of his short stories. His first glimpse of it was recaptured in *Youth*, written fifteen years later:

. . . now I see it always from a small boat, a high outline of mountains, blue and afar in the morning; like faint mist at noon; a jagged wall of purple at sunset. I have the feel of the oar in my hand, the vision of a scorching blue sea in my eyes. And I see a bay, a wide bay, smooth as glass and polished like ice, shimmering in the dark. A red light burns far off upon the gloom of the land, and the night is soft and warm. We drag at the oars with aching arms, and suddenly a puff of wind, a puff faint and tepid and laden with strange odours of blossoms, of aromatic wood, comes out of the still night—the first sigh of the East on my face.

After the sinking of the *Palestine* Conrad waited in Singapore for a berth, but finally embarked as a passenger on a steamer bound for London. There, on July 4, 1883, he passed his first mate's examination. He had not seen his Uncle Thaddeus for five years, since his duel in Marseilles, and on July 24 Conrad joined him at the Bohemian watering place of Marienbad, west of Prague. From the mineral springs spa of Teplitz, northeast of Marienbad, Conrad wrote a letter in Polish on August 14, 1883, to Stefan Buszczynski, an old friend of his father, who had looked after him in Cracow at the time of Apollo's death. Written when he was twenty-five, it is one of the earliest of Conrad's letters to have survived.

Dear and Esteemed Sir,
Uncle Thaddeus and I had hoped that we would be able to meet you here in Teplitz; but we found out after our arrival here that you had gone.

Well, being unable to present myself to you personally and to ask your indulgence for all my transgressions, I hasten to do it by letter and enclose a photo of myself—in the hope that, for the sake of the memory of the father's friendship, the son will receive your cordial remembrance, and his letter, though coming after such a long silence, a favorable reception.

Although away from my homeland for a long time, and perhaps, by appearances, forgetting those whose favors I received, I have actually never forgotten the homeland, the family, nor those who were kind to me; among them you, dear Sir, my tutor at the time I became an orphan, will always hold first place.

I take the liberty of asking you to remember me to dear Kostus. Certainly, I have given him the right to forget our friendship in Cracow; I myself have never forgotten, although it all seems so distant now! Perhaps he would be willing to recall those old times and accept my warm greetings and a friendly handshake.

I am leaving here for London in a few days; from there I don't know where fate will take me. In the last few years, since the time of my first examination, I have not been too lucky in my voyages. I was in a sinking and in a fire. Outside of that I am in good health, I have hope, a willingness to work, and am attached to my profession. I always remember what you told me before I left Cracow: "Remember"—you said—"wherever you go, you are taking Poland!"

I have not forgotten that and shall not forget it!

In the hope that my neglect will be forgiven, I commend myself to your kind memory, remaining with warm regards, gratitude and the highest esteem,

Your humble servant,

KONRAD N. KORZENIOWSKI

Back in London, Conrad left for India in September as second mate aboard the 1,500-ton sailing ship *Riversdale*. A dispute with his captain, L. B. McDonald, caused him to quit the ship in Madras. In Bombay chance put him on one as graceful as a yacht, the *Narcissus,* a beautiful sailing ship of 1,300 tons, built by a sugar refiner of Greenock, Scotland. Originally intended for the Brazilian sugar trade, she had been employed instead in the Indian Ocean and the Far East. Conrad left her in Dunkirk on October 19, 1884, the North Sea port where the nine-year-old ship was dismantled.

From his six months' voyage as second mate of the *Narcissus,* her last voyage, Conrad drew one of the finest and most complex of his books, *The Nigger of the Narcissus,* written twelve years later.

"Most of the personages I have portrayed," he said of that novel, "actually belonged to the crew of the real *Narcissus,* including the admirable Singleton (whose real name was Sullivan), Archie, Belfast, and Donkin."

As a vivid account of life on a sailing ship, as a study in group psychology, as a myth-like comment on life's ebb and flow and man's instability in its shifting currents, as the book of which Conrad said "as an artist striving for the utmost sincerity of expression, I am willing to stand or fall," *The Nigger of the Narcissus* has been subjected to unceasing appraisal. "Touch one wire, merely breathe on the lovely thing, and it wavers to a new form!" Albert J. Guerard summarized his view of Conrad's "mobile".

Six months after disembarking from the *Narcissus* at Dunkirk, Conrad left Hull, on April 24, 1885 as second mate on the *Tilkhurst*. A London sailing ship of 1,500 tons, she made her long crossing to Singapore, called at Calcutta, returning to Dundee in June, 1886.

After that voyage of more than a year Conrad spent seven months ashore. In London on August 19, 1886, he became a naturalized British subject and on November 11, 1886, passed his master's examination, eight years after entering the British merchant marine. During the next month he wrote his first story, "The Black Mate," submitted in a contest conducted by the magazine *Tit-Bits* for a prize it failed to win.

Though his master's certificate entitled him to the command of a ship, few such openings fell to young men of twenty-nine. When he was offered a chief mate's berth on the *Highland Forest* Conrad crossed over to Amsterdam on February 18, 1887, to supervise the loading of a cargo of general merchandise destined for Java. A month later, her cargo badly stowed due to Conrad's inexperience, the *Highland Forest* sailed for the East. During that passage of more than three months the ship was severely punished by gales.

Chapter XXII

THE hurricane "howled and scuffled about gigantically in the darkness," punching the *Highland Forest* with solid force, making her stagger "as a clubbed man reels before he collapses."

Four years after the sinking of the *Palestine* Conrad was in the East again, in the southern ocean approaching Java, when his ship underwent the brutal beating he wrote into *Typhoon*.

The gale struck with sudden, formidable power. Captain John MacWhirr, whose name, appearance and character Conrad gave to the master of the fictional *Nan-Shan* in *Typhoon*, was caught off guard by the storm's attack. He lunged for his shoes "gambolling playfully over each other like puppies" as they rolled from end to end of his cabin. Within five minutes of the warning rain dropping hard as molten lead, the ship was yanked about in rushes of the wind.

"There was hate in the way she was handled, and a ferocity in the blows that fell. She was like a living creature thrown to the rage of a mob: hustled terribly, struck at, borne up, flung down, leaped upon."

Towering waves, like a "column of water running upright in the dark, butted against the ship, broke short, and fell on her bridge, crushingly, from on high, with a dead burying weight."

Great chasms opened in the sea. The thousand-ton sailing ship balanced on the edge of running walls of water and, nose down, plunged over sheer cliffs in her dizzy rise and fall. Water fell in roaring tons on her deck, driving her under. Thumped and tossed, it seemed unlikely she could survive.

"Ultimately," Conrad wrote in *The Mirror of the Sea,* "some of the minor spars did go—nothing important: spanker-booms and such-like—because at times the frightful impetus of her rolling would part a fourfold tackle of new three-inch Manila line as if it were weaker than pack-thread."

During the gale a piece of one of those minor spars struck Conrad in the back, sending him sprawling along the main deck. Captain MacWhirr was puzzled by the "queer symptoms" of his resulting injury, subject as he was to "inexplicable periods of powerlessness, sudden accesses of mysterious pain." Even when the *Highland Forest* completed her voyage from Amsterdam and made her port of Samarang in Java in June, 1887, the Dutch doctor there was unable to give a medical reason for Conrad's baffling disablement. He advised him to leave the ship, to lay up for three months of total rest.

Conrad relinquished his first mate's billet and entered a hospital in Singapore. The strange injury that could not be diagnosed, that affected his leg with unexplainable pain, was one cause of his staying in the East for two years. Choosing that area's warmer climate and easier sea duty, he made the acquaintance in Borneo of the Dutch half-caste trader Olmeijer, or Almayer as British seamen said it. His first view of the pajama-clad trader on the jetty of the East Borneo river port of Berouw in October, 1887, was an important event in his life, for, as he told in *A Personal Record,* "if I had not got to know Almayer pretty well it is almost certain there would never have been a line of mine in print."

His injury, leading indirectly to his meeting with Almayer

and the resulting *Almayer's Folly,* kept Conrad in the Singapore hospital for two months. That prolonged neurasthenic illness—for which doctors could find no physical cause—occurred at the strikingly identical time as an outstanding event in Paula's life: her marriage.

Although Conrad wrote in *The Arrow of Gold* that he (as Monsieur George) lost touch with the girl he had loved in Marseilles—"The faithful austerity of the sea protected him from the rumours that fly on the tongues of men. He never heard of her"—some correspondent kept him informed of the turns in Paula's life. Either of two men could have sent him such news: Richard Fecht, the friend in Marseilles who loaned Conrad money during his gunrunning days, notified his Uncle Thaddeus of his dueling wound, and until 1882 handled his finances; or Adolf P. Krieger, a friend Conrad indicated he met in Marseilles, and to whom he dedicated *Tales of Unrest.* For five years, from November, 1882 to December, 1887, Krieger forwarded the allowance Conrad received from his uncle, sending messages and funds to the various world ports where Conrad's ships called.

Whether or not Conrad found a letter waiting in Samarang in June, 1887, telling him of Paula's marriage, both he and his biographer Jean-Aubry accented the psychic quality of his "strange indisposition" at that coincidental time.

For the five years following her break with Don Carlos Paula's life was that of an "heiress" without position. As Conrad had Mills predict in *The Arrow of Gold,* she had not found love, having "sacrificed that chance to the integrity of your life —heroically." In Paris in the spring of 1887, at twenty-eight, she contracted a *mariage de convenance* with a Spanish singer two years older than herself. Count de Melgar in his final report of the exotically beautiful girl whose star was to rise and fall so rapidly told how that marriage was arranged.

From Paula de Somoggy, telling me herself, I knew of her strong wish to find a husband.

"I am dominated," she told me, "by the fixed idea of associating with ladies; with ladies," she insisted, "not with just ordinary women, because up to now my society has been exclusively composed of men. Those who are willing to know me are not what I want and those whom I would like to meet refuse to accept me."

A few hours later Providence willed that this delicate problem should be solved in a most satisfactory and unexpected way.

That same night I was having dinner with some friends at a hotel that had just been built on the Avenue Kléber, those friends including an aide of Don Carlos, don José Ponce de Leon, who a short while before had married the widow, Countess de Campomanes. We were finishing our dinner when a valet brought Ponce de Leon a letter saying that the bearer was waiting in the lobby, asking at what time he could be received the following day.

Ponce de Leon opened the letter, which was from his cousin the Duke of Arcos, secretary of the Spanish embassy in Rome, who warmly recommended the bearer of the letter, a young baritone with a promising future, called don A. de Trabadelo, who had already sung with success in the principal theatres of Italy, La Scala in Milan, Le Fenice in Venice, the San Carlo in Naples, and who wished to further his studies in Paris.

Ponce asked to have the visitor brought to the smoking room where we went to take coffee with him. There we invited him to sit in on our card game, which he refused, explaining that he was not enough of an expert, but asking, if we would permit it, to let him look on.

This ended at midnight when Trabadelo sat down with us and we began to gossip.

We took advantage of this friendly interlude to question our compatriot about his plans and hopes. These could be reduced, according to what he told us, to obtaining a grant either from Ponce de Leon or from Don Carlos (Trabadelo had been in the Carlist camp during the war) to provide him with a means of existence.

"What I need," he added, "is not to be forced to fight for my daily bread, and to be able to dedicate myself for a couple of years to perfecting myself in my art, until I can start a singing course, since my preference is more toward teaching than the theatre."

Then one of us said to him:

"Would you be interested in a grant, one which would be at your disposal all your life? Would 15,000 to 20,000 francs be enough for you?"

"I think so," he answered, showing great amazement.

"And in addition to this income," this spokesman continued, "you can add the possession of a beautiful, distinguished, and good woman who will bring this dowry to you if you consent to marry her."

He appealed to us with no malice:

"Will you forgive me for asking a question? Are you not looking for an obliging husband who, for money, allows his wife to enjoy another?"

"Nothing of the sort. We will explain it all to you, throwing the cards on the table and showing you the whole play."

We described, in fact, the whole situation, which he listened to very attentively, seeming very flattered that his future wife had had such lofty connections.

"The situation," he said finally, "interests me very much and on principle I feel inclined to accept. I would like to contact her and after meeting her I will give my final answer."

"Exactly. This is her name and she lives in such and such a place. Go there tomorrow at 2:30 in the afternoon, to this address, and you will meet the person of whom we have been speaking."

At nightfall this gallant came to see me, threw himself in my arms, and exclaimed:

"Ah, my friend, what a jewel she is! How wonderful! What an enchanting woman! I am late in coming because in her house we both wrote, she to Hungary and I to Spain, asking that the necessary papers be sent for a marriage contract, and both of us beg you to be our best man."

The wedding took place in less than a month, with four best men being present, two for the bride and two for the groom: don Miguel de Marichalar, don José de Suelves, Viscount de Monserrat, Commander of Artillery Alvear, military attaché of the Spanish embassy in Paris, and myself. The evening before the ceremony the bride asked me to find a priest, preferably a Spaniard, to whom she could confess. I took her to don Manuel Barrena, who was then chaplain of the Spanish church on

Avenue Friedland. Afterwards I took her by carriage to her house, and when we crossed the Champs Élysées on that magnificent spring morning she smiled at the glances passersby directed toward us.

"What a world this is!" she said to me. "Everyone who looks at us believes that we are a pair of lovers returning from a morning walk in the Bois de Boulogne and they envy you for having made the conquest of such a well set up young woman."

That marriage lasted thirty years, until the year 1917 when she died, and was a very happy one. The artist's ambitions were realized in part; his theatrical career was very short, for soon after going to sing in the Royal Theatre in Madrid he developed a teaching method that was very successful in a singing academy very much in vogue for many years, competing with the famous Baldelli, and it had as alumni most of the great American singers who later achieved fame. He earned a great deal of money and lived in true luxury. He was always very good to his wife, and very proud of her past.

The career of Angel Trabadelo was, as the Count de Melgar indicated, one of success. As a gifted operatic singer he gave concerts not only in New York but in London, Paris, Berlin and St. Petersburg. Among those who studied with him when he later became a prominent teacher of singing in Paris were Caruso and Melba. Geraldine Farrar and Mary Garden studied with him from 1898-1900, Mary Garden paying a high tribute to his teaching method in the story of her own career.

In the town where he had been born, San Sebastian, Spain, Trabadelo died on February 24, 1939. He was then eighty-two.

Many years before that he received a coveted recognition, through the influence of Don Carlos, when the King of Spain conferred upon him the title of Marquis. As a Marquise, Paula was admitted to social circles which had previously refused to accept her. Her assumed name of Baroness de Somoggy forgotten, she was at last to move in a normal world, to meet "some woman soul that would have known, in which perhaps I could have seen my own reflection."

Chapter XXIII

◇◇◇◇◇◇◇◇◇◇◇◇◇◇◇◇◇◇◇◇

CONRAD succumbed to the "green sickness of late youth" as he neared his thirtieth birthday. Idle weeks in the Singapore hospital lying on his back with a mystifying injury had given him time to scrutinize his life. The day-long and night-long unrelenting labor of life at sea had brought constant action with no lull in the round for moody introspection; still days in the hospital had broken that peace of movement. "On men reprieved by its disdainful mercy, the immortal sea confers in its justice the full privilege of desired unrest," he summarized in *The Nigger of the Narcissus* the appeal of a seaman's life.

When he left the airy hospital ward with its windows overlooking the tops of palm trees he remained in the East, partly because the climate suited him, a convalescent, but also in hurried return to "that untempted life presenting no disquieting problems."

Still unwell and little as he cared for steamships, he sailed from Singapore on August 22, 1887, as first mate of the *Vidar*. For four and a half months he made the Borneo run on the 800-ton tramp steamer owned by an Arab, Syed Mohsin bin S. Al Jaffree. Under Captain James Craig she sailed the Java Sea and Macassar Strait, ranging as far north as Palawan in the

Sulu Sea and as far south as the Sumatra port of Palembang. As a pedlar of the sea the *Vidar* transported odds and ends of freight, leaving Singapore on September 30—according to bills of lading Conrad saved—with crockery ware bound for Berouw. Earlier the steamer carried fifty-eight bags of dammer, cat's eye resin used in incense, shipped by the Berouw trader Babalatchie to Sing Jimmung in Donggala.

There were but four white men on board the *Vidar*. In addition to Captain Craig and Conrad were the chief engineer James Allen, "young too, but very thin, and with a mist of fluffy brown beard all round his haggard face" who suffered from a liver ailment, and the second engineer John C. Niven, a sturdy young Scot with a smooth red face known as a "fierce misogynist." Two Malay petty officers, an eleven-man Malay crew, and eighty Chinese employed in loading and unloading cargo at isolated up-river trading stations were carried on each voyage.

Leaving Singapore, the *Vidar* called at Bandjarmasin, a primitive Venice in southern Borneo, steamed up Macassar Strait to the Celebes settlement of Donggala, crossed back over the Strait to the east coast of Borneo, stopping at such trading stations as Berouw—later named Tandjungredeb—on the Berouw, or Berau, River, retraced her route to Singapore. Making a "monotonous huckster's round, up and down the Straits," the *Vidar* covered 1,600 miles on each trip of thirty days. Conrad made five or six voyages on the steamer on her colorful, equatorial run.

The Borneo he came to know then—and was to use for background in such novels as *Almayer's Folly, An Outcast of the Islands,* and *The Rescue*—was a kettle of intense heat, of stifling humidity varying little day or night in any month of the year. The rainy season in November and December brought heavy pounding cloudbursts, less like rain falling than propelled.

Overnight mildew grew on clothes in the saturated and enervating air. Mosquitoes swarmed, oversize bats and moths came out of hiding with the dark. Brilliant short sunsets colored the sky with opal tones of rose and purple as night dropped quickly, releasing the jungle's early evening cries—the barking of monkeys, the staccato *taw-kay* call of the big tree lizard, the sharp human cough of the red-haired orang-utan, the Malayan *mias* that, with an arm span of seven feet, swung in the tangled branches of the trees, rarely touching the ground. Cobras, twenty-foot pythons, the deadly *ijzerslang* or iron snake resembling a piece of wire, wild pigs, deer, prehistoric-looking lizards moved through the matted growth. Laced and bound with lianas, trees of every shade of green fought to reach the light— coconut palms, the great *kajoe radja,* wild rubber trees, beefwood or *tjimara,* banana trees, giant ferns, sandalwood, camphor trees, ironwood, cashew, mangosteen and durian. Twining wherever the sunlight filtered through were wild orchids, lavender, tan, chartreuse. When the durian fruit ripened the jungle was heavy with a penetrating odor, a "sickly perfume as of decaying flowers."

In the interior of Borneo, coming to the trading stations when the twisting rivers were swollen with rain, were the Dyaks, a primitive race of warriors, head-hunters. Armed with short swords, the *parang* of their own making, blowpipes and poisoned arrows, they were the hunters of the jungle, rivermen who traveled the streams in dugout canoes. Dyak women, sarongs wrapped around their thighs, their ear lobes stretched by the weight of heavy silver rings, made the bark jackets of the tatooed men, their umbrella-sized palm leaf hats, their ceremonial headdress of Argus pheasant feathers. The Dyaks were an ancient, proud and intelligent race who had little use for the Mohammedan Asiatics or for the few scattered Europeans living in campongs along the coast.

On his trips in the *Vidar* to the up-river settlements of reed and bamboo houses built on posts rising high above the swampy ground, Conrad met the men who were to form part of the cast of *Almayer's Folly, Lord Jim, An Outcast of the Islands, The Rescue:* Tom Lingard, the skipper of a sailing ship trading in those seas; his nephew Jim Lingard, a trader at Berouw whose haughty airs brought the nickname of "Lord Jim" from the plain-spoken officers of the *Vidar;* Willems, a castaway drunken Dutch seaman at Berouw; Babalatchi and Lakamba, two natives of Celebes, traders in Berouw; and Almayer.

All along the Borneo run Conrad heard talk of Almayer. His name cropped up repeatedly on the *Vidar.* In *A Personal Record* he recalled the early mist-hung morning when his ship anchored at Berouw and he saw the trader for the first time.

It was really impossible on board that ship to get away definitely from Almayer; and a very small pony tied up forward and whisking its tail inside the galley, to the great embarrassment of our Chinaman cook, was destined for Almayer. What he wanted with a pony goodness only knows, since I am perfectly certain he could not ride it; but here you have the man, ambitious, aiming at the grandiose, importing a pony, whereas in the whole settlement at which he used to shake daily his impotent fist there was only one path that was practicable for a pony: a quarter of a mile at most, hedged in by hundreds of square leagues of virgin forest. But who knows? The importation of that Bali pony might have been part of some deep scheme, of some diplomatic plan, of some hopeful intrigue. With Almayer one could never tell. . . .

Leaning over the rail of the bridge, I looked at Almayer, who looked down at the wharf in aggrieved thought. He shuffled his feet a little; he wore straw slippers with thick soles. The morning fog had thickened considerably. Everything round us dripped—the derricks, the rails, every single rope in the ship— as if a fit of crying had come upon the universe.

Almayer was a man of such pretension that he not only imported a pony to the jungle where it could not run, he not only raised geese—the only geese on the coast—which he gave as a "sort of court decoration" to those he deemed worthy, he not only built a folly of a house in the intolerant jungle, his dreams of grandeur reached out from his Borneo mudbank in a rain-crying world to one final towering height. He would go, as Conrad wrote in *Almayer's Folly*, with his half-caste daughter to Amsterdam and there, in that most rigid of all European capitals, have her accepted by society. "They would be rich and respected. Nobody would think of her mixed blood in the presence of her great beauty and of his immense wealth."

The dream Conrad gave to Almayer in the first of his books to deal with the rescue of a girl with some mark on her came as an echo of his own love affair with Paula, for Paula, as the mistress of a prince in the Victorian world of 1878, bore a social stigma too. Yet in this year of 1887 another man had married the girl he had run away from in Marseilles.

Disgruntled with the crying world of rain, the endless rain, Conrad became bored with the Borneo run, weary of his own punishing thoughts. He grew increasingly restless on the *Vidar* and when the steamer returned to Singapore on January 5, 1888, he quit his job in the "inconsequential manner in which a bird flies away from a comfortable branch." His sudden, erratic move had the engineer Niven chaffing him, "Oh! Aye! I've been thinking it was about time for you to run away home and get married to some silly girl."

In *The Shadow Line*, his masterful story of "personal experience seen in perspective," Conrad gave a factual account of those first three months of 1888 and his reasoning in leaving the *Vidar*.

"My action, rash as it was, had more the character of divorce —almost of desertion. For no reason on which a sensible person could put a finger I threw up my job—chucked my berth —left the ship of which the worst that could be said was that she was a steamship and therefore, perhaps, not entitled to that blind loyalty which. . . . However, it's no use trying to put a gloss on what even at the time I myself half suspected to be a caprice."

Two weeks later he was waiting at the Officers' Sailors'

Home in Singapore with his mind half made up to return to England when he was suddenly appointed to his first command. The captain of the *Otago* had died on board his ship, a bark then in Bangkok due to be sailed back to her home port in Australia. Conrad, jubilant over his unexpected luck, was sent as a replacement. He found the ship moored in Bangkok, a high-class vessel beautifully proportioned, standing out in a line of larger craft like "an Arab steed in a string of cart-horses."

But the *Otago* proved a haunted ship. During her voyage down the Gulf of Siam the whole crew were stricken with fever. For days on end the ship lay unmoving, clutched in a dead calm. Conrad spent seventeen days on deck without relief and when the wind finally came he had only the cook, disabled by a faulty heart, and the fever-gaunt chief mate to help him sail his ship to Singapore. The unmanned ship was filled with wasting men in urgent need of hospital care. But the hospital was 900 miles away and the *Otago* took three weeks to crawl over the too-placid gulf.

When he brought his bark into Singapore, the last forty hours of the passage without sleep, Conrad felt, not tired, but old. To him the veteran seamen on shore looked like skittish youngsters who had never known a care in the world. At thirty, the youngest man on board his first command, he had pulled his ship and his crew through a crucial testing. He had crossed the shadow line where "the region of early youth, too, must be left behind."

From those first of his weeks on the *Otago* in Bangkok and the Gulf of Siam grew three stories—"Falk," and two of the finest he was ever to write, *The Shadow Line* and "The Secret Sharer."

The *Otago* left Singapore with a new crew in March, 1888, for Australia and for the next year Conrad sailed his first and only command about the Indian Ocean. He took her to Mauritius in September, 1888, and during a stay of two months at Port Louis became acquainted with a French girl, Eugénie

Renouf, the sister of a merchant marine officer he had met in Bombay. Contented with his ship and his life as a Captain and wishing to settle down in the East, he made a formal proposal of marriage. He knew the girl so slightly he was not aware she was already engaged, with a wedding arranged to take place in less than two months. He sailed back to Australia and in April, 1889, rather than return to Mauritius as the owners of the *Otago* insisted he do, he gave up his command. In June, 1889, he was back in London after two years spent in the East.

The summer passed without his securing a berth as master of another ship and in September, weary of idleness, he sat down at his table in a furnished room in Bessborough Gardens and began *Almayer's Folly*. His first novel, written in other idle moments in scattered parts of the world, was to take more than four and a half years to complete. Conrad was just under thirty-two when he began it, almost thirty-seven when he finished it.

In the same month that he started *Almayer's Folly*, with only a few pages of the novel written, he impulsively decided to go to Africa. Seeing a map of the Congo in the window of a book store on Fleet Street, he determined to travel to the David Livingstone country he had read about as a boy in Poland. He immediately applied to Brussels for a commission as captain of a Congo river steamer, but his appointment was long in coming—eight months.

Two of the winter months, from mid-February to mid-April, he spent with his Uncle Thaddeus in the Ukraine. Conrad received from him then the notebook titled "For the information of my dear nephew Konrad Korzeniowski." His uncle's reasons for keeping that twenty-year financial record were given in the opening paragraph.

"*Cher,* in order that you, having reached a mature age, should know all the experiences of your parents and their relations with the family, I want you to know in what way the little fund was created which is to serve as the basis of your further work and independence!! I undertake this tale, not to put forth my own merits in this matter—for your other relatives, as you will soon find out, did more for your parents than I could do with my relative means—but, chiefly, in order to let you know how we all loved your mother and, through her, also your father."

The ledger showed that from December 1, 1869, to February 4, 1890, Thaddeus Bobrowski had spent 17,454 rubles ($8,727) on his misadventuring nephew. He had been a costly young man to raise, extravagant and reckless. Dying before Conrad's writing career began, the complainingly giving—but always giving—"Uncle Thaddeus B." was never to have the satisfaction of knowing what use Conrad was to make of his wild years.

From his uncle's estate of Kazimierowka Conrad drove the fifty miles to the paradise of his boyhood, Nowofastow, his first visit there in twenty-three years. Passing through Poland, he stayed two days with relatives in Lublin. There Conrad came to know his married cousin, Maria Bobrowska Tyszkowa, a daughter of his uncle Casimir Bobrowski, with whom he was to correspond for many years.

From London he wrote to her on May 2, 1890, that his African plans were settled: "I could not write earlier. I was unspeakably busy and even now I have a great deal to do. I am leaving for the Congo in four days and I must get ready for a three-year stay in the middle of Africa; so you will easily understand how essential every moment of the day is to me. . . . Be my go-between with the family, Mariette. Embrace them all for me and ask them to think of the wanderer."

Conrad's command of a Congo river steamer had finally been put through—again he was to replace a captain who had died —and on May 6, 1890, he left for Africa.

Sailing on a French steamer from Bordeaux, he arrived at Matadi in the Belgian Congo on June 12, 1890. Construction of the railroad had just begun and he faced a walk of more than two hundred miles to reach his steamer at Stanley Pool. His march through equatorial heat with a caravan of thirty-one Negro bearers was a grueling trek of thirty-six days over mountains, through tall plains grass, along forest tracks, over streams crossed on crude bridges of lianas. Days of marching under a scorching sun, cold damp nights spent in pitched camps, Conrad crossed an empty country where there was "nobody, not a hut." The Africans, made into slaves whenever caught, kept well away from the caravan trail.

Conrad arrived in the Congo five years after Leopold II of Belgium had organized his private "International Association for the Exploration and Civilization of the Congo," when that part of the world was witnessing the most brutal period of exploitation history ever knew. The savagery of Leopold's treatment of the Africans created an international scandal and in 1908 he was forced to relinquish the area that had made him so fabulously rich.

The Congo abuses of the Belgian monarch brought outcries from men such as Mark Twain who labeled Leopold a "wild beast . . . who for money's sake mutilates, murders, and starves half a million of friendless and helpless poor natives in the Congo State every year . . . this moldy and piety-mouthing hypocrite, this bloody monster whose mate is not findable in human history anywhere."

Immediately upon his arrival in the Congo Conrad stepped into a world "where the merry dance of death and trade goes on." In words he gave to Marlow in "Heart of Darkness" he learned that the "conquest of the earth, which mostly means the taking it away from those who have a different complexion or slightly flatter noses than ourselves, is not a pretty thing when you look into it too much." Within his first few minutes on the African shore he met a Negro chain gang.

A slight clinking behind me made me turn my head. Six black men advanced in a file, toiling up the path. They walked erect and slow, balancing small baskets full of earth on their heads, and the clink kept time with their footsteps. Black rags were wound round their loins, and the short ends behind waggled to and fro like tails. I could see every rib, the joints of their limbs were like knots in a rope; each had an iron collar on his neck, and all were connected together with a chain whose bights swung between them, rhythmically clinking.

At Matadi, funneling point of a trade importing terror to Africa, exporting wealth to Brussels, he watched the exchange of products pass through, a "stream of manufactured goods, rubbishy cottons, beads, and brass-wire sent into the depths of darkness, and in return came a precious trickle of ivory."

The atmosphere of the trading stations was heavy with pretense. Under hypocritical terms of philanthropy, of civilizing the savages, the "pilgrims," as Conrad in bitter irony named the white traders so quick to beat and kill their black captives, trampled on each other to secure appointments to stations lush with ivory profits.

"The word 'ivory' rang in the air, was whispered, was sighed. You would think they were praying to it. A taint of imbecile rapacity blew through it all, like a whiff from some corpse."

After fifteen days spent in Matadi and five weeks on the sizzling walk to Stanley Pool, Conrad reached Kinchassa only to discover that the *Florida*, the tinpot steamer he had been sent out to command, was laid up for repairs. Wrecked a few days before, she could not be made ready for some months.

Another steamer, the *Roi des Belges* under Captain Koch, was about to depart on an upstream trip for ivory. On it Conrad, leaving Kinchassa on August 4, made his only voyage on the great river. The stern-wheeler burned wood and carried a crew of Africans to cut the jungle's trees. Unfed, they were paid each week with three pieces of brass wire.

Unless they swallowed the wire itself, or made loops of it to snare the fishes with, I don't see what good their extravagant salary could be to them. [Conrad had Marlow say in "Heart of Darkness"]. I must say it was paid with a regularity worthy of a large and honourable trading company. . . . Why in the name of all the gnawing devils of hunger they didn't go for us—they were thirty to five—and have a good tuck-in for once, amazes me now when I think of it.

The steamer made calls at the sparse trading stations as it covered a thousand miles of the empty river. By day only the clap of the paddles broke the silence of the forest. By night came the tom-tom of the jungle drums.

Trees, trees, millions of trees, massive, immense, running up high; and at their foot, hugging the bank against the stream, crept the little begrimed steamboat, like a sluggish beetle crawling on the floor of a lofty portico. . . . The reaches opened before us and closed behind, as if the forest had stepped leisurely across the water to bar the way for our return. We penetrated deeper and deeper into the heart of darkness.

At Stanley Falls, the farthest point of navigation on the 2,900-mile river and the center of the great continent, Conrad fulfilled his childhood promise—"When I grow up I shall go *there*." He had reached the heart of Africa. Instead of the land of a boy's dreams he found an ominous wilderness, rank with more than its own decay. He stood, lonely, looking into the blackness of midnight at the scene of the "vilest scramble for loot that ever disfigured the history of human conscience."

The company's agent at the outpost was a Frenchman, Georges Antoine Klein. He had been in the Congo less than two years when, like the great majority of white men daring the climate, he succumbed to tropical fever. Carried by stretcher on board the *Roi des Belges,* he died on the downstream journey. Conrad was in command of the return voyage since Captain Koch, too, had fallen ill.

Eight years after meeting Klein at Stanley Falls Conrad wrote him into "Heart of Darkness" as Kurtz. "His was an impenetrable darkness. I looked at him as you peer down at a man who is lying at the bottom of a precipice where the sun never shines."

In the character of Kurtz, who looked upon everything as "mine," Conrad personified Europe's gift of civilization to Africa. With talents so great he might have contributed in any field—as orator, writer, thinker, musician, political leader (of any party)—Kurtz was the most ruthless, and the most successful, of all the company's agents in extorting ivory from the black men whose decaying heads, when they opposed him, decorated his wilderness home. Symbol of a mankind depraved by greed, betraying its culture, Kurtz was Conrad's unforgettable portrait of a black god.

The haunting story "Heart of Darkness"—of a stature equal to "Youth," *The Shadow Line* and "The Secret Sharer"—and "An Outpost of Progress" were all the "spoil" Conrad took back from his six months in the Congo. For those stories he paid a great price, carrying the physical marks of his African adventure for more than thirty years, and only—by the good luck that pulled him through many narrow escapes—remaining alive.

Conrad, very like the desperate man his uncle chided him with being, had an uncanny faculty for challenging fate. In the course of six years, though injured each time, he escaped death in the shipwreck of the *Tremolino,* in his duel with Blunt, in the 1881 sinking of the *Anna Frost,* in the burning of the *Palestine.* The Congo supplied him with a new form of danger.

On the river journey in the *Roi des Belges* Conrad walked ashore one day from the temporarily tied-up steamer and wandered off alone. Within the jungle, a short distance from his ship, he stepped into a bog. Sinking to his armpits, he was unable to free himself or to make his calls heard. As the quagmire drew him slowly under he blew on the mate's whistle carried on a cord around his neck—a whistle he was to guard as a lucky piece for the rest of his life. The Negro crew on the steamer heard his signal and reached him in time.

When confronted with another of the Congo's hazards, Conrad was less fortunate. Tropical fever found him no more immune than the others, and struck early. Within two months he had four attacks. Critically ill during one attack, the Belgians assumed he would die and abandoned him. An old Negro woman found him in a native hut and, bringing him water day after day, nursed him through the fever.

"She saved my life," Conrad told Edward Garnett when working on "Heart of Darkness" eight years later. "The white men never came near me."

His health still shaky, Conrad was nevertheless determined to stay in the Congo when the *Roi des Belges* returned to its base at Kinchassa on September 24, 1890. On that day he wrote to his cousin Mme. Maria Tyszkowa, whose sister Zunia had recently married. Reaching out of his loneliness to those contented homes in Poland, he gave to his cousin the family term of "sister."

Beloved dear Mariette,

Today your letter with the photo reached me and I am replying instantly to explain the long interruption in our correspondence.

Well, I was on the Congo River, some 1300 miles from the seashore where the postoffice is, and I could neither hear of Europe nor let Europe know about myself. Your letter pleased but also somewhat saddened me. I have lived long enough to know that life is full of griefs and worries, and to know that no one can avoid them; nevertheless, I am saddened to think that those whom I love must suffer, and do suffer. I am gratified by the proof of your trust in writing me openly about your troubles. I truly do not deserve to be admitted into your hearts—for I am almost a stranger to all of you—so the words of fondness you wrote are all the more precious to me. I shall shelter them carefully in my heart, and the photograph in an album where I can take a look at my little sister every day.

You are now both married, your wishes fulfilled, and I hope that you may walk on the road of life in the sun, without the slightest cloud in your sky. Please assure your husband of my real esteem and friendly feelings. I gratefully accept your invitation and I promise you, my sister, to come to visit you as often as possible. I hope that Auntie's health will continue to improve. I have a letter from Uncle Thaddeus, who intended to visit you in August. He must have returned home by now.

I am very busy preparing for a new expedition on the Kasai River. In a few days I shall probably leave Kinchassa again for some months, perhaps a dozen months. So don't wonder if there is no sign of me for a long while.

I embrace dear Zunia and apologize for not having written. Please send me her exact address, also your new one.

I kiss dear Auntie's hands and hope you will remember me and keep me in your heart, Mariette. Do not forget me in the new circumstances and conditions of your life.

Your ever loving brother,
K. N. KORZENIOWSKI

The company's acting manager in the Congo, Camille Del-commune, took a dislike to Conrad and refused to honor his Brussels commission to command the *Florida*. For the Kasai River expedition the steamboat was put in charge of Captain Carlier—whose name Conrad gave to the dismal human discard of "An Outpost of Progress." Sickened by the moral decay of a wilderness corrupted, combatting fever, Conrad reacted to the final bitterness of the violation of his contract by the "Managing Director of the Great Civilizing Company." He left Kinchassa in a dugout canoe, too sick to care whether or not he survived the dangerous trip down the rapids.

In January, 1891, he was back in England and for a year went through recurring bouts of fever and the rheumatic gout which were to afflict him for the rest of his life.

Unmarried at thirty-three, he was finding single life increasingly lonely, as he told in his letter from London of April 15, 1891, to Maria Tyszkowa, herself so happy with her husband Theodore.

Your letter of February 24 found me so ill, and this illness has dragged on so, that it has been impossible for me to answer until now. Do not accuse me of indifference, or even of laziness. I spent two months in bed. I got up a short time ago and for three weeks walked around with my hands so swollen that only

with the greatest difficulty could I write a few lines to Uncle. . . .
As for worries, who doesn't have them? But you, who are cared
for by the kind and gentle Theodore, can stand them more
easily than those who have to stumble over life in solitude.

Melancholy, ill and brooding, he pulled himself out of his
dejection to sail as chief officer on the *Torrens,* leaving Plymouth on November 25, 1891, for a 95-day passage to Australia.
He returned to England on September 3, 1892, and five days
later wrote to his cousin Maria, mother of a new baby.

I congratulate you both on your daughter and I shall try to
come as soon as possible to have the joy of meeting her. But
I'm afraid I won't be able to manage it until next year. You
don't say what name you gave to the young person. . . .
I returned from Australia the 3rd of this month and I sail
on the same ship on October 20 again to Australia. I shall
probably return from this voyage at the end of July and will
take a 6-week leave to visit Uncle and all of you. In the mean-
time I will live in the hope of finding you in better health
and happier than this past year. My health is not bad now, but
quite uncertain—and the less we speak about happiness, the
better. From that kindly soul Thaddeus I have had a letter,
also written in May like yours. I am answering him today. I
thank your husband for his kind thoughts and send him a
cordial handshake. A brotherly embrace to you and many kisses
to Miss Tyszkowa.

As he wrote his Polish cousin, Conrad sailed for a second
trip on the *Torrens.* On the homeward passage from Australia
he became acquainted with one of the passengers, John Galsworthy, who was to remain a lifelong friend.

When the sailing ship docked in London on July 26, 1893,
Conrad, at thirty-five, stepped ashore from his final long voyage
as a seaman.

Chapter XXIV

◇◇◇◇◇◇◇◇◇◇◇◇◇◇◇◇◇

IN HIS London lodginghouse at 17 Gillingham Street Conrad wrote with a favored steel pen, his fingers drumming during long, absentminded pauses. It was March 29, 1894. Working on *Almayer's Folly*, he broke into his story of Borneo to tell the woman he called "Aunt," Madame Marguerite Poradowska, the feelings of a beginning author.

I begrudge each minute I spend away from paper. I do not say "from pen," because I write very little, but inspiration comes to me in looking at the paper. Then there are soaring flights; my thought goes wandering through vast spaces filled with shadowy forms. All is yet chaos, but, slowly, the apparitions change into living flesh, the shimmering mists take shape, and— who knows?—something may be born of the clash of nebulous ideas.

The widow of a distant Polish cousin and not an aunt, Mme. Poradowska was a Frenchwoman, a novelist, living in Paris at 84 rue de Passy. After the death of her husband in Brussels in 1890, she moved to Paris and from 1892 to 1910 remained in the same apartment in the corner of Passy where Don Carlos had had his Pavilion, where Paula had lived—and, half a mile away, still lived.

With but two women, Paula and Mme. Poradowska—the latter an attractive woman nine years older than himself—did Conrad have close personal ties in the years before his marriage. Both were associated with the France for which he had such deep attachment, and by the strange chance that brought Paula repeatedly back to his mind, for more than eighteen years they shared the same quarter of Paris.

Even though his Uncle Thaddeus reproved him for flirting with his aunt and showed concern about their relationship in its early days in 1890, when she was forty-two and Conrad thirty-three, his feelings for his French relative by marriage were never stronger than affection. As a novice in the writing field they shared, he leaned on her for guidance.

A month after reporting his "clash of nebulous ideas," he completed the novel whose inked pages he had carried about with him for almost five years—to the Ukraine, the Congo, Switzerland, Australia, Poland. The weatherbeaten sheets had been with him on ships, on trains, on sleighs, in a dugout canoe; they had gone with him through winter snows, through equatorial heat. Now, as he wrote Mme. Poradowska on the spring morning of April 24, 1894, that much-traveled novel was finished.

It is my sorrowful duty to inform you of the death of Mr. Kaspar Almayer, which occurred this morning at three o'clock.

It's finished! A scratch of the pen writing "The End," and suddenly that whole company of people who have spoken in my ear, moved before my eyes, lived with me for so many years, becomes a troop of phantoms, who are withdrawing, growing dim, and merging—indistinct and pallid—with the sunlight of this brilliant and sombre day.

Since awakening this morning it seems to me that I have buried a part of myself in the pages lying here before my eyes. And yet I am happy—a little.

When, in July, he sent the manuscript to the London publisher T. Fisher Unwin he signed it with the pseudonym "Kamudi," the Malay word for rudder. He had so little confidence in it that he withheld his own name, yet for three months waited fretfully for some news of its reception. Between sieges of illness, still thinking of returning to the sea, he searched for a ship to command.

On October 4 Conrad received the first typewritten letter of his life. The book was accepted. He was given a total of £20 or $100 for it, copyright included, and *Almayer's Folly* came out under his author's name of Joseph Conrad on April 29, 1895, in an English edition of two thousand copies. The New York edition the same year was a small 650 issue. At thirty-seven his new career as a writer had begun.

He took that career more seriously than he cared to admit. A month after sending Fisher Unwin the manuscript of his first book—and two months before learning the outcome—Conrad began *An Outcast of the Islands*. He wrote of his plans for it to Mme. Poradowska on August 18, 1894, from Champel, Switzerland where he had gone for a second series of hydropathic treatments to relieve the arthritis in his hands and feet.

I want to sketch in broad outline, without shading or detail, two human wrecks such as one meets in the forsaken corners of the world. A white man and a Malay. You see that I can't get away from Malays. I am devoted to Borneo. What bothers me most is that my figures are so real. I know them so well that they fetter my imagination. The white man is a friend of Almayer; the Malay is our old friend Babalatchi before he arrived at the estate of prime minister and confidential adviser to the Rajah. There it is.

By October 29, back in London, he was into the story and told his aunt of its theme.

"The theme is the boundless, mad vanity of an ignorant man who has been successful but is without principles or any motive other than the satisfaction of his own vanity. Nor is he faithful even to himself. Whence the fall, the man's sudden descent into physical enslavement by an absolutely savage woman. I have seen that!"

An Outcast of the Islands required more than a year to write. A third of it composed at Champel, the rest took shape in his rooms at 17 Gillingham Street. It was a slow struggle, as he wrote to Mme. Poradowska on December 6, 1894.

I have burnt nothing. One talks like that and then courage fails. People talk this way of suicide! And then something is always lacking; sometimes it is strength, sometimes perseverance, sometimes courage. The courage to succeed or the courage to recognize one's impotence. What remains always indelible and cruel is the fear of finality. One temporizes with fate, or tries to outwit desire, or attempts to juggle with his life. Men are always cowards. They are afraid of "nevermore." I believe that only women have true courage.

I am working a little. I agonize, pen in hand. Six lines in six days.

He was still working on *An Outcast of the Islands* in August, 1895, when he made three trips to Paris to help a friend in Johannesburg, "a very good fellow called Rorke," out of financial trouble. Rorke owned South African gold claims and was being shabbily treated by a German-owned syndicate. To straighten out Rorke's tangled affairs Conrad went to Paris and, for the assistance they could give him, looked up old acquaintances he had known in Marseilles and had not seen since—Jules Guesde, member of the Chamber of Deputies, young Jullien who had become a Paris banker, and Pascalis, a journalist on *Le Figaro*.

It was more than likely from Pascalis that he learned his most recent news of Paula, for *Le Figaro*, a right-wing newspaper and an earlier Legitimist organ, had closely followed the affairs of Don Carlos and those around him.

Returning from Paris, Conrad completed *An Outcast of the Islands* on September 16, 1895. With thoughts of Paula restirred by his talks with Jullien and Pascalis, by reminiscences exchanged of Marseilles, by news of her current life—she, a Marquise, then lived but four blocks from *Le Figaro*—Conrad began work on the first of his attempts to write her story, *The Sisters*.

It was his story, too, one he was finally to tell twenty-two years later in *The Arrow of Gold*. Slightly changing the actual time and setting, from 1877 in Marseilles to 1875 in Paris, he began it with the childhood of Rita and, writing himself into the character of Stephen, described the Ukraine lands of his own early years. In the opening pages Conrad showed he was prepared to deal no less brusquely with the West than he had done with the East in his just-completed story of Willems.

For many years Stephen had wandered amongst the cities of Western Europe. If he came from the East—if he possessed the inborn wisdom of the East—yet it must be said he was only a lonely and inarticulate Mage, without a star and without companions. He set off on his search for a creed—and found only an infinity of formulas. . . .

The western life . . . was full of endeavor, of feverish effort, of endless theories, of preconceived hates, of misplaced loves. It was all limited, hard, sharp in outline, unlovely in form. And so were the men.

Though he worked on *The Sisters* for five or six months he wrote but ten thousand words. The story, too small a fragment to judge its theme, ended suddenly. On it last page Rita, an orphan raised in the mountains by her uncle, a fanatical village priest, was still an adolescent. She was about to meet Stephen when Conrad, as if divorcing a love haunting him so long, abandoned the story—the evening before his wedding.

He had met an English girl in London eighteen months before when mutual friends introduced him to Jessie George, an attractive girl of twenty-two. She was the second child in a family of nine and, the father having died, helped to support her younger brothers and sisters through her secretarial job with the American firm Calligraph. She was "a little person who is very dear to me," Conrad wrote his Polish cousin Charles Zagorski, conceding that "nobody is more astonished than I am" by his getting married at the late age of thirty-eight.

His Uncle Thaddeus, the one person steadfastly close to him in twenty years of wandering, had died in February, 1894. More than ever after that loss Conrad felt the loneliness shadowing "those who have to stumble over life in solitude."

Mrs. Conrad in her two books *Joseph Conrad As I Knew Him* and *Joseph Conrad and His Circle* described his shy and jerky courtship. Months of silence passed after their first meeting; suddenly he sent her flowers and a note inviting her and her mother to dinner; again months went by with no word from him, followed by another unexpected and formal call. The sea captain and author fifteen years older than herself, a man of courtly and foreign manners who gave an impression of "continual restlessness," seemed frightened of a serious tie. On a walk during a day of streaming rain when he dashed with her for the shelter of the National Gallery, he blurted out, "Look here, my dear, we had better get married and out of this. Look at the weather. We will get married at once and get over to France."

He told her he wanted no children, that, though he had little time to live, they should be able to have a few good years together. Engaged in February, they were married six weeks later, on March 24, 1896. It was a marriage that lasted more than twenty-eight years, until his death in 1924.

His was not a happy nature, his wife admitted. He was at times exceedingly charming, at others, hypersensitive, broodingly reserved. With his acute imagination he lived life as a novel, exaggerating small trifles, soaring into absorbing talk as he paced the room, dramatizing his thoughts with picturesque gestures.

Conrad did not allow his marriage to interrupt his writing. On his honeymoon in Brittany, where his wife was "a very good comrade and no bother at all," he wrote "The Idiots," "An Outpost of Progress," "The Lagoon," began *The Rescue* which he was not to complete for twenty-three years, wrote the first pages of *The Nigger of the Narcissus*. In those five months in Brittany he maintained an intense author's pace.

In spite of almost continual ill health and harassing finances —never, until the success of *Chance*, out of debt in nineteen years—he produced almost a book a year for thirty years. Debts, with his expensive tastes, Conrad was used to; he had always had them. Until he was thirty he received an allowance from his Uncle Thaddeus, yet it had never been enough. In Marseilles he had borrowed so heavily from Richard Fecht that his debts were still being repaid by his uncle five years after Conrad left the port. Regardless of how costly Monte Carlo had proved to him then, he still had a speculator's hopes of fortune. The March, 1896, failure of a South African gold mining company, in which Conrad had sunk the inheritance left him by his uncle, almost caused him to cancel plans for his marriage. Only the financial help of friends, a state grant, and the later backing of his agent J. B. Pinker, enabled Conrad to write novels that showed increasing scope as he experimented with ways of telling what seemed tales of adventure, but which carried a depth of comment on man's attempts and failures to live with himself and his world.

They were novels which immediately won high praise. Although H. G. Wells criticized Conrad's style, declaring his sentences to be not unities but "multitudinous tandems," he credited *An Outcast of the Islands* with being perhaps the finest piece of fiction published in 1896, as *Almayer's Folly* was one of the finest published in 1895. In his review of *An Outcast of the Islands* in the May 16, 1896, issue of *The Saturday Review* of London, Wells compared Conrad's second novel with the usual dismal fare of that time:

It is hard to understand how the respectable young gentlemen from the Universities who are engaged in cutting out cheaper imitations of the work of Mr. Stanley Weyman and Mr. Anthony Hope can read a book like this and continue in that industry. Think of the respectable young gentleman from the University, arrayed in his sister's hat, fichu, rationals, and cycling gauntlets, flourishing her hatpin, and pretending, in deference to the supposed requirements of Mr. Mudie's public, to be the deuce and all of a taverning medieval blade, and compare him with Willems the Outcast.

The new author offering the Outcast to a public attuned to fichus was as strange to England as reviewers found his books to be. Smaller than the average man, Conrad was outstandingly gallant. Bowing stiffly from the waist, extravagantly flattering, the hand-kissing, monocle-wearing continental was a startling figure to meet. Yet the storybook "Count" could drop his effusive manner in a flash, and his dark, almost black, eyes would burn with intensity in a speedy turn of mood. To Edward Garnett he seemed to have two natures, interwoven: "one feminine, affectionate, responsive, clear-eyed, the other masculine, formidably critical, fiercely ironical, dominating, intransigent."

Brooking neither insolence nor abuse, highly sensitive to either, Conrad's temper flared with quick fury. In hotheaded response to some cutting barb, he had quarreled with M. Delestang in Marseilles, with the captain of the *Mavis,* with Captain McDonald of the *Riversdale,* with Camille Delcommune in the Congo. He had fought one duel in Marseilles and in 1895 was prepared to send a challenge to a stranger at the National Liberal Club in London. Over Mr. N.'s slighting remarks Conrad would have fought again had the country been France.

At sea, reading Shakespeare, carrying a gold-headed cane, he had created an impression of refined gentleness—upon which the forecastle learned not to presume, since his courage was high. On one ship, armed with only a short stick, he had driven an enraged razor-wielding Negro ashore, forcing his assailant along a ten-inch plank to the wharf. From Australia, choosing a route too hazardous for other captains, he had taken the *Otago* on a daredevil race through Torres Strait, a shipwreck-strewn passage insurance companies considered too dangerous for normal rates. He had brought the ship through, if somewhat strained, from one more foolhardly contest with the sea.

Along with his truculence, so quick to evaporate, went a charm and a warmth of affection which endeared him to his friends, giving him, almost without exception, lifelong ties. His memory, for injuries or favors, was a long one, and his feeling for a place or a person never lost its force. To an area still sharp with meaning for him, the Basque country beyond Marseilles, he planned to take his bride on their honeymoon, eighteen years after parting there with Paula.

A spendthrift still with luxurious tastes—twenty years of lectures from his uncle had had no effect upon him—Conrad determined that, new author though he might be, he would never spin out his days in an attic. Living in country homes, with comforts he could ill afford, he wrote to exhaustion, flailing himself to get the words, the right words, for stories that were so much, in the term he often used, confessions.

In the first of those homes in the country, a semi-detached house at Stanford-le-Hope, Essex, Conrad finished his third novel, *The Nigger of the Narcissus*. He was thirty-nine. Having been born "too far East, where not many cultivate the virtue of reticence," he was rushing into print where, as he wrote E. L. Sanderson, "my sentimentalism, my incorrect attitude to life—all I wish to hide in the wilds of Essex—shall be disclosed to the public gaze!"

The Nigger of the Narcissus came out at the end of 1897 in an unusually small English edition of 1,500 copies—half that of *An Outcast of the Islands*. His third novel but his first tale of the sea took eight months to write and brought him only $500. It was slow to win favor.

"Let it be unpopular, it *must* be," he wrote to Edward Garnett, his editor and friend, while still working on it. "But it seems to me that the thing—precious as it is to me—is trivial enough on the surface to have some charm for the man in the street. As to lack of incident, well—it's life. The incomplete joy, the incomplete sorrow, the incomplete rascality or heroism —the incomplete suffering."

His collection of short stories *Tales of Unrest* came out in 1898, appearing in America a month before English publication and evidencing in its New York issue of 1,250 copies a still-reluctant public.

Conrad was forty when he wrote one of his most famous stories, "Youth." He was a new father hearing the wails and chortles of his five-month-old son Borys, born January 15, 1898, when he reached back to those days of his own "silly, charming, beautiful youth" on board the luckless *Palestine*. He produced his "feat of memory" more quickly than any other piece of his work, writing it in a few days at the end of May and beginning of June, 1898. He, his wife and young son were living at Ivy Walls Farm at Stanford-le-Hope, Essex, in a lath-and-plaster Elizabethan farmhouse which Conrad rented for £20 a year.

Immediately after finishing "Youth," he began *Lord Jim* which took two years, until July, 1900, to complete. The largest part of that best known of all Conrad's books was written in another rented farmhouse, Pent Farm, at Stanford, near Hythe, Kent. The third in the long procession of homes he leased in a restless wandering over the English countryside, he lived in it nine years at an annual rental of £27. How he finished *Lord Jim* in a "steady drag of 21 hours" alone in the house with Escamillo, the black-and-white hound given to his son by Stephen Crane, Conrad described in a letter of July 20, 1900, to John Galsworthy.

I sent wife and child out of the house (to London) and sat down at 9 A.M. with a desperate resolve to be done with it. Now and then I took a walk round the house, out at one door in at the other. Ten-minute meals. A great hush. Cigarette ends growing into a mound similar to a cairn over a dead hero. Moon rose over the barn, looked in at the window and climbed out of sight. Dawn broke, brightened. I put the lamp out and went on, with the morning breeze blowing the sheets of MS. all over the room. Sun rose. I wrote the last word and went into the dining-room. Six o'clock I shared a piece of cold chicken with Escamillo (who was very miserable and in want of sympathy, having missed the child dreadfully all day). Felt very well, only sleepy: had a bath at seven and at 1:30 was on my way to London.

Seven months before that rushed ending of *Lord Jim* Conrad had written "Heart of Darkness," the Congo story taking shape during a month of English winter at Pent Farm. *Typhoon,* another tropical story, grew in the winter of 1900. "The End of the Tether," "Falk," "Amy Foster," "Tomorrow," were all completed by 1903, as were two novels in which Conrad collaborated with Ford Madox Hueffer, *The Inheritors* and *Romance.*

Twenty months of nerve-destroying concentration were given to his most difficult novel, *Nostromo.* From December, 1902, to September, 1904, Conrad lived in his fictional South American world, building a revolution from his short view of the 1876 uprising in Colombia.

No author could have worked under greater stress, with more paralyzing handicaps. During 1903 he was continually ill, with five attacks of gout in eleven months. His wife showed signs of heart trouble and in January, 1903, he took her to doctors in London. In a December 15, 1904, letter to Mme. Poradowska Conrad told of the harassing conditions under which *Nostromo* was written and of the accident to his thirty-one-year-old wife which was to cripple her for life.

. . . just as we were getting ready to return home to Pent Farm she had a terrible accident, a fall in the street dislocating both her knees! After six weeks of agony in London, we spent a miserable summer in the country; she, hardly able to drag herself about, I, writing night and day, so to speak, to finish my wretched book. . . . During all this while I have been in a pitiable state of mind. Unable to work for a whole year, fearful as to the future, struggling with financial difficulties. . . . At last I am coming out of this, shaken, jolted, but having regained a little hope.

Having published seven novels and three collections of short stories in ten years at a driving pace, Conrad was physically and nervously exhausted, "at the end of my tether." In January, 1905, he left England with his ailing wife and seven-year-old son Borys for a four-month stay in Capri.

For the return in May he elected to travel by freighter from Naples to Marseilles. He wanted to enter the harbor he had not seen in twenty-seven years, to sail into the Vieux Port as he and Dominic had done in long ago gunrunning days. He was forty-seven. Again he registered at the Hôtel de Genève, the waterside hotel in Marseilles that had known him, the Monsieur George of nineteen. On the familiar rue Cannebière memories of his youth and of Paula came flooding back.

He had started *The Mirror of the Sea* in February, 1904, and it was nearly finished. Late in 1905 newspapers carried what turned out to be a false report of Paula's death. With that, and with Marseilles fresh in his mind, Conrad wrote the "Tremolino" chapter of *The Mirror of the Sea,* telling of Paula under the name of "Rita," recalling Dominic, Blunt, and the balancelle on which he had run contraband arms for the Carlists in Spain.

Bringing back that time in his life induced the anguish he described in a letter of October 20, 1905, to H. G. Wells.

I stick here fighting with disease and creeping imbecility—like a cornered rat, facing fate with a big stick that is sure to descend and crack my skull before many days are over. . . . The damned stuff comes out only by a kind of mental convulsion lasting two, three or more days—up to a fortnight—which leaves me perfectly limp and not very happy, exhausted emotionally to all appearance, but secretly irritable to the point of savagery.

He was "very much down" with a new attack of neurasthenia and, as he wrote Norman Douglas, had been having "a deucedly hard time of it lately," just managing to keep his head above water.

Although Blunt, the American who had given Conrad his almost fatal dueling wound, had died "in a Balkanian squabble, in the cause of some Serbs or else Bulgarians," Paula still lived, as did Don Carlos and the Englishman, Henry C——. To veil the real gunrunning occurrences involving them, Conrad somewhat fictionalized the facts in his autobiographical "Tremolino" chapter, making *The Mirror of the Sea,* as he told his publisher, "an imaginative rendering of a reminiscent mood." As a result of the mistiness he purposely gave it, critics saw the shadowy record of those events in his life as "symbols of one knows not what sacred ritual taking place behind the veil."

In *The Mirror of the Sea* Conrad varied far more from the facts than he did in his novel *The Arrow of Gold,* written twelve years later when none of the principals in the Marseilles story were living or could be embarrassed by his disclosures. He identified Blunt in the earlier and supposedly factual account only by the initials J.M.K.B., a "North Carolinian gentleman." More truthfully in *The Arrow of Gold* he gave his name as John M. K. Blunt and his home as South Carolina.

Making the facts nebulous enough for publication in *The Mirror of the Sea* was difficult work. "It is surprising how much time was taken up in putting it into some shape," he wrote his London agent J. B. Pinker on March 5, 1906, as he finished the revision of the book in Montpellier, France.

The second and last of Conrad's children, John Alexander, was born in London on August 2, 1906. Conrad, nearly forty-nine, was happy about his new son, a "quiet, unassuming, extremely ugly but upon the whole a rather sympathetic young man," he wrote to the Galsworthys to announce the news. Borys at eight was quick to accept his young brother. "Besides half of his dog Borys has been busy making over a large share of his property to Brother Jack. I have (as head of the family) sanctioned all these arrangements, which come into force immediately."

Conrad was a devoted father, affectionate and worried about his boys, however little time—and little knowledge—he had for play. His wife was the mainstay; good natured, an excellent cook, an understanding mother, she both typed his manuscripts and ran the home in a way to save him from distractions.

From his fourth home in eleven years, a house called Someries near Luton, Bedfordshire, Conrad wrote to Mme. Poradowska on January 15, 1908 of a father's pride in his boys. He, at fifty, was writing *Chance*. Borys was ten, John a year and a half.

Borys is at the Luton school . . . his health still requires close attention . . . He is a very fine boy; very loyal, a little melancholy, and of rather uneven temper, but with a great store of love for his family. He adores John Alexander, who reciprocates in his own way. Poor child, he was very ill in Switzerland with whooping cough. For three months he was like a corpse, between frightful fits of coughing. The least little complication would have carried him off. Now he is a sturdy rascal, and beginning to walk, though he doesn't yet talk much. He is much more boisterous than his elder brother ever was. Everyone finds him very charming. I too think he is very nice. He has light chestnut hair (a little coppery), dark brown eyes, very black lashes, and big pink cheeks. We spoil him badly. That's fatal. Everyone does it, including his papa.

Although he had been writing in English for over twenty years, it was, as he told his aunt, "still a foreign language to me, requiring an immense effort to handle." Yet his books came at a steady pace: *The Mirror of the Sea* published in 1906; *The Secret Agent* in 1907; *A Set of Six* in 1908; *Under Western Eyes* in 1911; *A Personal Record* and *'Twixt Land and Sea* in 1912; *Chance* in 1913; *Victory* and *Within the Tides* in 1915; *The Shadow Line* in 1917.

But there was still one book to write that had long been in

his mind: his own love story. His novels had carried the theme of guilt, of that troubling other-self of "A Secret Sharer." Eminently loyal and honest, a man of extreme integrity, his own life was an untarnished record. He was the rare sailor who never drank in twenty years of drifting through the waterfronts of the world. Yet his persistence in dealing with guilt— equally true of Sophocles—led critics to guess at its underlying cause, some supposing he carried a lasting remorse as a result of leaving Poland. The continuing puzzle caused Jean-Aubry to make a search of his sea life, writing in *The Sea Dreamer,* "A personal scrutiny of all the 'sea papers' relating to Joseph Conrad has convinced me that never throughout his maritime career, either as an ordinary seaman or as an officer, did he fail in his duty."

Conrad's "literary obsession with remorse," as Jean-Aubry phrased it, had little to do with an occurrence at sea. It's seed time, rather, dated from the introspective weeks of Conrad's hospital stay in Singapore, from the nine months of his early manhood spent in the Malay Archipelago, an area where social distinctions were acute. Stories acclaimed among his greatest grew from those days of intensive self-study in, as he wrote in *The Shadow Line,* "that part of the Eastern Seas from which I have carried away into my writing life the greatest number of suggestions."

In his first book, written of those seas, he took up the theme of a woman "outside the organized scheme of society," the half-caste girl Nina in *Almayer's Folly.* Again in his second novel, *An Outcast of the Islands,* Conrad gave to Willems the same dream of social acceptance sought by Almayer, telling of it in the Outcast's thoughts:

"A man of his stamp could carry off anything, do anything, aspire to anything. In another five years those white people who attended the Sunday card parties of the Governor would accept him—half-caste wife and all!"

In *Victory,* again written of those seas, the waif Lena, "almost a child of the streets," cried out to Heyst "I didn't know that you wanted anybody ever to see me," as if she guessed his shame.

The theme of a man socially rejected because of a connection with an unapproved girl was to recur in "A Smile of Fortune." In that story Jacobus, equal in heritage to any of his fellows, became an untouchable through one rebellious move: he raised his illegitimate daughter in his own home. The two, ostracized, were a lonely pair of castaways in the Pacific island port whose people, descendants of early colonists passing their days in "dull, dignified decay," found the girl's mere presence an outrage even after eighteen years.

Conrad was a sober worker, both as seaman and author, with a keen feeling for responsibility and a horror of losing his "sense of full self-possession." Yet his men of fiction, strong men, repeatedly lost it and in their floundering betrayed some trust. His literary pattern of ideals lost in crisis, of loyalties betrayed, led such critics as the Polish writer Madame Marie Dombrowska to conclude about Conrad that "something in his life posed a lasting contradiction to his instinct of fidelity and loyalty."

Over and over the heroes of his books, out of some inner weakness, brought added disaster to the ill-starred women they wished to protect. The drumbeat of this theme and the tormenting guilt shrouding it was an indication of how much of Conrad's dwelling on remorse had its roots in Marseilles—"a city I shall always love with a very special feeling"—where his own emotions had been so involved in an affair mystifyingly brusque in its ending.

When *The Arrow of Gold* was published critics found its conclusion, of Monsieur George piously accepting Rita's disappearance, a "chilling, dissipating douche to the story's illusion." The London *Times* expressed the general discontent with a hero so passionate and daring—until the final crisis.

"Monsieur George, it is true, wins at last to those white

arms; but at no excessive expense of mind or spirit; and, for no clear spiritual reason, he is sentenced to, and rather frigidly survives, his renewed banishment."

The *Times* published its reproof of Monsieur George in 1919. But the 1877-78 days of Conrad's romance had been less tolerant. The ultra-righteous, ultra-Victorian *Le Correspondant* of Paris could then extol La Vallière—more than two centuries after her career as the mistress of Louis XIV had ended— as "the only truly interesting one among those women who have loved sovereigns," finding her memory, so long after the event, creating "a profound feeling of sympathy . . . mixed with admiration and respect."

But the same journal that honored La Vallière for "a passion so persistent, so sad and so saintly expiated," was less gentle with contemporaries. In its next issue, of March 10, 1877, it denounced such a girl as the eighteen-year-old mistress of Don Carlos as "one of those creatures one doesn't name."

That courage and guilt became accented themes in Conrad's work may well have resulted from the fear that restrained him —in a moral climate where the double standard was religiously upheld—from trying for a permanent life with the girl he loved in Marseilles. A girl of integrity and superior intelligence, Paula was nevertheless then exposed to the tongues of gossips, to the scarifying terms of Véron, the well-known Paris journalist so powerful in the France of 1878. To undertake marriage with "one of those creatures one doesn't name" would have been the highest test of courage for a youth with Conrad's background. He was twenty then and under the scrutiny of watchful, critical relatives—of the man closest to him, his Uncle Thaddeus, whose letter he had before him with the reminding words "if I should ever turn silent from '*anger*,' which would depend entirely on you, then it would probably be forever."

The magnitude of his own problem in Marseilles found Conrad, two years after meeting Almayer, writing into his first book an impossible social hurdle for the trader. To that end he altered the true facts for the emphasis of fiction. In actual life Almayer was a half-caste, married to a Malay woman. He had, not the one prized Nina that Conrad gave him, but eleven children—five sons and six daughters.

If Conrad bore a personal guilt, stemming from adolescence, he was like other men. Developing that theme in realistic terms, he challenged the hatpin-and-fichu standards of the 1890's and gave impetus to modern psychological fiction.

In the more candid climate brought by World War I, and out of the mellowness of his older years, he looked back on his youthful romance. Aware that, as he wrote Colvin, "the critics will have a chance to say that J.C. has turned over still another leaf," he was to write of it, with little masking, as it happened.

In *The Shadow Line*, which he sub-titled "A Confession" and defined as exact autobiography, his ship, the *Otago*, was becalmed in the Gulf of Siam. Burns, the crazed chief mate, believed the bark to be paralyzed by the ghost of her ex-captain. The haunting spirit had to be sternly faced if the ship were to be freed. "Skulking's no good, sir," he insisted. "Boldness is what you want."

A few months after *The Shadow Line* was published in 1917 the time arrived when Conrad could release a memory haunting him for forty years.

Chapter XXV

◇◇◇◇◇◇◇◇◇◇◇◇◇◇◇◇◇◇

COLVIN stood with his back to the fire on an evening in early spring, recalling Gambetta and the dramatic 1870's in France as Conrad paced the room in the excitement of eager talk. Sir Sidney Colvin, scholar, well-known critic and biographer of Keats, was down from London on an overnight visit to Conrad's home, Capel House at Orlestone in Kent. It was April, 1917, and the two friends in their older years—Colvin seventy-two and Conrad sixty—reminisced about their youth in the France both loved.

Colvin had met Gambetta in Paris in the winter of 1873-74 and saw him often during the next four years when he had become "in all men's eyes incontestably the chief personage in France." Through his long career as a man of letters Colvin had made such friends as Robert Louis Stevenson, Robert Browning, Henry James, George Eliot, Tennyson, and Victor Hugo, but in this evening's talk with Conrad his thoughts centered on the statesman prominent in the France of his youth.

Then, during hectic days when the republic was tremblingly new, when Marshal MacMahon perpetuated his *coup d'état*, dismissing the Republican ministry of Jules Simon and appointing one of violent reaction under De Broglie and Fourtou, this one man had stood out, fighting almost alone. For Gambetta, a Frenchman of the south, the most impassioned of political orators and a great leader, Colvin had immense admiration. The election won by Gambetta in 1877 was to Colvin "decisive for the whole future of France."

Conrad was stirred by the talk of a year so vital in his own life. It had been the year in Marseilles when his love for Paula had sent him on dangerous voyages to Spain, twelve months of "profound emotion, continuous and overpowering."

Long as Colvin had known Gambetta, often during eight years visiting at the statesman's Paris home, yet, as he told Conrad and later wrote in *Memories & Notes of Persons & Places,* he had no inkling of the well-kept secret in Gambetta's life.

I never saw nor suspected—but in this I was practically at one with all except the very nearest of his intimates—the existence of the tie which had been through all those strenuous years the governing fact and secret inspiration of his life. Since one of his friends [Francis Laur in *Le Coeur de Gambetta,* Paris, 1907] has made public the story of his relations with Mademoiselle Léonie Léon, and the determined self-abnegation which kept that devoted woman from consenting, until almost the very end, openly to share the life which all the while she was secretly guiding and inspiring, the new halo of a great romantic passion has been added to Gambetta's ever-growing fame as a statesman.

At the end of Colvin's account of Gambetta's great love and of the woman who inspired it, Conrad spoke of the story of such a love, "dealing with facts," which he one day intended to write. He recalled that April promise in a letter to Colvin two years later when *The Arrow of Gold* was published.

You never suspected your close association with this book. And yet it is a fact that you are not the first but the only man to whom I spoke of it some months before I put pen to paper. It was at Capel. You stood with your back to the fire. But I did not lay a particular stress on my intentions and later I noticed that the circumstance had escaped your memory. And no wonder. I was very inarticulate that day—and on that subject too.

To no one but Colvin had Conrad mentioned the story that had been in his mind since his first attempt to write it as *The Sisters* in 1895. But seven months after listening to Colvin tell of the hidden love in Gambetta's life an event occurred which allowed Conrad to write of his own. On November 18, 1917, *Le Figaro* carried a small item in its column of death notices:

The death is announced of the Marquise de Trabadelo (née Baroness de Somogyi) who died in her home in Paris at 4 rue Marbeuf. Following her expressed wish, the funeral service was held in strict privacy, with no one invited to attend.

Receiving word of Paula's death, Conrad immediately began the story of his love for her, *The Arrow of Gold*. She had died at fifty-nine in a quiet slipping-away hauntingly lonely. Her last home on the rue Marbeuf was in the same fashionable quarter as the one on the rue Pauquet, three blocks away, where she had lived forty years before as the glamorous mistress of Don Carlos. The years between had been strangely silent. The celebrated beauty and magnetic "heiress," for a time so much in the blaze of notice, had sought the shadows.

She had ended her life as Conrad described it, a woman "who might have been a very brilliant phenomenon but has remained obscure, playing her little part in the Carlist war of '75-6 and then going as completely out of the very special world which knew her as though she had returned in despair to the goats of her childhood in some lonely valley."

Conrad gave that description to his American publisher in 1918 in a supposed portrait of Rita in *The Arrow of Gold* he was then writing. But that ending of her life, so true of Paula, never came into his book.

Like Léonie Léon, the shadowy figure in Gambetta's life, Paula had remained a mystery in Conrad's, concealed from everyone, an inspiration to the author who drew upon her for the heroines in so many of his stories—where, in a slight variation of Paula's name, they had appeared as Nina, Rita, Lena, Flora, Freya.

Romantic eastern settings had enabled him to write more easily in his earlier novels of socially-marked girls so nearly rescued by men who loved, yet failed them, but when Conrad undertook to tell the story of his love for Paula in its factual setting of Victorian Marseilles he found it difficult to frame. Though it would have an *"intime"* quality, as he wrote Sir Sidney Colvin on May 17, 1918, while still working on the novel, "the proprieties however won't be outraged, at least no more than is inherent in the subject."

Using a narrative device to present the story, he offered it as a supposed answer to a letter received from his Polish cousin Tekla, the "austere" girl who had been the second of his schoolboy loves, giving that introduction in pages of "The Laugh" dropped from the final version of the book.

"He is writing to a woman whom he has not seen for something like five and thirty years. When they last saw each other they were not only very young but I may say youthful. . . .

"And he answers: 'Had time stood still with you, were you still as I remember you at eighteen, I would never dare to begin; but I must believe that by now you have added indulgence to your other perfections.'

"He then begins the story with the episode preserved here. It concerns the third woman of his experience, as far as numbers go. In truth, she might well be called the first. The other two were young girls; and by no stretch of imagination (different as they are) could they have been expected to understand the woman about whom he writes. They had their place in the world. But of the two it is perhaps the austere one that was more fit to hear. If the tale had to be told at all."

Feeling that the tale had to be told, Conrad struggled for weeks to begin it. His hesitation in disclosing that intimate history showed in deleted portions of *The Arrow of Gold* where he endeavored to make the story of his love for Paula acceptable to the "uncompromising Puritan" of his boyhood.

"Even in the most careful rendering I can give it (that is with all its subtleties) you may find it hard to accept—just as some prosperous people are unwilling to be made to lay a finger on some great misery. For you at any rate have not suffered from moral destitution. I take the precaution of saying all this not for my own sake you may believe me, but partly for yours, for I don't want you to be gratuitously shocked, and partly for the sake of her whom our Dominic used to invoke as La Señora in a tone as near to awe as it was possible for that lawless man who, I am convinced, believed in the Devil but certainly did not fear him. It would take an uncommon woman to impress Dominic who believed in them very much in the same way he believed in the Devil. They did not see each other more than three times altogether but from the first she had pronounced him a perfect man, *'mais il est parfait cet homme,'* in her best grande-dame manner. That woman of whose awful destitution it is difficult to give you an idea (I am not alluding to lack of money here) had something of a grande dame in her; not because she could put on 'an air' (she was terribly natural) but because I suppose that to be on top of the scale is in a sense the same sort of thing as being outside of it altogether, when one can also judge men and things with absolute independence, from a strictly personal standpoint, in utter freedom as a great lady would."

His gout-crippled hand preventing him from continuing with a pen, Conrad began dictating *The Arrow of Gold* at the end of December, 1917, and completed it June 14, 1918. To Sir Sidney Colvin who, unknowing, had had such a close association with the book, he revealed how strongly affected he was still—a man nearing sixty-two—by the recall of his early love.

The fact is, between you and me (and Lady Colvin of course), that I have never been able to read *these* proofs in cold blood. Ridiculous! My dear (as D. Rita would have said) there are some of these 42-year-old episodes of which I cannot think now without a slight tightness of the chest—*un petit serrement de coeur*. What a confession!

An author widely acclaimed and with a reputation solidly established by 1919, he feared the public's disapproval of his early romance no less than when an unknown youth of nineteen. When Colvin prepared to write a review of *The Arrow of Gold* for the London *Observer* Conrad shied from having the autobiographical nature of that story revealed.

A man of your *savoir-faire* [he wrote Colvin on August 7, 1919], your sense of literary *convenances* and your *homme-du-monde* tact, is best fit to judge how the autob'al note, if struck, may affect the world—and the man.

With all deference then I venture to suggest that the view of its being a study of a woman, *prise sur le vif* (obviously, you may say) and also the story of young, very young love told with a depth of emotion pointing to experience is what you perceive, what impresses you—which makes the "quality" of the book. This said with your authority will amount to a confession—a sufficient confession to a not particularly delicate world.

Conrad's handwritten inscription in the copy given his friend Richard Curle, to whom he dedicated *The Arrow of Gold,* indicated how much he continued to be troubled by his affair in Marseilles. In a poignant phrase drawn from the last sentence of the book he was still asking himself an old question about that long ago, abandoned love:

". . . what could he have done with it?"

A strong strain of autobiography ran through all of Conrad's work, yet his sense of personal privacy was agonizingly acute. He drew his own experiences repeatedly in his fiction, wrote close to reality, so much so that, rare among authors, he retained the true names of people he knew—Lingard, Willems, McWhirr, Beard, James Wait, Babalatchie, Dominic, and Blunt among them. Other names he changed but slightly—from Klein to Kurtz, from Sullivan to Singleton, from Born to Burns, from Véron to Versoy, from Olmeijer to Almayer—requiring a close association of sound to focus on the real men and factual episodes he wove into stories. Invention, he maintained, was difficult for him.

Pulling from his memory such actual happenings as those given in "A Smile of Fortune," Conrad wrote with so much self-identification that his stories were told with the inevitable and recurring "I." Their pertinence to his own life was so marked that he sketched remembered settings and people as he worked: a map of his boardinghouse on the rue Sylvabelle inked on a page of "The Laugh"; Doña Rita of *The Arrow of Gold* in the pose of a girl in dishabille curled up in bed, a seductive drawing he proposed as the only illustration he would consent to have in the book; presenting her again as the Byzantine Empress Theodora on a jacket he designed for that novel.

More almost than any writer, Conrad produced highly subjective fiction. Yet, with his openness in writing, went a personal seclusion. He carried within himself a "double" with much the same unease as the captain in "The Secret Sharer." A rebel in the mold of his captain, defying an intolerant society so ready to place the brand of outcast on any erring or nonconforming member, he retreated, at thirty-eight, from a too-constricting world.

For twenty-eight years after his marriage Conrad lived an isolated existence in the English countryside, moving from one rented house to another, rarely persuaded by his wife to visit anyone, allowing only his closest friends, two at a time, to come to him. He shunned the public, avoided the press, rejected lecture offers. He had almost a phobia for destroying personal letters and, in consequence, very few were found among his papers after his death.

His mother's letters, which his Uncle Thaddeus had saved for thirty years—letters so largely responsible for his father's apprehension by the Czarist police, his exile, and the resulting family tragedies—Conrad burned when on a visit to the Ukraine in 1893. Perhaps those letters, innocently written, brutal in effect, instigated the practice of destruction he carried to such extremes.

Burning letters became a mandate with him. He directed his wife to set fire to every scrap of paper bearing his signature on communications he had sent her before their marriage. Early drafts of his work suffered the fate referred to in an unused portion of "The Laugh": "it all went into the fire, which is the best way to dispose of dead emotions—and of old papers the very indiscretions of which have lost their glory and their shame."

On their honeymoon in Brittany Conrad ordered all the papers in his trunk to be thrown into the flames. Secretly disobeying him and winning his later displeasure for it, his young bride spent lonely hours in the attic while her husband wrote downstairs, sorting out sheets of manuscript from the condemned bundle, thereby saving the unpublished and only copy of *The Sisters* as well as his handwritten drafts of *Almayer's Folly* and *An Outcast of the Islands*.

Conrad's letters written to his uncle in the course of his twenty years at sea—the only firsthand account of those important years of his life, describing events as they occurred—disappeared. Undoubtedly Conrad destroyed them, too, after his uncle's death in 1894. No trace of them was found as far back as 1904 when, through the increasing fame brought by *Lord Jim, Nostromo,* "Youth," *The Nigger of the Narcissus,* and *Typhoon,* Conrad letters already had high value.

Of straight autobiography, Conrad wrote only two volumes, small ones, which could be classed as such—*The Mirror of the Sea* and *A Personal Record.* Both were mystifyingly vague and unrevealing, so much so that E. M. Forster described the clouded quality of *A Personal Record* in the baffled complaint that Conrad lets us "into the severe little compartment that must, for want of a better word, be called his confidence."

Though often urged to write of his childhood, of his first seventeen years in Poland, he refused to do so, insisting he would not expose his wounds for the public to stare at his scars.

In an angry letter, rare for a man so courteous, Conrad rebuked Richard Curle for revealing too much of his private life in a proposed article "Joseph Conrad in the East."

"Didn't it ever occur to you, my dear Curle," he wrote on April 24, 1922, "that I knew what I was doing in leaving the facts of my life and even of my tales in the background? Explicitness, my dear fellow, is fatal to the glamour of all artistic work, robbing it of all suggestiveness, destroying all illusion."

By withholding map points, place names, dates, costume, all the confining facts of specific instance, Conrad expanded his stories into experience universally shared. He went below the surface of events easily forgotten to the pains, sorrows, vanities, ambitions, loves, and passions mankind is moved by, endowing his tales with the authentic stress of life. A strain of symbolic meaning ran through his work as he reached toward that art he defined in a 1918 letter to Barrett H. Clark. "All the great creations of literature have been symbolic, and in that way have gained in complexity, in power, in depth and in beauty."

Life he saw as a ceaseless and courageous contest. Because of "the duality of man's nature and the competition of individuals," he wrote in his essay on Henry James, "the life-history of the earth must in the last instance be a history of a really very relentless warfare." His view of that warfare lay in his comment, "mankind is delightful in its pride, its assurance, and its indomitable tenacity. It will sleep on the battlefield among its own dead, in the manner of an army having won a barren victory. It will not know when it is beaten."

A man with a "private gnawing worm of my own," Conrad devoted his writing life to making readers see both into the troubled hearts and minds of the characters he drew and the environments fostering pain. His range was as wide in human problems as the physical world of his settings. At sixty he created the tempest of a youth's first passionate love with a reality that made the story fade, the shared experience remain; he probed the murky purpose of anarchy in *The Secret Agent,* knowing "almost nothing of the philosophy, and nothing at all of the men."

He attacked prejudices, challenged convictions, "the disguised servants of our passions." Of Daudet he wrote, "his small distinction, worth many a greater, was in not being in bondage to some vanishing creed." From early years spent with a father extreme in his political and religious beliefs grew Conrad's admiration for the sane view of life and his hostility to political and religious extremists whom he exposed in *The Secret Agent, Under Western Eyes, The Sisters,* and *The Arrow of Gold.* In an echo of his childhood his troubled men of fiction were, like himself, sons deprived of mothers, raised by fathers with fixed ideas: Heyst, son of an embittered writer in *Victory;* Anthony, the poet's son of *Chance;* Jim of *Lord Jim,* son of a pious rural parson possessing his "certain knowledge of the Unknowable"; Charles Gould in *Nostromo,* son of a mine-obsessed father; Leggatt in "A Secret Sharer," son of a Norfolk parson sure to be unforgiving of his son's crime.

Beyond personal disasters lay "the poignant miseries and passionate credulities of a mankind so tragically eager for self-destruction," the greater tragedy of war. He fiercely condemned the autocracy of Czars and Kaisers, their abjectly obedient subjects; turned scathing comments on wars of imperialism, the Boer War, the Spanish-American War, the action of "Yankee Conquistadores" in Panama.

Dark as his stories often were they were freed of the macabre pessimism of Dostoevsky to whom he was often compared. "What one feels so hopelessly barren in declared pessimism is just its arrogance," Conrad wrote in *Notes on Life and Letters.* "To be hopeful in an artistic sense it is not necessary to think that the world is good. It is enough to believe that there is no impossibility of its being made so." His novels carried a strong underlying purpose, to bring readers to "look with a large forgiveness at men's ideas and prejudices, which are by no means the outcome of malevolence, but depend on their education, their social status, even their professions." Yet he did not propose universal absolution, for in that "benevolent neutrality towards the warring errors of human nature all light would go out from art and from life."

What Conrad gave through the illusion of his stories was the convincing tone of reality. The human storms and those of the sea were acutely vivid, and for that his tales have lasted. Despair was in them, and hope. His pictorial image of hope took the form of emerging sunshine. The strongest wish he could give was to "walk on the road of life in the sun, without the slightest cloud in your sky." It was a theme heard like a musical chord at the end of *The Nigger of the Narcissus.*

"The roar of the town resembled the roar of topping breakers, merciless and strong, with a loud voice and cruel purpose; but overhead the clouds broke; a flood of sunshine streamed down the walls of grimy houses. The dark knot of seamen drifted in sunshine."

Chapter XXVI

◇◇◇◇◇◇◇◇◇◇◇◇◇◇◇◇◇◇◇

CONRAD, at sixty-six, was looking for another house, one more remote. His wife, in bed recovering from another of the long series of operations on her knee, listened in quiet good humor to his restless longing to move again, away, farther away. They were then, in the summer of 1924, living in the eighth of the rented homes of their marriage, Oswalds at Bishopsbourne, near Canterbury in Kent. Conrad was a grandfather, his married son Borys twenty-six, his younger son John a youth of eighteen learning French with a family in Le Havre. But neither age nor illness—the previous eighteen months had brought him continual sessions of gout and bronchitis—diminished Conrad's yearning for some perfect retreat. "His whole attitude to life" was, as his wife said, "opposed to any idea of rest."

For ten years he had been free of financial worries. The sale of his books had, at fifty-six, begun to bring him a living. The most recent, *The Rover,* was proving a great success in New York. Honors of all kinds were pouring in upon him. The universities of Oxford, Edinburgh, Liverpool and Durham had offered him honorary degrees but, "determined to have nothing to do with any academic distinction," he had declined them.

He had been offered the honor considered highest in England, the bestowal of a knighthood. In gentle refusal he had written Prime Minister Ramsay MacDonald on May 27, 1924, of his inability to accept it.

Sir:
It is with the deepest possible sense of the honour H.M. The King is graciously willing to confer on me on your recommendation, that I beg leave to decline the proffered knighthood.

In conveying to you my sincere thanks I venture to add that, as a man whose early years were closely associated in hard toil and unforgotten friendships with British workingmen, I am specially touched at this offer being made to me during your Premiership.

I have the honour to be, with my greatest regard

Your obedient servant
Joseph Conrad

Over that proffered title—"ever since this happened Jessie has been teasing me"—he had sworn his friends to secrecy, not wishing a whisper of it to reach newspapers in England or America. Of public attention he had had more than enough on his trip to the United States the previous year when he had spent six weeks from April 30 to June 2, 1923, on the only visit he ever made to this country, the last of his sea voyages. Beyond a nine-day motor trip to Boston and New England, he had seen only New York, made but one semi-public appearance. On the evening of May 10 in the New York home of Mrs. Curtiss James he had read to two hundred guests parts of *Victory*, "a book in which I have tried to grasp at more 'life-stuff' than perhaps in any other of my works."

A battery of newsmen greeted him, an unaware celebrity, when he had arrived in New York on the *Tuscania*. Shaken by the onslaught of photographers, he had written his wife, "to be aimed at by forty cameras held by forty men is a nerve-shattering experience." He was deluged with telegrams, invitations to dinners, banquets, swept up in a storm of attention. Though New York sought to lionize him, he clung to the shelter of the Oyster Bay home of his publisher, F. N. Double-day, where he was "looked after like an infant." Each day he had to rely on office help to cope with the flood of letters sent by a clamoring American public. The strength of his popularity astounded him and in amused awe he wrote home, "I am made to feel I am a considerable person."

Three weeks of such attention was too much for a shy man. "I must confess that I am heartily sick of all this infinite kindness," he told his "very own dear Jess." He longed to be out of it and home. "Don't imagine, my dearest, that the delights of this country make me forget my home,—which is where you are: and indeed is nothing to me but you, you alone wherever you may be . . . I can't give you the slightest idea how impatient I am to get back to you. I think of nothing else. The time seems interminable and yet the visit is a success."

And so he had gone home and in his Kentish countryside had set to work writing. He had said when he finished *The Arrow of Gold* that the people of that story, whom he had been moved to go and seek in the shadows, would from then on rest undisturbed. Yet he found it impossible to leave them. In his new story *Suspense,* left unfinished at his death, the setting was the Mediterranean. There was a harbor like Marseilles filled with sailing ships; a youth named Cosmo, a signorino like himself at nineteen; an older seaman, the conspirator Attilio, a man like Dominic; and a beautiful, tall, intelligent French girl with dark blue eyes, a seductive voice, a gift of familiarity, a disturbingly appealing girl named Adèle—like Paula. The three were together again and the time was youth.

On August 2, 1924, Conrad had a sudden heart attack from which he seemed to recover. Early on the morning of the 3rd, feeling better, he sat at his table writing. His invalid wife in the next room heard the familiar tapping of his fingers on the arm of his chair as his mind soared into the regions of memory, of fancy. A few minutes later he slumped from his chair, dead.

A great cast of unforgettable men were left behind—among them Monsieur George, Marlow, Jim, Heyst—voices of Conrad wandering the world, lonely, "whispering their pain softly—only to themselves."

Bibliography and Acknowledgments

WORKS OF JOSEPH CONRAD

Complete works published by Doubleday, Doran & Co., 26 vols. New York: 1938.

Almayer's Folly, An Outcast of the Islands, The Nigger of the Narcissus, Tales of Unrest, Lord Jim, Typhoon, Youth, Nostromo, The Mirror of the Sea, The Secret Agent, A Set of Six, Under Western Eyes, A Personal Record, 'Twixt Land and Sea, Chance, Victory, Within the Tides, The Shadow Line, The Arrow of Gold, The Rescue, Notes on Life and Letters, The Rover, Tales of Hearsay, Suspense.

Last Essays. London: J. M. Dent & Sons, 1926.

The Sisters. New York: Crosby Gaige, 1928.

Preface to *Into The East* by Richard Curle. London: The Macmillan Co., 1923.

LETTERS OF JOSEPH CONRAD

Letters of Conrad in *Joseph Conrad: Life and Letters* by G. Jean-Aubry, 2 vols. New York: Doubleday, Page & Co., 1927.

Lettres Françaises, (ed.) G. Jean-Aubry. Paris: Gallimard, 1930.

Letters of Joseph Conrad to Marguerite Poradowska, translated from the French and edited by John A. Gee and Paul J. Sturm. New Haven: Yale University Press, 1940.

Letters from Joseph Conrad: 1895-1924, (ed.) Edward Garnett. Indianapolis: Bobbs-Merrill, 1928.

Conrad to a Friend, (ed.) Richard Curle. New York: Doubleday, Doran & Co., 1928.

POLISH DOCUMENTS AND WORKS

"For the information of my dear nephew Konrad Korzeniowski," a notebook of 22 pages handwritten by Thaddeus Bobrowski, being a financial record kept by him between December 1, 1869, and February 4, 1890, of funds sent to Joseph Conrad, his expenses and activities during those years; also information on the marriage and subsequent life of his parents.

"Information which may be useful to you," a handwritten page by Thaddeus Bobrowski prepared for his nephew, Joseph Conrad. Family data, including date and place of Conrad's birth.

Poem of Apollo Korzeniowski on the birth of his son Conrad.

Letters of Apollo Korzeniowski to Casimir Kaszewski written in the years 1865-1868.

Letter of Conrad's grandmother, Mme Teofila Bobrowska, to Casimir Kaszewski written after the death of Conrad's father.

(The manuscript letters and documents above are in the Jagellon Library, Cracow, Poland.)

Letters of Apollo Korzeniowski to Stefan Buszczynski written in the years 1868-1869.

Letter of Joseph Conrad to Stefan Buszczynski of August 14, 1883.

Five letters of Joseph Conrad to his cousin, Mme Maria Tyszkowa, written May 2, 1890, May 6, 1890, September 24, 1890, April 15, 1891, September 8, 1892. Letter from Joseph Conrad to A. M. Jasienski of April 25, 1905. Published in *Ruch Literacki*, 1927, 1-10, pp. 138-141. Warsaw, Poland.

(The manuscript and published letters above are in the Pan Library, Cracow, Poland.)

Letters written to Joseph Conrad by his uncle and guardian, Thaddeus Bobrowski, during the years 1869-1893.

Two letters written to Joseph Conrad by his uncle, Casimir Bobrowski, of March 18, 1882 and August 8, 1884.

(The manuscript letters above are in the Narodowa Library, Warsaw, Poland.)

"Polskie Lata Conrada" ("The Polish Years of Conrad") by Zdzisław Najder in November, 1956 issue of *Twórczość*. Warsaw, Poland.

"Niedrukowane Wiersze A. Korzeniowskiego O Buncie Chłopskim Na Ukrainie" ("Unpublished Poems of Apollo Korzeniowski on the Peasants' Uprising in the Ukraine") by Roman Taborski in *Pamiętnika Literackiego.* Rocznik XLVI, 1955, z.1. Wroclaw, Poland.

"Polityczna I Literacka Działalność Apolla Korzeniowskiego W R. 1861" ("Political and Literary Work of Apollo Korzeniowski in 1861") by Roman Taborski in *Pamiętnika Literackiego.* Rocznik XLVI, 1955, z.4. Wroclaw, Poland.

WORKS OF OTHER AUTHORS

Cadby, Carine, "Conrad's Dislike of the Camera, and How it was Conquered by Will Cadby." London: *The Graphic,* November 1, 1924.

Cecil, Lord David, *The Fine Art of Reading and Other Literary Studies.* New York: Bobbs-Merrill, 1957.

Colvin, Sir Sidney, *Memories & Notes of Persons & Places, 1852-1912.* New York: Charles Scribner's Sons, 1921.

Conrad, Borys, "A Famous Father and His Son." *The New York Times,* December 1, 1957.

Conrad, Jessie, *Joseph Conrad As I Knew Him.* London: William Heinemann, 1926.

Conrad, Jessie, *Joseph Conrad and His Circle.* New York: E. P. Dutton & Co., 1935.

Conrad, Jessie, "Conrad's Skill as an Artist." *The Saturday Review of Literature,* April 10, 1926.

Curle, Richard, "Conrad in the East." *Yale Review,* April, 1923.

Curle, Richard, *The Last Twelve Years of Joseph Conrad.* New York: Doubleday, Doran & Co., 1928.

Daudet, Alphonse, *The Nabob.* Translated from the French by Lucy Hooper. Boston: Estes and Lauriat, 1878.

Ford, Ford Madox, *Joseph Conrad: A Personal Remembrance.* Boston: Little, Brown & Co., 1925.

Forster, E. M., "Joseph Conrad: A Note" from *Abinger Harvest.* New York: Harcourt, Brace & Co., 1936.

Galsworthy, John, "Reminiscences of Conrad," from *Castles in Spain and Other Screeds.* London: William Heinemann, 1927.

Garnett, Edward, "Joseph Conrad: Impressions and Beginnings," and "Joseph Conrad: The Long Hard Struggle." New York: *The Century Magazine*, February, March, 1928.

Gautier, Judith, *Le Second Rang du Collier*. Paris: Felix Juven, 1904.

Gordan, John Dozier, *Joseph Conrad, the Making of a Novelist*. Cambridge, Mass.: Harvard University Press, 1940.

Guerard, Albert J., "The Nigger of the Narcissus." *The Kenyon Review*. Gambier, Ohio: Spring, 1957.

Guerard, Albert J., "The Voyages of Captain Korzeniowski." New York: *The Reporter*, March 21, 1957.

Hackett, Francis, "Back to Conrad" from *The New Republic*. New York: August 6, 1956.

Hamilton, Lord Frederic, *The Vanished Pomps of Yesterday*. New York: George H. Doran Co., 1921.

Haugh, Robert F. *Joseph Conrad: Discovery in Design*. Norman, Okla.: University of Oklahoma Press. 1957.

Hastings, W. S. (ed.) *Balzac's Letters to His Family, 1809-1850*. Princeton: Princeton University Press, 1934.

Henao y Melguizo, J. M. and Gerardo Arrubla. *History of Colombia*. Chapel Hill: University of North Carolina Press. 1938.

Herzen, Alexander, *Memoirs*, 5 vols. New York: Alfred A. Knopf, 1924.

Hewitt, Douglas, *Conrad, A Reassessment*. Cambridge, England: Bowes & Bowes, 1952.

Huneker, James, *Promenades of an Impressionist*. New York: Charles Scribner's Sons, 1910.

Jean-Aubry, G., *Joseph Conrad: Life and Letters*, 2 vols. New York: Doubleday, Page & Co., 1927.

Jean-Aubry, G., *Vie de Conrad*. Paris: Gallimard. 1947. Translated by Helen Sebba as *The Sea Dreamer*. New York: Doubleday & Co., 1957.

Jean-Aubry, G., "La Jeunesse de Conrad." *Revue de Paris*. Paris: May, 1947.

Jean-Aubry, G., Introduction to his translation, *Le Miroir de la Mer*. Paris: Gallimard, 1946.

Joseph Conrad: A Sketch. Booklet published by Doubleday, Page & Co. Garden City, New York, 1925.

"Joseph Conrad Today," a symposium with contributions by Oliver Warner, John Wain, W. W. Robson, R. Freislich, Tom Hopkinson, Jocelyn Baines, Richard Curle. *The London Magazine*. London: November, 1957.

Keating, George T., *A Conrad Memorial Library*. New York: Doubleday, Doran & Co., 1929.

Knopf, Alfred A., *Joseph Conrad: the Romance of His Life and of His Books*. New York: Doubleday, Page & Co. (booklet), April 20, 1914.

Knopf, Alfred A., "A Footnote to Publishing History." Boston: *The Atlantic Monthly*, February, 1958.

Kunitz, Joshua, *Russia, The Giant That Came Last*. New York: Dodd, Mead & Co., 1947.

Lair, Jules, *Louise de la Vallière*. New York: G. P. Putnam's Sons, 1908.

Laur, Francis, *Le Coeur de Gambetta*. Paris: Payot et Cie. 1921.

Lohf, Kenneth A. and Eugene P. Sheehy, *Joseph Conrad at Mid-Century*. Minneapolis: University of Minnesota Press, 1957.

Louis-Lande, L. *"Trois Mois de Voyage dans le Pays Basque."* Paris: *Revue des Deux Mondes*, October 15, 1877.

Maude, Aylmer, *The Life of Tolstoy*, 2 vols. New York: Dodd, Mead & Co., 1911.

Maurois, André, *Prophets and Poets*. New York: Harper & Bros., 1935.

McClintock, Captain, R. N., *The Voyage of the "Fox" in the Arctic Seas*, a Narrative of the Discovery of the Fate of Sir John Franklin and His Companions. London: John Murray, 1859.

Melgar, el Conde de., *Veinte Años con Don Carlos*, Memorias de su Secretario el Conde de Melgar. Madrid: Espasa-Calpe, 1940.

Mencken, H. L., "Joseph Conrad" from *A Book of Prefaces*. New York: A. A. Knopf, 1918.

Milosz, Czeslaw. "Joseph Conrad in Polish Eyes." Boston: *The Atlantic Monthly*. November, 1957.

Morf, Gustav, *The Polish Heritage of Joseph Conrad*. London: Sampson Low, Marston & Co., 1930.

Morley, Christopher, "Storms and Calms." *The Saturday Review of Literature*, New York: April 25, 1925.

Moser, Thomas C., *Joseph Conrad: Achievement and Decline.* Cambridge, Mass.: Harvard University Press, 1957.

Review of *An Outcast of the Islands* by H. G. Wells from *The Saturday Review.* London, May 16, 1896.

Review of *The Arrow of Gold* in *Revue des Deux Mondes.* Paris, October 1, 1919.

Review of *The Arrow of Gold* in *The Times,* London. August 7, 1919.

Rogers, Woodes, *A Cruising Voyage Round the World.* Reprinted from the original of 1712. London: Cassell & Co. Ltd., 1928.

Rothenstein, Sir William, *Men and Memories.* London: Faber and Faber Ltd., 1932.

Roux, Jules Charles T., *Le Cercle Artistique de Marseille.* Paris: A. Lemerre, 1906.

Russell, Bertrand, *Portraits from Memory and Other Essays.* New York: Simon and Schuster, 1956.

Scruggs, William L., U. S. Minister to Colombia and Venezuela, *The Colombian and Venezuelan Republics.* Boston: Little, Brown & Co., 1900.

Silbert, José, *Raymond Allègre, 1857-1933.* Booklet published by the Comité des Amis de Raymond Allègre. Paris: 1933.

Tomlinson, H. M., *The Face of the Earth.* New York: Bobbs-Merrill, 1950.

Troyat, Henry, *Firebrand,* the Life of Dostoevsky. New York: Roy Publishers, 1946.

Valras, Le Comte de., *Don Carlos VII et L'Espagne Carliste,* 2 vols. Paris: J. Fechoz, 1876.

Washburne, E. B., *Recollections of a Minister to France, 1869-1877,* 2 vols. New York: Charles Scribner's Sons, 1887.

Wiley, Paul L., *Conrad's Measure of Man.* Madison, Wis.: University of Wisconsin Press, 1954.

Woolf, Virginia, "Joseph Conrad" from *The Common Reader.* New York: Harcourt, Brace & Co., 1925.

Zabel, Morton D., (ed.) *The Portable Conrad.* New York: Viking Press, 1947.

Zévaès, Alexandre, "*Clovis Hugues: Sa Vie, Son Oeuvre Littéraire.*" *Nouvelle Revue,* Série 4, Tome 94, Paris, 1928.

Zweig, Stefan, *Balzac.* New York: Viking Press, 1946.

NEWSPAPERS, PERIODICALS, DIRECTORIES, MANUSCRIPTS

The Times, London: 1863, 1876-1883, 1909, 1917, 1924.

New York Times: 1863, 1876-1883, 1909, 1917, 1924, August 15, 1937.

Le Figaro, Paris: 1880-1883, 1909, 1917.

New York Herald, Paris edition: 1880, 1909, 1917.

Almanach de Gotha. 1876-1879.

Annuaire-Almanach du Commerce. Didot-Bottin. Paris: 1879.

Le Correspondant, fortnightly journal. Paris: 1877.

Le Monde Illustré, weekly journal. Paris: 1877, 1878.

Manuscript of "The Laugh," typescript of *The Arrow of Gold,* manuscript letters and documents of Joseph Conrad in the Yale University Library, New Haven, Conn.

Manuscript letters, documents and drawings of Joseph Conrad in the Berg Collection, New York Public Library, New York.

LETTERS AND DOCUMENTS RECEIVED BY JERRY ALLEN

Letters from el Conde de Melgar of March 14, 1956, April 5, 1956, June 2, 1956, September 24, 1957, October 31, 1957.

Letter of June 9, 1957 from Professor Marcel Clavel, Faculté des Lettres, Aix-en-Provence, France.

Letters from M. André Villard, Archivist of Bouches-du-Rhône Department, France, of April 6, 1957, and June 17, 1957.

Letters from William B. Rodman, Jr., Attorney General, State of North Carolina, of January 23, 1956 and February 1, 1956.

Copy of death certificate of Angel Trabadelo. Cemetery of Polloe, San Sebastian Town Hall, San Sebastian, Spain.

ACKNOWLEDGMENTS

For material drawn upon in this biography I should like to express my warm gratitude to: Doubleday & Co. for permission to quote from the works of Joseph Conrad; the Polish Embassy in Washington, D.C., and the Institute of Literary Research in Warsaw, Poland, for microfilm copies of the original manuscript letters of Conrad's family now in the Jagellon Library of Cracow, the Pan Library of Cracow, and the Narodowa Library of Warsaw, Poland; el Conde de Melgar for information on the life of Paula de Somoggy, the photograph of her, and for permission to quote from the memoirs of his father; the Trustees of the Conrad Estate for the use of extracts from Conrad's unpublished manuscripts and letters; Yale University Library for unpublished material drawn from its Conrad collection; the Berg Collection of the New York Public Library for permission to reproduce the Joseph Conrad letter to Prime Minister Ramsay MacDonald; Professor Marcel Clavel, André Villard, and E. Baratier for data concerning the Marseilles period of Conrad's life; Zdzisław Najder for studies on Conrad and his father recently published in Poland; Olga Scherer-Virski of the faculty of Yale University for translations of the Polish letters of Conrad and his family; the many correspondents in North and South Carolina who aided in the (unfortunately unsuccessful) effort to trace John M. K. Blunt, and the many others in France, England, Spain, and Sweden who answered inquiries about Conrad's life; Susie E. Allen, Francis Drake, Juan Ribot, W. T. McKeown, and Rachel MacKenzie for personal help so generously given.

J.A.

Index

Acapulco Ship, 89, 90
"Aesthetic Movement," 66
Affaire Morin, L', 81
Aigle, L', 80
Alamosa, 170
Alaska, whaler, 176
Alexander II, Czar, 20, 31, 131-32
Alfonso XII, King, 71, 100, 102, 125, 132
Al Jaffree, Syed Mohsin bin S., 192
Allègre, Raymond, 78-79, 82
Allen, James, 193
Almayer's Folly, 8, 10, 15, 29, 79, 82, 188, 193, 195, 196, 198, 207-09, 213, 221, 232
Alsagoff, Seyyid Muhammad, 175
Alvear, Commander, 190
American Revolution, 31
Amie du Roi, L', 110
Amsterdam, 185
"Amy Foster," 217
Anna Frost, ship, 176, 203
Antioquia, 88
Aragon, 74
Archangel, 20
Arlesienne, painting, 83
Around the World in Eighty Days, 144
Arrow of Gold, The, 10, 61, 77, 79, 81, 83, 91, 99, 102, 105, 107, 108, 109, 110, 112, 115, 117, 118, 122, 131, 133, 136, 138, 140, 141, 151, 152, 162, 163, 167, 168, 173, 188, 211, 219, 222, 226-30, 231, 234, 238
Art Circle, 82
As You Like It, 48

Australia, 172, 176, 197, 206
Austria, 119, 120

Babalatchi, 193, 195, 209
Baffin Bay, 52
Balaton Lake, 122
Baldelli, 191
Balzac, Honoré de, 24, 25-26, 33
Bandjarmasin, 193
Bangkok, 197
Barcelona, 102
Barrena, Manuel, 178, 190
Basle, 144
Beard, Captain, 180, 181
Beaumont College, 177, 178
Because of the Money, 21
Belgian Congo, 15, 16, 50, 158, 199-205
Bendz, Ernst, 86
Berdichev, 26, 45
Berg, General, 35
Berlin, 34
Berouw, 187, 193, 195
Bezak, Governor-General, 46
Birth of a Tragedy, The, 144
Bishopsbourne, 236
"Black Mate, The," 185
Bleak House, 68
Blount, Thomas, 105
Blount, John M. K., 103-04, 105, 116, 126, 137, 141, 161, 163, 203, 218, 219
Blunt, Key, 103
Blunt, Mme. Key, 104-05, 141
Bobrowska (Korzeniowski), Evelina, 20, 26-29, 30, 32-33, 41-42, 46
Bobrowska, Josephine, 44-45, 48, 49, 57
Bobrowska, Zunia, 204, 205

Bobrowski, Casimir, 39, 181, 199
Bobrowski, Joseph, 27
Bobrowski, Nicholas, 53
Bobrowski, Stanislas, 32
Bobrowski, Stefan, 30, 34
Bobrowski, Thaddeus, 26, 43, 44, 45, 46, 48, 56, 57, 58, 60, 64, 67, 75, 83-85, 96-97, 139, 154, 162, 164-65, 166, 167, 169-70, 176, 181, 183, 188, 198-99, 205, 208, 212, 213, 223, 231
Boer War, 94
Böet, General, 119, 131
Bohemia, 56
Bombay, 184, 198
Bonnard, M., 164
Book of Prefaces, A, 9
Borneo, 187, 192, 193-95
Boston, 237
Bourbon, Margaret de, 73
Boyer, Marie, 136
Boyer, Monsieur, 77
Boyer trial, 136
Brittany, 212-13, 232
Browning, Robert, 225
Bruce, James, 54
Bucharest, 131
Buszczynski, Stefan, 49, 165, 166, 183

Caesar, Julius, 101
Calcutta, 185
Campbell, George, 175
Campomanes, Countess de, 189
Campou, Raymond de, 138
Canada, 173
Cape Guardafui, 174, 175
Cape Horn, 176
Cap Haitien, 66
Capri, 218
Captain Singleton, 91
Carlier, Captain, 205
Carlism and the Carlists, 70-75, 102-07, 116, 129, 132, 160
Carlist Wars, 71, 88, 102, 119, 123
Carlos, Don, Duke of Madrid, 70, 71-75, 102, 106-07, 110, 115-16, 117, 119-25, 129-30, 131-32, 150, 152-53, 159-60, 163, 164, 167-68, 173-74, 177, 178-79, 189, 191, 219
Carol I, King, 121, 131
Cartagena, 86, 87, 88, 89-90, 91, 93
Carthage, 101
Caruso, Enrico, 191
Catalonia, 74, 160, 173
Catherine the Great, 30
Cauca Valley, 88
Central Committee, Polish, 31, 34
Cervoni, César, 93, 128, 156, 157
Cervoni, Dominic, 91-93, 125, 127-28, 156-58, 218
Cézanne, Paul, 141
Chabert, Mme., 133

Chaix-Bryan, B., 137
Chamber of Deputies, French, 80, 81, 144, 146, 148, 173, 210
Chambord, Count de, 73, 120, 145, 173
Champel, 209, 210
Chance, 168, 213, 220, 234
Charles III, King, 72
Charles IV, King, 72
Château d'If, 63, 64
Chatterton, 48
Chernigov, 41, 42, 46, 47, 48
Cinque Ports, 91
Civil War, American, 34, 74, 103
Cjaz (the *Times*), 51
Clark, Barrett H., 233
Clavel, Marcel, 133
Coeur de Gambetta, Le, 226
Colombia, 87-89, 92, 94, 104, 137
Colorado, 170-71
Colvin, Sir Sidney, 142, 151, 224, 225-27, 228, 229, 230
Comedy, A, 21
Comedy of Errors, A, 48
Compiègne, Marquis de, 148
Compleat Gentleman, The, 105
Conrad, Borys, 216, 218, 219, 236
Conrad, John Alexander, 219-20, 236
Conrad, Joseph, ancestry, 21-24; Australian voyages, 172-76; autobiographical strain in writings, 230-31; birth, 28; Bohemian set, 76-85; boyhood, 51-60; Borneo venture, 192-96; British subject, 185; Carlism and, 70-75, 102-07; childhood, 38-39, 41-42, 43-50; children, 216, 218, 219-20, 236; collaboration, 217; Congo venture, 199-205; death, 238; duel with John Blunt, 161, 165-66, 214; exiled from Poland, 19-21, 32-33, 36, 38-39, 41; extravagances, 83-85; first command, 197-98; gun-running experiences, 86-97, 118, 125, 127-29, 135, 153-54; honors, 236-38; indebtedness, 165; illnesses, 32, 48, 192, 205, 187-88, 192, 217, 218-19, 236; letters, 38, 56, 183-84, 204-05, 206, 208, 209, 210, 216-17, 218, 220, 231-33, 237; literary obsession with remorse, 221-24; loves, boyhood, 14, 59; Marseilles romance, 60, 109-18, 124-25, 150-54, 160-63, 227-30; marriage, 211-12; parents, 20, 21, 23-24, 26-33; pilot duty at Marseilles, 61-66; Polish name, 15; pseudonyms, 140, 208; *Saint-Antoine* voyage, 86-98; schooling, 49-50, 56-57, 59-60; shipwreck, 118, 176, 180-83; *Tremolino* enterprise, 128-30, 133, 135, 139, 140, 154, 155-58; wish to go to sea, 58-59, 60; wreck of the *Palestine,* 180-83

"Conrad Enigma," 134
Constantine, Grand Duke, 34
Copernicus, 58
Corneille, 68, 73
Corporation of Pilots, 63
Correspondant, Le, 223
Cossacks, The, 36
Count of Monte Cristo, 64-65
Court Ladies, painting, 77
Court of the Princess, The, painting, 77
Cracow, 51-60
Cracow University, 56, 57, 58
Craig, James, 192, 193
Crane, Stephen, 216
Crazy Horse, Chief, 67
Crime and Punishment, 23
Crime of Sylvester Bonnard, The, 142
Cronista, 160
Cruising Voyage Around the World, A, 91
Curle, Richard, 8, 230, 233
Custer, General, 67

Daime, Joseph, 80
Daudet, Alphonse, 81, 82, 142, 143, 234
De Broglie, 225
Decembrists, The, 36
Declaration of Independence, 67
Defoe, Daniel, 91
Delcommune, Camille, 205, 214
Delestang, Monsieur and Madame, 67-70, 85, 86, 103, 139, 214
Delestang & Son, C., 67, 128, 133, 139
De Lesseps, 89
Descartes, René, 73
Deutschland, ship, 66
Dickens, Charles, 68
Didot, Firmin, 140
Dombrowska, Marie, 222
Donggala, 193
Dostoevsky, 21, 30, 32, 36-37, 40, 234
Double, The, 40
Doubleday, F. N., 238
Dover, 91, 174
Drake, Sir Francis, 90
Dram-Shop, The, 142
Duchess, ship, 90
Duels, 148, 161, 165-66
Duke, ship, 90
Duke of Sutherland, clipper ship, 172
Dumas père, Alexandre, 64
Dunkirk, 184, 185
Durand, Mlle., 45
Duteil, Captain, 166
Dyaks, 194
Ecuador, 90
Edward the Confessor, 91
Égalité, L', 80

Eliot, George, 225
Emancipation Proclamation, 34
"End of the Tether, The," 217
England, 91, 169, 174
Entrance to the Port, painting, 79
Erebus, ship, 52
Escarras, Captain, 139, 162, 164, 165, 166
Estella, battle, 74
Exiles, Polish, 38-41

"Falk," 197, 217
Falmouth, 181
Farrar, Geraldine, 191
Fathers and Sons, 142
Fecht, Richard, 139, 162, 165, 166, 167, 188, 213
Fehbuts, C. J., 163
Félebres de la Mer, 83
Ferdinand VII, King, 71
Fernandez, Juan, 91
Ferronays, Comtesse de la, 130
Figaro, Le, 106, 122, 139, 210, 227
Fishau, 35
Fishburne, Robert, 148
Flaubert, Gustave, 142
Floral Games, 149
Florida, steamship, 201, 205
Fogas, Mme., 132-33
Fontaine, La, 73
Forster, E. M., 232
Fort Meyer, 70
Fort St. Jean, 63
Fourier, 22
Fourtou, 225
Fox, ship, 52, 53
France, 140-43, 144, 145
France, Anatole, 142
Francesca, 43, 44
Franco, Francisco, 74
Franco-Prussian War, 76, 144-45
Franklin, Sir John, 52, 54
Franz Josef, Emperor, 120
French Revolution, 64, 101
Frétigny, "Prax," 100
Frohsdorf, 120
Furca Pass, 59

Galsworthy, John, 8, 97, 150, 206, 216, 219
Gambetta, Léon, 81, 144-45, 146-48, 225-27
Garden, Mary, 191
Garland, 171
Garnett, Edward, 8, 56, 110, 204, 214, 215
Garrapata, 88
Gautier, Judith, 104
Gautier, Théophile, 104, 105

Gelu, Victor, 81
"Geography and Some Explorers," 54, 60
George, Jessie, 211-12, 220, 232, 236, 237
Gettysburg, battle, 33, 36
Gilbert, W. S., 171
Gladstone, William, 170
Gonzalez, Marquis de, 129
Gould, J. B., 137
Gounod, Charles François, 83
Grabowski, Count, 34
Graham, R. B. Cunninghame, 137, 166
Grant, Ulysses S., 170
Gratz, 120, 130, 153
Greeley, Horace, 22
Greenland, 52, 53
Guadeloupe, 66
Guayaquil, 90
Guerard, Albert J., 185
Guesde, Jules, 14, 81, 210
Gulf of Mexico, 66, 94
Gulf of Rosas, 129
Gulf of Siam, 197

Haiti, 66, 87, 97
Hamilton, Lord Frederic, 131
Hanska, Anna de, 25-26
Hanska, Evelina de, 26
Harley, Walter S., 148
Hastings, 91
Havana, 90
"Heart of Darkness," 10, 200, 201, 202-03, 204, 217
Heine, Heinrich, 21
Hernani, 29
Herzen, Alexander, 39, 40
Highland Forest, ship, 185, 187
House of the Dead, The, 37
Howard, Henry Fitzalan, 106-07
Hudson Bay, 54
Hueffer, Ford Madox, 217
Hugo, Victor, 21, 29, 47, 80, 142, 146, 225
Hugues, Clovis, 79-81, 82
Hull, 185
Huntress Diana, The, painting, 79
Hythe, 91, 216

Importance of Being Earnest, The, 17
Impressionists, 66, 130-31, 140-41
India, 81, 184
Indian Ocean, 197
Infected Family, The, 36
Inheritors, The, 217
International Association for the Exploration and Civilization of the Congo, 200
Isabella II, Queen, 71, 155, 160

Jaime, Don, 74, 106, 107, 120, 130, 177-78
Jamaica, 90
James, Henry, 225, 233
James, Mrs. Curtiss, 237
James Westoll, ship, 65
Java, 186, 187
Java Sea, 192
Jean-Aubry, Georges, 133, 134, 188, 221
Jeddah, steamship, 174-75
Jeune République, La, 80
Johannesburg, 210
Joseph, coachman, 45
Joseph II, Emperor, 30
Joseph Conrad and His Circle, 212
Joseph Conrad As I Knew Him, 212
"Joseph Conrad in the East," 233
Jours de Combat, Les, 80

Kaposvar, 122
Kasai River, 205
Kazan, 39
Kazan University, 23-24
Kiev, 45, 46, 48, 162
Kinchassa, 201, 204, 205
King William Island, 54
Klein, Georges Antoine, 202
Koch, Captain, 201, 202
Korzeniowski, Apollonius Nalecz, 20, 21, 23-24, 26, 27, 28-32, 38, 41, 46, 47-48, 49, 51, 54, 56, 57-58
Korzeniowski, Conrad, see Conrad, Joseph
Korzeniowski, Hilary, 22, 34
Korzeniowski, Robert, 22, 34
Korzeniowski, Theodor, 21-22, 48-49
Kosciusko, Thaddeus, 31
Kraszewski, Joseph, 28
Krieger, Adolf P., 188

"Lagoon, The," 212
La Guaira, 87
Lakamba, 195
Landlady, The, 40
Laur, Francis, 226
La Vallière, Louise de, 113, 177, 223
Lee, Robert E., 103
Légende des Siècles, La, 29
Legitimist Principle, 108
Legitimists, 75, 120, 125, 138, 145
Le Havre, 66
Léon, Léonie, 147, 226, 227
Leopold II, 200
Lettres de mon moulin, 82
Lincoln, Abraham, 34
Lingard, Jim, 195
Lingard, Tom, 195
Lisle, Rouget de, 101

Lithuania, 35
Little Big Horn, battle, 67
Livingstone, David, 50, 55, 198
Loch Etive, ship, 175-76
London, 13-18, 34, 36, 124, 155, 167, 169, 171, 172-73, 174, 176, 179, 183, 184, 185, 198, 199, 206, 209, 211, 219
London *Observer,* 230
London *Times,* 35, 72, 106, 107, 119, 129, 136, 146, 155, 169, 170, 173, 174, 175, 179, 222, 223
Lord Jim, 10, 175, 195, 216-17, 232, 234
Los Chances, 88
Louis XIV, King, 68, 72, 73, 109, 114, 177
Lowestoft, 167, 169, 171
Lublin, 199
Luther, Martin, 73
Luton, 220
Lwow, 49, 51, 59

Macassar Strait, 192, 193
MacDonald, Ramsay, 237
MacMahon, Marshal, 74, 130, 132, 145-46, 225
MacWhirr, John, 186, 187
Madras, 184
Mancini, Maria, 109
Manet, Edouard, 141
Mardi Gras, Marseilles, 99-100
Marguerita, Doña, 168, 179
Marichalar, Miguel de, 190
Marienbad, 183
Marseillaise, 101
Marseilles, 10, 11, 14, 60, 61-66, 67, 69, 71, 74, 75, 76, 79, 80, 81, 83, 97-98, 99-108, 116, 125, 126, 129, 134, 135, 138-39, 141, 148, 149, 159, 160, 161, 162, 164, 213, 218, 226
Martinique, 65, 66, 87, 95
Marx, Karl, 81
Massalia, 62
Matadi, 199, 201
Maupassant, Guy de, 142
Mauritius, 197
Mavis, ship, 167, 169
Maximilian, Emperor, 88
Mayard, Pierre, 133
McClintock, Captain, 52, 53, 54
McDonald, L. B., 184, 214
Medellin, 88
Melba, Frances, 191
Melgar, Count de, 121, 124, 125, 154-55, 167, 174, 177-79, 188-91
Melgar, Count Francisco de, 121
Melville Bay, 53
Memories & Notes of Persons & Places, 226
Mencken, H. L., 9

Ménerbes, 80
Metropolitan Museum of Art, 77
Metz, 145
Mexico, 88, 90
Meyer, Mr., 148
Mickiewicz, 21, 28
Milan, 153
Mirabeau, Count, 64
Mireille, 83
Mireio, 83
Mirror of the Sea, The, 83, 91, 92, 103, 105, 128, 156, 172, 187, 218, 219, 220, 232
Mistral, Frédéric, 81, 82-83
Mniszek, Count Georges, 25, 26, 57
Mniszek, Count Ladislas, 57
Molière, 73
Monarchists, 73, 145, 146, 173
Monde Illustré, Le, 130
Monserrat, Viscount de, 131, 190
Mont-Blanc, ship, 65, 66, 68, 128, 166
Monte Carlo, 166, 213
Monte Cristo, 63
Monticelli, Adolphe, 76-78, 79, 82
Montpellier, 219
Morin, lawyer, 81
Moscow, 32
Moscow University, 40
Much Ado About Nothing, 48
Muraviev, governor in Lithuania, 35

Nabob, The, 142, 143
Napoleon III, Emperor, 36, 88, 104, 132, 145
Napoleon IV, 145
Narcissus, ship, 184-85
Nassau, 90
Newcastle, 169, 180
New Orleans, 66
New Republic, The, 10
New York, 237-38
New York *Daily Tribune,* 130
New York *Herald,* 106
New York Times, The, 10, 73, 119
New York *World,* 11
Nicholas I, Czar, 22, 23, 39, 40
Nietzsche, Friedrich, 144
Niger River, 55
Nigger of the Narcissus, The, 10, 91, 172, 184-85, 192, 213, 214, 232, 235
Nihilist, The, 36
Ninety-Three, 142
Niven, John C., 193, 196
Nizhni Novogorod, 33
North Sea, 180
Northwest Passage, 54
Nostromo, 10, 86, 91, 93, 137, 232, 234
Notes on Life and Letters, 52, 171, 234
Nowofastow, 43-46, 48-49, 199
Numancia, 102

Olmeijer (Almayer), 15, 187, 195-96, 223-24
Omsk, 40
Oratov, 27, 28
Orléanists, 145
Orléans, 145
Orlestone, 225
Otago, bark, 197-98, 214, 224
Othello, 48
Outcast of the Islands, An, 16, 193, 195, 209-10, 213-14, 215, 221, 232
"Outpost of Progress, An," 203, 205, 212

Palawan, 192
Palembang, 193
Palestine, bark, 180-83, 186, 203
Panama, 94
Paris, 14, 34, 36, 66, 73, 79, 102, 115, 121, 122, 123, 125, 128, 130, 133, 140, 141, 144-45, 149-50, 153, 155, 159, 167, 179, 207, 210
Paris, Count of, 145
Paris Commune, 80, 145
Park, Mungo, 54, 55
Parra, Aquileo, 88
Pascal, 73
Pascalis, 14, 210
Peary, Robert E., 53
Peasant revolts, 31
Pension Georgeon, 56, 57
Perm, 32, 39
Perm Province, 39
Personal Record, A, 47, 58, 187, 195, 220
Petilhon, Gustave, 133
Philadelphia Centennial Exposition, 67
Philip V, King, 72
Pianello, Jean, 136
Pianello, Spiridion, 136
Pilgrim ships, 174-75
"Pinafore, H. M. S.," 171
Pinker, Eric, 123
Pinker, J. B., 213, 219
Pirates, 90-91
Pirondi, Dr., 162
Plate Fleet, Spanish, 89, 90
Ploesti, 131
Plymouth, 206
Poland, 20, 22, 28, 30, 34-37, 199
Polikoúshka, 36
Polish insurrection, 34-37, 49
Ponce de Leon, José, 189
Poor Folk, 40
Poradowska, Marguerite, 38, 39, 82, 207-08, 209, 220
Port-au-Prince, 87, 97
Port Louis, 197
Portraits from Memory, 8
Potter, Frank W., 137

Pripet Marshes, 47
Proudhon, 22
"Publications," 29
Pueblo, 171
Puerto Cabello, 87
Pulmann, Adam, 57, 58-59, 60
Pygmalion, 123

Quartel Real, 71, 72, 105, 121, 123

Racine, 73
Raigecourt-Goyon Prize, 79
Rambouillet, Marquise de, 68
Raymond, Dr., 168
Recollections of a Minister to France, 104
Red Sea, 175
Renouf, Eugénie, 197-98
Rescue, The, 193, 195, 212
Revue des Deux Mondes, 30, 168
Rita, Doña, *see* Somoggy, Paula de
Riversdale, ship, 81, 184
Rochefoucauld, La, 68
Rogers, Woodes, 89, 90-91
Roi des Belges, steamship, 201-03, 204
Romance, 217
Rome, 148
Romney, 91
Rorke, Mr., 210
Rosas, 102
Roses, Jean, 133
Rothenstein, Sir William, 8
Rover, The, 10, 91, 168, 236
Royalists, 69, 70, 79
Russell, Bertrand, 8
Russia, 19, 20
Russo-Japanese War, 94
Russo-Turkish War, 120-21, 132
Rustchuk (Ruse), 121

Saint-Antoine, ship, 85, 86-98, 100, 103, 128, 137
St. James's Theatre, 17
St. Petersburg, 31, 36, 40
St. Petersburg University, 23, 31, 57
St. Pierre, 66, 87, 95, 96
Saint-Simon, Claude Henri, 22, 40, 73
St. Thomas, 66, 87, 95, 96
Salic Law, 71
Samarang, 187, 188
Samaritaine, The, painting, 79
Sanderson, E. L., 215
Sandwich, 91
Sanguszko, Prince Roman, 48-49
San Sebastian, 191
San Stefano, Treaty, 121
Saturday Review, The, 213

Savannah, 148
Schiller, ship, 65
Scilly Islands, 65
Scruggs, William, 88
Sea Dreamer, The, 221
Second Rang du Collier, Le, 104
Secret Agent, The, 220, 234
"Secret Sharer, The," 10, 197, 203, 221, 234
Selkirk, Alexander, 90-91
Semipalatinsk, 40
Serfdom, 31
Set of Six, A, 220
Sévigné, Mme. de, 68
Shadow Line, The, 10, 98, 196, 197, 203, 220, 221, 224
Shakespeare, William, 47, 48
Shaw, George Bernard, 123
Siberia, 40
Simon, Jules, 225
"Simple Heart, A," 142
Singapore, 174, 175, 182, 183, 185, 187, 188, 192, 193, 196, 197, 221
Singapore Steamship Company, 174
Sing Jimmung, 193
Sisters, The, 16, 110, 211, 227, 232, 234
Sitting Bull, Chief, 170
Skimmer of the Seas, The, 169
"Smile of Fortune, A," 222, 231
Sobanska, Melanie, 22, 28
Soirs de Bataille, Les, 80
Solary, Baptistin, 64
Somoggy (Somogyi), Paula de ("Rita"), 13, 14, 107, 108, 109-18, 121-25, 126-27, 130-31, 132, 133, 141, 150-51, 152-55, 160-61, 162-64, 165, 167-68, 173, 174, 177, 178, 188-91, 196, 210-11, 218, 219, 223, 227-30
Sophocles, 221
Spain, 70, 71, 72, 74, 102, 103, 155, 159
Spanish-American War, 70, 94
Spanish civil war (1936-39), 74
Squire, J. C., 160
Stanford-le-Hope, 215, 216
Stanley Falls, 202
Stanley Pool, 200, 201
Stevenson, Robert Louis, 225
Stoke Newington, 173
Story of a Crime, 146
Stradling, Captain, 91
Stuart, William, 175
Suelves, Don José de, 121, 122, 190
Sullivan, Arthur, 171
Sumatra, 193
Suspense, 58, 91, 238
Sutherland, W., 169, 171
Switzerland, 59
Sydney, 172, 175
Syroczynska, Tekla, 59
Syroczynski, Antoine, 164, 165

Tales of Unrest, 188, 216
Tandjungredeb, 193
Temps des Cerises, Le, 80
Tennyson, Alfred Lord, 7, 225
Teplitz, 183
Terror, ship, 52
Third Company, 63, 64, 65
Third French Republic, 71, 101, 146, 147
Three Tales, 142
Tierra Firme, 89
Tilkhurst, ship, 185
Time, 30, 36-37
Tit-Bits, 185
Tobolsk, 39
Toilers of the Sea, 47
Tolima, 88
Tolosa, 71, 72, 105, 121, 123
Tolstoy, Leo, 23-24, 36, 45, 46-47
Tolstoy, Sergius, 36
"Tomorrow," 217
Tomsk, 23
Torrens, ship, 206
Torres Strait, 214
Tours, 145
Toussaint, Albert de, 139, 164, 165
Trabadelo, Angel de, 189-91
Tremolino enterprise, 128-30, 133, 135, 139, 140, 154, 155-58, 203
Triana, Perez, 137
Turgenev, 23, 142
Turin, 153
Tuscania, steamship, 237
Twain, Mark, 200
'Twixt Land and Sea, 220
Two Gentlemen of Verona, The, 47
Typhoon, 186, 217, 232
Tyszkowa, Maria Bobrowska, 199, 204

Ukraine, 22, 24, 49, 57
Uncle Tom's Cabin, 171
Under Western Eyes, 220, 234
United States, 237-38
Untimely Opinions, 144
Unwin, T. Fisher, 208, 209
Ural Mountains, 20, 32

Valencia, 74
Van Gogh, Vincent, 83
Veinte Años con don Carlos, 121
Venice, 60, 119, 124, 153
Vera Cruz, 90
Verne, Jules, 144
Véron, Pierre, 130-31, 223
Versailles, 146
Vesuvius, Mount, 170
Victoria, Queen, 67
Victory, 94-96, 151-52, 168, 220, 221, 234, 237

Vidar, steamship, 192-96
Vienna, 36, 58, 120, 124, 131, 153
Vigny, Alfred de, 48
Villefranche, 166
Virgin Islands, 95
Vitalis, Léon, 136
Volhynia, 22, 24, 25, 46
Vologda, 20-21, 33, 38-39, 41-42
Vologda River, 42
*Voyage of the "Fox" in the Arctic
Seas,* 52
Vyatka, 39

Walewska, Countess, 177
War and Peace, 24, 36
Warsaw, 20, 21, 30, 31, 32, 34, 35
Washburne, E. B., 104, 143

Washington, George, 31
Wells, H. G., 10, 213-14, 218
West Indies, 65, 68, 85, 86-97
White Sea, 19, 21
Wierzchownia, 25-26
Wilde, Oscar, 17
Within the Tides, 220
World War I, 224
Wright, Orville, 70

Yásnaya Polyána, 36
"Youth," 10, 176, 180, 182-83, 203

Zagorski, Charles, 211
Zambesi River, 55
Zhitomir, 21, 23, 29, 34, 49
Zola, Émile, 82, 142